my eyes feel
they need to cry

my eyes feel they need to cry

STORIES FROM THE **FORMERLY HOMELESS**

MARTHA ALADJEM BLOOMFIELD

Michigan State University Press • East Lansing

☺ The paper used in this publication meets the minimum requirements of
ANSI/NISO Z39.48-1992 (R 1997) (Permanence of Paper).

Michigan State University Press
East Lansing, Michigan 48823-5245

Printed and bound in the United States of America.

19 18 17 16 15 14 13   1 2 3 4 5 6 7 8 9 10

LIBRARY OF CONGRESS CATALOGING-IN-PUBLICATION DATA
Bloomfield, Martha Aladjem.
My eyes feel they need to cry : stories from the formerly homeless / Martha
Aladjem Bloomfield.
pages cm
Includes bibliographical references.
ISBN 978-1-61186-091-7 (pbk. : alk. paper)—ISBN 978-1-60917-383-8 (ebook)
1. Homelessness—United States. I. Title.
HV4505.B526 2013
362.5'92092273—dc23
2013003032

Book design by Charlie Sharp, Sharp Designs, Lansing, Michigan
Cover design by Erin Kirk New

The title for this book, *My Eyes Feel They Need to Cry*, comes from the poem "Are
You Willing to Open Your Heart?" by Lewis, one of the participants in "Your Story
and Mine: A Community of Hope." The full text appears in chapter 5.

The painting on the cover of the book is by David, another participant, and shows
him singing and playing the guitar at an open mike night in Lansing, Michigan.

The majority of the author's net proceeds from this book will go to the literacy
programs at Advent House Ministries, Lansing, Michigan.

Michigan State University Press is a member of the Green Press Initiative and
is committed to developing and encouraging ecologically responsible publishing
practices. For more information about the Green Press Initiative and the use
of recycled paper in book publishing, please visit *www.greenpressinitiative.org*.

Visit Michigan State University Press at *www.msupress.org*

If we each look honestly, consciously, and deeply into ourselves

without censorship, we will see that at one time or another, either we

ourselves, a relative, or a friend has suffered from mental illness,

drug or alcohol abuse, violence, self-abuse, and/or homelessness.

None of us are exempt on our journey through life.

—————————————————————

MARTHA ALADJEM BLOOMFIELD

To my sons, Avi and Simi—
May you always have a home and
Help others to have one, too.

And to all the people who willingly, courageously, and graciously dared to share their life stories through words and paintings—their pain and sorrows, their hopes and dreams—to help themselves and their families, and others who can learn from them. They are truly our mentors!

As I came to the end of writing this book, I remembered a series of three pictures I had painted many years ago reflecting images that appeared in my mind one day. While the images are simple and rather stark, they exemplify the essence of longing, trauma, courage, hope, dreams, sadness, and resilience.

In the first painting, a pretty blue bird sways gently on a red swing in his cage, wistfully looking out through the bars and through the window beyond to an orange-yellow setting sun, purple clouds, and an autumn leafless oak tree. He yearns for freedom from the shackles of the cage and house so he can return home to the outdoor world.

In the second painting, the blue bird does the unthinkable and flies out through the cage and the window. The glass shatters. While in flight, he injures his wing, causing it to bleed. He falls to the earth.

In the third painting, the bird sees a never-ending orange-red staircase on a green mound of grass that goes up to the sky. Unable to fly, but also refusing to stay limp on the ground, he begins to climb the steps one by one towards his home in the sky, to the soothing setting sun and clouds, towards freedom.

Time passes. The blue bird develops perspective on his life as he looks down on the earth and reflects on his journey.

Both the bird and the homeless are resilient, but all carry a heavy burden deep within, passed on through generations. They understand now that their task is to lighten their loads for themselves, their children, and their grandchildren.

Contents

Foreword

Susan E. Cancro

E very one of us wants a place to call home. Finding, sharing, and keeping a home can be manageable or overwhelming. For some, home means the old family homestead, full of tradition and memories that span generations. For others it means a place chosen outside of family tradition, shaped to express a different life path. At times, for a group of individuals and families, home means not a "place" but a "process" of gaining information and experiences, finding temporary oases of safety and support, redesigning themselves and their understanding of how to live a productive life. Among those in this last group are the men, women, and children who struggle with homelessness.

People become homeless for a broad range of reasons, including loss of a job, loss of a wage-earning family member, loss of original housing due to natural disaster or fire, loss of income and basic stability due to domestic violence, substance abuse, physical or mental illness—to name a few. Considering this, it is clear that any one of us could become homeless. With the support of family and friends, we might avoid seeking help from strangers and staying at a shelter; however, there are also many who do not have this resource and need outside assistance.

In the eighteen years I have worked with the homeless, and the almost thirty years assisting those in need, I have found that most who seek outside assistance do not have a safety net other than the broader community. Particularly among those who have grown up in generational poverty, family and friends are poorly housed or homeless themselves. When this is the case, there are few resources immediately available, and sometimes little support for the fragile stability that is gained later on. The best tools we can give those who face the obstacles of homelessness and long-term poverty—and also those who come into homelessness with greater personal stability—are experiences that build both academic and social literacy, as well as honing the skills necessary to self-advocate effectively. The projects referenced in this book were an effort on the part of a group of Advent House Ministries' volunteers and staff to do just that.

Each year Advent House Ministries serves over 3,000 people, providing assistance with immediate basic needs, such as food and shelter, and opportunities to build lifelong literacy and employment skills. Of those who come to us, 75 percent have experienced generational poverty; 45 percent are homeless and referred from area shelters, including approximately 8 percent who are chronically homeless; and 60 percent are those who are not homeless but are living in substandard housing. Most often, these are individuals who have been unsuccessful in navigating traditional education and work settings, coming to believe that they are bound to fail.

Advent House Ministries' provides a flexible, nontraditional environment in which to learn and build self-sufficiency. Food and all-day shelter is offered every weekend of the year through our Weekend Shelter Program. Each year we serve over 34,000 meals to more than 2,100 people—an average of 130 people each day. Transitional shelter and case management services are provided through our Shelter Home Program, addressing the needs of more than 15 homeless families and 50 individuals working toward permanent stable housing. Our literacy program is bridging the education gap for more than 180 persons every year, providing open learning sessions and individual tutoring, as well as more than 3,000 meals (ensuring that our students have adequate nourishment and the positive companionship that comes with sharing meals is critical to their success). Employment assistance, including life skills training, résumé development, interview preparation, job search and placement services, and general job coaching helps more than 150 homeless and at-risk adults each year. Adding self-development tools, such as art and writing classes similar to those described in this book, allows each participant to have the experience of unique accomplishment that is crucial to building confidence and gaining long-term stability.

All of the programs described above are dependent on our partnerships with other area shelters and agencies in our community. Advent House Ministries has been an active member of the Greater Lansing Homeless Resolution Network for over twenty years. This group of dedicated private and public organizations focuses on addressing the causes of and working toward an end of homelessness. The member agencies of the network work closely together to maximize the impact of services. As a result, Advent House Ministries has increased the effectiveness of our services by 60 percent in the last 15 years, moving from providing only basic services to 1,800 persons to providing comprehensive stability-building services to over 3,000 persons in our programs today. Building trust with partners and participants is key.

To address homelessness, a hope-filled environment must be provided using the cornerstones of kindness, fairness, generosity, and faith. In the "Your Story and Mine: A Community of Hope" project, for example, each person was invited to share his or her story of the journey of homelessness. These stories were recorded and transcribed, and the tremendous value of each person and their story was communicated throughout the project. Each person in the project was given time and resources to tell his or her story through multiple means of expression. Each person knew from the outset that our staff and volunteers believed in and valued each one's input. This is a small practical application of the formula we use in all of our programs.

As an individual or family comes to us, we reach out with respect and an open mind, listening to the stories that come with each person. We frame this comfortable environment with solid case-management practices and an informed understanding of current resources available in our community. This approach is fairly standard among human services organizations. What is unique about our approach is the real-life learning activities that are the foundation of our programming. We walk with our guests through key life experiences, identifying critical learning opportunities with each one. These activities may be as simple as going shopping for interview clothing in our employment programs, or drawing and painting in our art programs, or cleaning a room in our shelter programs. They may be as complex as sharing stories of great personal loss in one of our life-skills groups, or a discussion with a parent of the best way to handle a rebellious teenager in our shelter programs, or celebrating a new job and discussing the next steps in our employment programs. Experiences such as these build an amazing level of trust—a bond that gives strength to our guests and to our organization.

I truly believe that it is essential to move beyond the traditional clinical approach to assisting those in need. We must let down our guard and realize that our stories are not that different one from the other. We must avoid doing "to" and "for" and strive to do "with." As we find a good balance of the personal and the professional in this work, we draw on the strength of shared human experience and thereby build a strong bridge to stability, a way to come "home."

Acknowledgments

I wish to thank all the many, many people who supported the creation and implementation of "Your Story and Mine: A Community of Hope" that gave birth to this book, a reflection of this project. It continues to be a "never-ending story." First, I am grateful to all the participants in the project who willingly, graciously, and honestly shared their painful, difficult memories and stories in so many different ways—through words, art, and music. They are all remarkable human beings in their own special ways. They each honored their commitment to the project from the beginning to the end. They are truly my mentors: Wynette, Lewis, Robert, David R., Jackie, Bill, Dora, Loren "Smokey," Brandy, LaKashia, LaKeya, and Robin. Others also came to classes occasionally and we are grateful for their participation.

I wish to thank all the members of our dedicated team who gave everything they could to make this project work for everyone. Their energy, enthusiasm, patience, intellectual expertise, unique life experiences, talents, wisdom, strength, and humor are remarkable and profound. You will have the opportunity to hear their voices throughout this book, which is merely a small reflection of all the work they did. Furthermore, they were unequivocally supportive of my endeavors to share our story as a book with the world at large. *My Eyes Feel They Need to Cry* is merely a reflection of everyone's collaboration—both mentors and mentees.

Susan E. Cancro, executive director of Advent House Ministries (AHM) and a member of the Greater Lansing Homeless Resolution Network, was responsive and supportive from the moment I called her to initiate a partnership between the Michigan Historical Museum and Advent House Ministries. She nurtured the original project and then suggested that the participants paint a mural of their life experiences. This idea mushroomed rapidly into an even larger endeavor.

Toni Townshend, literacy director at AHM, became and continues to be my mentor and role model for working with the guests at Advent House Ministries. Her unassuming, calm, positive, nonjudgmental, understanding approach helped me develop confidence to work with these people who were so unfamiliar to me. She continuously feeds me positive reinforcement and always thoughtfully answers my million questions. Without Toni inviting me to her jobs class way back when we wanted to initiate the pilot project, I do not believe that I would have ever found a way to be comfortable, feeling so at home with the homeless and those looking for homes! Looking back on that morning, I think it is almost like a dream, and yet this whole "never-ending story" of "Your Story and Mine" is like a never-ending dream of laughter, smiles, and tears.

Allyson Bolt, LLMSW, director of the Employment Program, AHM, originally came to us as a graduate student intern from Michigan State University. Within an hour of our talking on the telephone about the internship opportunity at the museum to work on "Your Story and Mine," Allyson came to the museum to meet and brainstorm with me. She was a godsend who jumped right in to help. Upon receiving her master's degree in social work, Allyson became a regular staff member at Advent House Ministries.

Erika Magers, artist, muralist, and art therapist in training—another amazing human being—guided the participants on their journey of telling their stories through painting. She always encouraged them calmly and respectfully—listening to their questions and comments, responding positively and wisely. With her gentle, quiet demeanor, she always sought a way for them to express their stories in the ways in which they wanted and needed to. While continuing her studies at Wayne State University, she also teaches art classes at Advent House Ministries and works on innumerable other community art projects, often helping youth express themselves.

Marion Kennedy Heider worked for many years for Ingham County Family Planning, in the mental health unit of St. Lawrence Hospital, and then as a friend of the court for Ingham County. Once retired, she became a volunteer docent at the Michigan Historical Museum and gave her time graciously, willingly, and humbly—first working with me on an immigration program and then on this project. She sat next to each participant and provided each one with unending individual compassion. She was such a joy to have on the project; her calm, kind, patient, encouraging support greatly helped the participants and the other mentors. We are all grateful for her unqualified involvement and help.

Peter Frahm, "Your Story and Mine: A Community of Hope" video producer, is an adjunct instructor in Communication, Media and the Arts at Lansing Community College (LCC), and volunteered many hours to videotape the oral history interviews at LCC, as well as art classes at Advent House. He also conducted and recorded a roundtable discussion with all the mentors.

Chris Dancisak, now retired, was the director of community relations at the Michigan Historical Museum. He now volunteers as the assistant director, Literacy Programs, at Advent House Ministries. I wish to thank him as my wonderful colleague, former boss, mentor, and good friend. He encouraged and worked with me to develop the partnership between the Michigan Historical Museum and Advent House Ministries to create the program "Your Story and Mine: A Community of Hope." He believed with both his mind and heart that this project was the right thing to do in the realm of museum community outreach. He also believed in the book and read, reread, and edited many drafts of the manuscript. His sensitive insights, organizational suggestions, and understanding of my thought processes empowered me to communicate positively and effectively. He let me bounce my ideas off him about homelessness, poverty, and "life" over many breakfasts at Dmitri's in Lansing.

Daniel Jones, job-developer case manager at Advent House Ministries, helped the participants develop employment and life skills so that they can find and maintain employment. He also made agency referrals and helped clients with their clothing and transportation needs.

"Your Story and Mine: A Community of Hope" was dedicated to Pam Fulton, who came from New York in the late 1980s to become the associate pastor of Westminster Presbyterian Church. She and members of the church organized a neighborhood outreach program, which eventually became Advent House Ministries. She died on May 7, 2009.

Geneva Wiskemann, Michigan Humanities Council consultant and the founder and secretary of the Michigan Oral History Association, acted as advisor for the oral history component for "Your Story and Mine." She also strongly encouraged me to give a paper about the project at the Michigan Oral History Conference in September 2009 and at the International Oral History Conference in Prague, the Czech Republic, in June 2010. She has been a true mentor and friend for many years.

I also organized a symposium at the U.S. Embassy in Prague on homelessness in 2010. I thank Ilja Hradecký, founder and director of the nongovernmental organization Naděje ("Hope") in the Czech Republic, his colleague Aftab Hladikova, a social scientist, and Helena Vágnerová, Public Affairs Officer at the U.S. Embassy in Prague, who all helped organize this event.

Others who were also helpful in teaching the classes to the participants include

Laurie Catherine Perkins, education department, Michigan Historical Museum; Julie Meyerle, State Archives of Michigan; Dean Anderson, the state archaeologist; and Kris Rzepczynski, Library of Michigan. I also thank Mary L. Ploor, retired museum educator and Web curator, Michigan Historical Museum, who encouraged me over lunches and cups of coffee to write this book.

Student interns who also played key helpful roles include Jacob Hemingway, Michigan State University; Joe Pfeiffer, Eastern Michigan University; Mattie Dugan, Michigan State University; Laura Boyd, Oakland University; Sarah Anne Buranskas, University of Michigan; and Danielle Culberson, Northwood University.

Special thanks go to the Michigan Humanities Council for a $15,000 grant for "Your Story and Mine: A Community of Hope"; Lansing Community College, Department of Media, Art, and Information Technology for providing production facilities; and O'Leary Paints for a generous donation of art supplies and technical advice.

Thanks go to the Lansing City Hall, which first hosted the exhibit, and the many libraries, historical societies, museums, and organizations where we presented talks, including: the Capital Area District Library and the Michigan Historical Museum in Lansing; the Hoyt Main Library and the Historical Society of Saginaw County—Castle Museum & Annex in Saginaw; the Peter White Public Library in Marquette; the Otsego County Library and the Otsego Area Historical Society in Gaylord; the Otsego Housing & Homeless Coalition and the Otsego Human Services Network in Otsego County; the Grand Rapids Public Library; the Kalamazoo Public Library; the Traverse Area District Library; and the Manistique School and Public Library.

I also wish to thank my mentor, Linda Wallace, who guided and empowered me through many years of my own personal trauma, grief, loss, transformation, and creativity. She inspired me to draw what I saw inside myself to complement my writing, and rejoiced with me in my own personal, profound transformation.

I thank Jim Heavenrich, another of my mentors, who helped me discover and confront my own "ghosts in the nursery" (Selma Fraiberg)—to put them to sleep and to break the cycle as best I could for my sons, Avi and Simi.

I wish to acknowledge my many friends from Michigan, elsewhere in the United States, and other countries, some of whom I have known for more than thirty years— some almost fifty years! Many, but not all, are therapists of one kind or another who have devoted their lives to help others deal with grief, loss, illness, and resilience. Others have been engaged in making the planet a better place in which to live—environmentally, legally, socially, and artistically. Their consistent support and friendship, as well as that of all their families, contributed profoundly to helping me navigate the illness and premature death in 2003 of my first husband, Jacob J. Climo, at age fiftyseven just at the brink of coming into his own. Through such an unbelievable support system during that sad, difficult time, they were also "aunties, uncles, and cousins" to my two sons, Avi and Simi, and helped me become emotionally stronger for them as well as for me. Their love and support empowered me to develop a capacity to rebuild my life and move forward—in other words, to become resilient.

When I was thirteen years old, I had profound difficulties expressing myself clearly in writing. I thank my high school English teacher Sally McGuire Muspratt, who told me that if I wanted to learn to write well, I needed to read a lot, write a lot, and keep a diary. She inspired me so much that I followed her advice literally and improved my grades dramatically. Many other high school English teachers also helped me navigate those difficult years while I was learning to write clearly and concisely. One history teacher also told me that since I had experienced every possible writing problem, one day I would probably teach writing. For several years, I was an adjunct writing instructor at Michigan State University's School of Journalism, and I also spent a year teaching at the University of Pittsburgh's English Department. I taught regular undergraduate students and nontraditional adult students in both universities.

In 1987, I worked as an editor on contract for Betty Tableman with the Michigan Department of Mental Health, and with infant mental health specialist Deborah Weatherston, for a manual to train infant mental health specialists to work with at-risk parents and infants. This experience provided infinite knowledge and wisdom about how to look at family dynamics, how we repeat unhealthy patterns of our parents and grandparents, and the profound importance and necessity of interrupting that cycle to help new mothers to develop healthy coping skills.

I wish to thank Associate Professor Gail Vander Stoep, Department of Community, Agriculture, Recreation and Resource Studies, Michigan State University (MSU), and six of her students— David Dilworth, Ju Hyoung Han, Eric Bailey, Jayne Goeddeke, Eun Jeong Noh, and Anna Stein—for conducting evaluations of "Your Story and Mine: A Community of Hope" as part of their course requirements. They all willingly gave their time and effort by attending classes with the participants, researching the project, analyzing their findings, and presenting written and oral reports.

I am grateful to Darlene A. G. Groomes, associate professor for Human Development and Child Studies, Oakland University, for providing me the opportunity to talk with her, and for sharing with me her wisdom about resilience and adaptation.

I also wish to thank Julie Loehr, assistant director and editor-in-chief at Michigan State University Press, for her support, insights, and editorial suggestions to help mold my original manuscript with the raw oral history interviews into a book. I also thank her staff and collaborators for their hard work, patience, and sensitivity: Kristine Blakeslee, Elise Jajuga, Barbara Fitch Cobb, Annette Tanner, Julie Reaume, Travis

Kimbel, and Marla Koenigsknecht. I also thank Erin Kirk New for designing the cover so beautifully and Charlie Sharp, Sharp Des!gns, for a lovely book design.

I thank my family for their continued long-term support. In particular I am grateful to my two sons, Avi C. Climo and Simi I. Climo, with whom I have weekly and sometimes daily conversations "about life" even though they live far away in other parts of the country. Through all the challenges we encountered as a family, they have evolved into two wonderful, sensitive, generous human beings. I am so proud of both of them! I also thank my late husband, Jacob J. Climo, professor of anthropology at Michigan State University, author, and editor, who continues in his own special way to encourage me on a journey of lifelong writing, fieldwork, interviews, and exploration of ideas about cultures.

I thank my current husband, Alan J. Bloomfield, a criminal lawyer for indigent people and book lover. He provides a nurturing, quiet, peaceful home and encourages me to pursue my dreams from adolescence to read and write. So often, when I asked him about a reference to an author in a book I was reading, he said, "Oh, I have that book in my library downstairs" and immediately went down to get it! Alan willingly traveled with me over the Upper and Lower Peninsulas in Michigan as we discovered new libraries. He helped me set up the exhibit of the participants' artwork, stories, and poetry to create greater awareness and promote dialogue about homelessness in all the local communities. In 2010, Alan traveled with me to Prague.

I also thank my mother-in-law, Betty Bloomfield Soffin, who has faith in me. She positively reinforces me daily and says that everything will work out! She is a true gift and role model for how to live life gracefully and determinedly and navigate the aging journey through all its ups and downs.

Finally, I thank my parents, Albert Tchelebi Aladjem and Henrietta Hirsch Aladjem, for their unmatched courage, strength, fortitude, and determination in life, and their encouragement for me to pursue my goals. They had the foresight and insight to immigrate to the United States from Bulgaria at the beginning of World War II. They believed strongly in the importance of education, social awareness, world events, creative ideas, cultural and artistic endeavors, and good health. They have been profound role models, and continue to be so ever since they died many years ago.

Introduction

Life ultimately means taking the responsibility to find the right answer to its problems and to fulfill the tasks which it constantly sets for each individual . . . These tasks, and therefore, the meaning of life, differ from man to man, and from moment to moment. Thus it is impossible to define the meaning of life in a general way. Questions about the meaning of life can never be answered by sweeping statements. "Life" does not mean something vague, but something very real and concrete, just as life's tasks are also very real and concrete. They form man's destiny, which is different and unique for each individual. No man and no destiny can be compared with any other man or any other destiny. No situation repeats itself, and each situation calls for a different response.

—Viktor E. Frankl, *Man's Search for Meaning*

What intrigues me about adults who have lived in poverty and/or were homeless and at risk and somehow found the inner motivation to change the course of their lives in a positive direction and find their way off the streets? When and how do those who have suffered from homelessness; poverty; profound loss, grief, and pain; abuse; trauma; mental, emotional, and physical illness; jail or prison, find inspiration and courage to break the seemingly endless cycle of hopelessness, to dare to change their lives and become self-sufficient? How and why do they realize that enough is enough? What emotional price do they pay to make these changes after years of repeating old, familiar, destructive patterns? How do they learn to trust new people in their lives to help guide them on their new journey when so many others have disappointed them so many times?

These people have a vision for change. They understand that they are still poor, with many layers of problems, and live from crisis to crisis—but they do have shelter, work for pay, or volunteer. They have found new ways to cope with their fragile lives so that they are more productive, self-sufficient, contributing members of society. They still find it difficult to maintain a stable existence. Even if they improve their situations, they know how easily they could revert to their old ways at any moment. It takes tremendous fortitude to change, maintain a new lifestyle, and not slip back into old worlds and patterns. Perhaps we will never understand exactly what inspired each of them to change their lives—but we do know that they each made a profound choice for their own reasons and took giant steps to move their lives forward.

While working as the community outreach liaison at the Michigan Historical Museum in Lansing, Michigan, for many years, I developed programs with nontraditional groups of people, including adolescent teenage delinquents, the homeless, and at-risk adults and children. I curated an exhibit about immigrants and migrants based on oral histories I conducted throughout the state. I realized that all people—not just famous ones—have a story to share that involves not just facts and dates, but significant people, critical events, milestones, thoughts, and emotions. I also wrote many grants to fund our projects. Traveling on my own inner life journey—exploring family stories and issues, painting pictures and writing poetry based on images I saw within me that I could not photograph—further validated the importance of helping others to discover and share their personal stories.

Everyone has a story and no one can take that story away! Regardless of our life experiences—whether we are blessed, injured, or imprisoned, our homes and possessions destroyed or stolen—we all carry memories deep within us. We can discover our stories through talking with family members and old friends, or through our personal artifacts, historical documents, and family photographs. Sometimes society, individuals, and even our own families try to repress our stories out of fear that we will implicate them in some way. Sometimes we censor our own stories and they remain latent—perhaps the memories are too painful, frightening, or intense, or we fear rejection or reprisal. In discovering and understanding our personal histories and heritage, we become stronger, more confident individuals, more comfortable with ourselves, and can develop a deeper sense of self-value and purpose. By not living in denial, we create the opportunity to self-actualize and become more authentic. By learning about other people's stories, we become more inclusive, accepting, and less biased. Furthermore, by remembering and sharing our stories, by grieving and laughing, we can lighten our emotional and sometimes our physical burdens, and heal our innermost, vulnerable wounds.

One day in 2007, I contacted Susan Cancro, the director of Advent House Ministries (AHM), a faith-based organization and a day shelter for homeless and at-risk poor people in the greater Lansing area, to see if we could collaborate. In our discussion, we realized we could create a history program based on personal stories, artifacts, documents, and family photographs to help marginal, fragile adults, who were most at risk of losing their identity, to discover and explore their histories—similar to the programs the museum already offered to mainstream populations.

The proposed project I discussed with Susan Cancro and literacy director Toni Townshend would complement educational, job-skills, and life-skills programs, including General Education Diploma (GED) classes that participants already attended as an alternative to a high school degree program, at Advent House Ministries. Through such a partnership, the day-shelter staff could expand the opportunities it provided to their guests. The Michigan Historical Museum staff could redefine its role in community outreach to create a more inclusive society—by reaching out to all peoples. The most important ingredient that allowed such a program to develop and evolve was the trust that staff at Advent House Ministries had established with their guests.

Compared to more mainstream populations, perhaps, these people have a disproportionate number of problems, layers upon layers with which they have struggled for many years. They were born into their worlds and have dealt with their issues the best they could in childhood, young adulthood, and middle age—often with little or no intervention to break up the unhealthy, counterproductive cycles and patterns of living. However, now they are seeking assistance. Sadly, other people whose families have abandoned them are too ill and disabled mentally and/or physically to even begin to fathom how to access help.

According to author and professor of human relations James D. Wright, "The most important fact about homeless people is that they are, indeed, *people*—each with their own biographies, their own problems, and their own resources. The next most important fact is that they are *poor* people, the poorest of the poor, who live as they do largely because they lack the means to live any other way" (Wright 1989, xiv).

High-functioning people who have benefited from a good education; sufficient income, food, and shelter; with greater self-knowledge and self-esteem, are more effective in their personal and professional lives. Helping the Advent House Ministries' guests discover their life stories and those of others would not give them a diploma or a job. However, by acquiring "soft skills"—interpersonal skills or people skills—they could gain insight and confidence to become more self-respecting, secure, and independent as they pursue their education and job search.

When conceptualizing this project with my colleagues at the museum and the day shelter, I tried to research on the Internet comparable programs at other institutions for helpful ideas. While libraries and museums have special arts programs for at-risk individuals, particularly children, I had a difficult time finding existing partnerships between museums—in particular, history museums—and homeless shelters. Historical museums have the capacity to help at-risk people develop a sense of personal and community history, a sense of individual and family identity in the broader context of the state and country in which they live. It appeared that the program we would develop was unique.

What started out as a small community pilot project, "Your Story and Mine" grew into a bigger, multifaceted, innovative project designed to give voice to and empower current and formerly homeless adults in transition. The program soon took on a life of its own and traveled far. It provided an opportunity for self-expression through personal oral-history stories, art, poetry, photography, and song. The project used literacy through personal history and the arts as tools for those struggling with poverty and homelessness, and therefore most at risk of losing their identity in the community.

ProLiteracy, the largest nonprofit organization dedicated to advancing the cause of adult literacy and basic education programs in the United States, states: "Literacy is the ability to read, write, compute, and use technology at a level that enables an individual to reach his or her full potential as a parent, employee, and community member" (ProLiteracy 2012). Literacy improves the lives of adults and their families, communities, and societies. It can help end poverty, injustice, discrimination, and violence. It empowers adults to make a better life and world for themselves and their families, and to raise children who read and do better in school and life. It helps families become healthier so they can become better citizens, support themselves through work, and create a more fair and just society.

A New Partnership

Little did I know or imagine when I called Susan Cancro at Advent House Ministries, back in November 2007, what a partnership was in the making between a day shelter for the homeless and a state historical museum.

Advent House Ministries, founded in 1987, has served the economically disadvantaged in the Lansing community with invaluable services, including food, temporary housing, employment assistance, literacy programs, family services, and mental and physical health services. They also help those with disabilities to access Social Security income. Rooted in a tradition of community outreach from a faith-based perspective, over time Advent House Ministries' staff have built a solid relationship with those in need in the community. AHM's mission is "to bring together people of many faiths to build a community of hope for those who struggle with poverty and homelessness in the Lansing area. Through our programs, we provide respite from life's struggles and create opportunities for children and adults to fulfill their potential."

The Michigan Historical Museum, established in 1913, has been devoted to telling the story of Michigan's peoples and cultures through artifacts (three-dimensional objects that hold stories), photographs and documents, and oral history as shared through exhibits, hands-on activities, and educational community programs. In turn, the museum staff helps others to discover their own stories. We realized the necessity to develop educational community programs based on history for all peoples—mainstream and at-risk—and to affirm that we are here for everyone.

When I sat down to talk with Chris Dancisak, the director of community relations at the museum, to explain how I would like to develop the partnership with the day shelter, he listened intently, thought for a few minutes, and then said, with a twinkle in his eyes, "Go for it. This is important, innovative, and rare community outreach work that the museum needs to engage in. However, realize that other museum staff might be nervous to work with this population." Shortly thereafter, I began to work with Toni Townshend and Allyson Bolt at Advent House Ministries to create, develop, and implement a program we called "Your Story and Mine."

Toni later said that

> Our vision for "Your Story and Mine" was to clear the stereotypical perception of homelessness and to create community dialogue about the struggle of the poverty-stricken. With the help of our team, we exceeded our own high expectations in fulfilling that vision. The program participants were the most important element of the entire program. Before a video camera, they spoke honestly and courageously of the hardships they had endured. Each story about addiction, mental illness, abuse, physical impairment, was unique and riveting. They looked upon their artwork as a way to express themselves and help the community to understand them better.

A history-museum setting for classes is an ideal learning environment for these people to discover their past, as they can move freely through the galleries. No one instructs them to sit down at desks, fill out work sheets, and read uninspiring texts. In 1983, Howard Gardner, PhD, a professor of education at Harvard University, developed a theory about multiple intelligences—including, but not limited to, linguistic, logical-mathematical, spatial, bodily-kinesthetic, musical, interpersonal, intrapersonal, and naturalistic intelligences. He writes:

> Human cognitive competence is better described in terms of a set of abilities, talents, or mental skills which I call intelligences. All normal individuals possess each of these skills to some extent; individuals differ in the degree of skill and in the nature of their combination. . . . This theory of intelligence may be more humane and more veridical than alternative views of intelligence and . . . it more adequately reflects the data of human "intelligent" behavior. Such a theory has important educational implications. (Gardner 1993, 6)

Learning in a museum setting complements Gardner's theory about the importance of multiple intelligences. Individuals who are not traditional learners have greater opportunities to maximize the learning experience when they are not required to sit at a desk in a traditional classroom setting and can explore other learning skills.

We designed the program so that participants would come to the museum every two weeks, and tour the exhibits led by museum staff to learn about other people's past through observing artifacts, documents, and photographs. In turn, they learned to discover their own stories and their importance. They learned how to interview each other about their life stories. They toured behind the scenes in the State Archives, where they examined original documents and records. They learned how to discover their family and genealogical history at the State Library of Michigan. We introduced them to archaeology and the history of Native Americans—the first peoples in Michigan. They also learned about the differences between drawing from imagination, memory, and what they see. They went on field trips to Michigan State University's museum and art gallery, and to Old Town in Lansing, where they took photographs and had a picnic lunch.

In assisting these formerly homeless adults in transition to gain a sense of personal history, develop a deeper understanding and appreciation of their heritage, identify key facts about family history, and reinforce understanding of personal value within the community, this project's goal, at its foundation, was to engage nontraditional groups of people in creating a more inclusive society. It specifically used the building blocks of history—personal oral history, artifacts, historical documents, and family photographs.

Participants became more aware of the importance of their lives, developed a deeper understanding and appreciation of their heritage and a better sense of themselves, learned to share their stories orally and through written words, and became more empowered as they traveled on their life journeys. They developed a deeper sense of self-value and life purpose, a better concept of their heritage, and a consciousness of their place in history. They began to understand past social challenges and solutions, and evaluated their present experiences in order to seek positive resolutions for the future.

We could safely assume that the participants were nervous about sharing their stories. However, we were also afraid and not completely sure of our path, not knowing if we could or would realize our vision. While the participants generously shared their stories through a variety of media, we too benefited profoundly from this opportunity—much as Steve Lopez did when he wrote *The Soloist*, a true story (which became a movie) about his relationship with a musician, Nathaniel Ayres, who was homeless. Repeatedly, participants showed each of us the way we needed to go and how we needed to get there.

Early on during a sharing time in the original pilot project "Your Story and Mine," one person provided much inspiration and impetus that profoundly validated what we hoped to accomplish. As a forty-five-year-old woman, she shared a story about her 109-year-old grandmother, whose parents had been slaves on a plantation in Marvel, Arkansas. Her grandparents had then become sharecroppers on the same farm. The story had appeared in an alternative newspaper, the *Lansing (Michigan) Star*, in the 1970s. She had fond memories of regular family visits with "Grandma." She had kept the article for some time, but it burned along with all her other family photographs and memorabilia when a fire ravaged her apartment. As soon as class was over that day, I went to the stacks in the Library of Michigan on the other side of the museum building. There, I found a copy of the newspaper with the story.

The article not only had the photograph of her grandmother, but of her father as well. Our museum exhibit designer, Steve Ostrander, laminated the article and we presented it to her at the next class. She laughed. She cried. She yowled, "Daddy, I now have a photograph of my Daddy. I had lost my family photographs in my fire."

At the time of the fire in her apartment, I can only imagine what great loss and devastation she must have felt. What an amazing sense of fulfillment and satisfaction she must have had that day when seeing the two photographs of her father and grandmother once again. She was the first, but certainly not the last, participant to lead us on our new journey. Unknowingly, she also empowered us to realize the importance of our work together.

When I shared the story with my husband, Alan, he noticed that the now well-known writer Alex Kotlowitz had written the article. Apparently, Kotlowitz's first journalism job after graduating from Wesleyan College, in Connecticut, was to work for the *Lansing Star*. Kotlowitz has since written several books about poverty, beginning with his first one, *There Are No Children Here: The Story of Two Boys Growing Up in the Other America.*

Sociologist Kai Erikson wrote about the uprooted community of people who lost their homes and personal belongings in an Appalachian flood when a dam broke in Buffalo Creek, West Virginia, in 1972. Many died or were severely injured. Many witnessed the deaths of their family and friends.

> People lost possessions of considerable meaning to them. . . . Objects such as family Bibles or photographs, a father's favorite gun or a mother's proudest embroidery, had a place in the household almost like holy relics, and their loss was deeply mourned. They were a link to the past. . . . These goods are more than a form of decoration or a cushion against want; they are . . . the furniture of self. . . . To lose a home or the sum of one's belongings . . . is to lose evidence of who one is and where one belongs in the world. (Erikson 1976, 175–77)

Another middle-aged woman who came to "Your Story and Mine" said that her mother had forbidden her to fill out any information sheets about her life history at the museum because we were a government agency and would use the information against her as she had "done time" in prison. She loved classes and said that she learned things she never would have gotten a chance to learn—such as the fact that she was named after her great-grandmother. She was dutiful to her mother, but we realized then that maybe she would be willing to draw some of her life stories and share her history without compromising her integrity. Furthermore, when a local newspaper reporter from Lansing's *City Pulse* came to visit the class and interview different participants, she readily agreed to talk with him. She further validated our decision to use art as an option for self-expression when we conceptualized the larger project.

We concluded the initial program with a celebratory full-course luncheon at the museum, with complimentary catering by Old Country Kitchen, a for-profit caterer, in Lansing. Participants read their stories to the class—many of whom had never spoken before a group. Brandy, a music savant who plays half a dozen instruments and performs in her church weekly, sang a spiritual song to the group.

Chris Dancisak said,

> What inspired me at the celebration luncheon was the big joy in the eyes of the participants. Some of them cried that they had accomplished something in an educational vein that they probably had never accomplished before. I

suspected that the struggle of those who participated that day and read some of the materials that they had written probably was the first time that they ever had communicated to a group of people of any size about anything that they had ever actually written.

I suspect that many of the folks did not participate in the classroom when they were in school, and certainly if they did it was about what year was the Declaration of Independence signed or something like that, but nothing to do with any feelings from the heart and the soul. And I think what they were doing that day was expressing their heart and soul in the way that they communicated to the folks who were there. Part of that may have been that they were dealing with a smaller group setting than they were in a classroom, but I suspect there was a lot more than that. I think that they were focused on their own lives and the lives of the people around them and whatever they found in that soul-searching effort.

Building on Success

When our program ended, we were both sad and happy. We all realized we had only barely begun our new journey together. Susan Cancro asked me about the possibility of having the participants paint a mural of their life stories for the walls at Advent House Ministries. I told her that it was a great idea, but suggested that they paint the mural on a separate canvas so that it would be permanent and so we could take it on tour. If they painted their images directly on the wall, tomorrow someone could paint over it. Our momentum resumed!

We applied for and received a grant from the Michigan Humanities Council to implement "Your Story and Mine: A Community of Hope." The project involved several main components: (1) oral history interviews with participants; (2) a DVD of the oral history interviews; and (3) a mural that would include the participants' paintings, poems, and photographs. The exhibit of their creative endeavors then went on tour to libraries and local history organizations throughout Michigan.

The Oral Histories

Advent House Ministries staff and volunteers establish a trust with those people who attend their programs. This fosters good will, and it facilitated the participants' willingness and ability to share their life stories with us, knowing also that others would listen to their stories. Allyson and I conducted these oral history interviews. Their stories have become the foundation material for this book. Video producer/technical writer Peter Frahm videotaped each interview at Lansing Community College and made a DVD based on them that is in numerous local libraries throughout Michigan.

In the interviews, the participants all talked about growing up in poverty in their families of origin, challenges they faced as children and adults, precipitating factors that caused them to become homeless in the past, and how they found their way out of homelessness. Willingly, openly, and honestly, they shared their stories about their lack of resources—monetary, emotional, psychological, physical, and/or educational—without personal, familial, or social support. Some had served in the military. They acknowledged problems with hunger, lack of shelter, abuse, grief and hopelessness, trauma, drug and alcohol addiction, and encounters with the law.

Sometimes they chose to leave home. Sometimes other people, including family members, evicted them. While growing up in their family of origin, they had no mental health intervention. Once they became adults and began their own families, their overwhelming, complex emotional and psychological issues compounded. While one ultimate crisis might have pushed them out on the streets as adults, it was often the culmination of years of child and/or adolescent trauma, homelessness, mental and emotional illness, job loss, low self-esteem, poverty, grief and loss, abuse (including self-abuse), drug and/or alcohol addiction, and trouble with the law—or a combination of any of these variables. Through the years, they had not developed the internal psychological and emotional skills to cope with multiple extraordinary life events, nor had they benefited from any professional support. Their lives are still very fragile, and they know that they could fall back into that unpredictable world at any given time.

As adults, they each acknowledged they needed help and wanted to follow their inner voices to make positive changes. When and how do they ask for help and access human social services? How did they understand that literacy was the major key to break the endless, hopeless cycle? They wanted to become literate, to study for their GEDs, to learn new life skills and job skills, to find transitional housing and employment so that they could become independent and self-sufficient. They accessed social services to help break the cycle of poverty and hopelessness and to make a better life for themselves and their children. Specifically, they discovered Advent House Ministries, their staff and programs.

Because of their vulnerable feelings of low self-esteem and failure, which they had had for years, they did not know how or if they could alter the direction of their lives in a meaningful way. Some were estranged from their families. Their lives at home had been very painful emotionally. Some had graduated from high school; others had not. Some had dropped out as teenagers and left home to go to work. Some had spent time in a juvenile detention center, jail, or prison.

By participating in "Your Story and Mine: A Community of Hope," these individuals had an opportunity to share their stories at length and in depth, and to understand that they are important and valuable. Toni announced the project to many attendees at programs at Advent House Ministries. The people who actually decided to participate to tell their stories through words and paintings were self-selected. They trusted their mentors and had great courage and inner strength that empowered them to take this giant step to share their stories through a variety of media. Having understood that telling their stories was important to them, to us, and ultimately to the community at large, and knowing that it would not be an easy endeavor, they agreed to participate for the year and did so honestly, graciously, and consistently. The idea behind the project was that if they could take new steps and tell and share their stories, they could develop inner confidence that could empower them to take new steps in other spheres of their lives. Their involvement in this project reflected an unusually profound resilience that fostered a determination and courage to move their lives forward.

Psychologist Donald Meichenbaum wrote:

> Resilience, "the ability to rebound from adversities" is tied to the ability to learn to live with ongoing fear and uncertainty, namely, the ability to show positive adaptation in spite of significant life adversities and the ability to adapt to difficult and challenging life experiences. . . .
>
> In short, resilience turns victims into survivors and allows survivors to thrive. Resilient individuals can get distressed, but they are able to manage the negative behavioral outcomes in the face of risks without becoming debilitated. (Meichenbaum 2012)

These people all had hopes, dreams, and goals for the near and distant future. Their dreams came in all forms, shapes, and sizes—some concrete, some abstract. Many had an almost wistful, longing tone in their voices as they shared their stories. Sometimes, their eyes glowed as they smiled. Like all people, they dream of the future but do not know for sure if they can attain their goals. During the program, some individuals attained short-term goals. Some were surprised and overjoyed that they had achieved them. Sometimes, one success created a ripple effect. Some shared their sense of humor.

> Progress can be hard to recognize, especially if our expectations are unrealistically high. If we expect our negative attitudes or unhealthy behavior to change

quickly and completely, we are likely to be disappointed—progress is hard to see when we measure ourselves against idealized standards. Perhaps it would be better to compare ourselves only to where we had been in the past. . . . Today I am no longer seeking perfection; the only thing that matters is the direction in which I'm moving. (*Courage to Change* 1992, 76)

The Traveling Exhibit

Under the guidance of Erika Magers, professional artist, muralist, and art-therapist-in-training at Wayne State University, participants attended art classes at Advent House Ministries. Our team of mentors, along with several university interns, supported and validated the participants and their work. The classes culminated in their painting pictures on canvases of their experiences with homelessness. Erika then sewed their paintings into a large mural.

The exhibit *Your Story and Mine: A Community of Hope* opened at a private celebration at Perspective 2 Gallery in Old Town, Lansing. Participants, mentors, Advent House Ministries board members, and donors attended. We honored the artists with certificates of completion for their participation in "Your Story and Mine: A Community of Hope." Two participants, David R. and Brandy, also performed music.

The exhibit formally opened at City Hall in Lansing, Michigan, in November 2009, during National Homelessness Month. It included the mural, additional paintings, photographs, six individual panels with excerpts from the oral histories and photographs, and a fifty-minute DVD with segments from the oral history interviews.

Then, numerous libraries, historical societies, and museums—including those in Lansing, Gaylord, Saginaw, Marquette, Charlevoix, Petoskey, Grand Rapids, Kalamazoo, Traverse City, and Manistique—hosted the exhibit for a month at a time where we presented talks. We also asked that each site invite an individual from the community who works on poverty issues to stimulate a discussion and awareness of homelessness. Our team also developed an educational guide, available on the website for Advent House Ministries for other communities to replicate or adapt.

In anecdotes from libraries and historical societies, and through a simple questionnaire evaluation completed at library sites we observed many positive outcomes. The Saginaw Public Library created booklets for children and adults to work on together at a community shelter. The Peter White Public Library in Marquette partnered with the Marquette County History Museum on a project to involve middle-school students, who did oral histories with the elderly in their community and then displayed their stories with the exhibit. An English teacher at the Manistique Public Library asked students to view the exhibit and write their thoughts and feelings in their journals about what they had seen and read. The local newspaper then published their journal entries. Gaylord's Otsego County Library created the "Shine the Light Project." They asked a number of sponsors to purchase lamps, and held a creative workshop on decorating lampshades. Those who participated in the workshop then donated the lamps to the local shelter so that each family in the shelter received a lamp. Additional communities continue to host the exhibit. The possibilities to expand this project are infinite, as "everyone has a story!"

EVALUATION OF THE PROJECT

We cannot scientifically prove if, how, and to what extent "Your Story and Mine" positively affected these people with regard to literacy, critical thinking, and problem-solving skills, but we do have evidence that this project contributed to their personal life successes—based on staff observations as well as a more formal qualitative assessment. Some program participants already had begun to make changes in their lives prior to participating in this program. Nevertheless, "Your Story and Mine" provided one more avenue that they chose to pursue on their journey of hope, and served as both a facilitating and reinforcing experience.

Two classes of graduate students, under the direction of Associate Professor Gail Vander Stoep from the Department of Community, Agriculture, Recreation, and Resource Studies at Michigan State University, evaluated the project as part of course requirements for ACR 873: "Culture, Communities and Tourism," which further validated our endeavor. In the first year, they used a multipronged, qualitative approach to develop a conceptual framework based on content analysis of grant language, project reports from museum staff, and other relevant written documents. Potential impact factors were structured within a literature-based conceptual framework that included three progressive stages of impacts: knowledge and awareness; personal attitudinal and behavioral change; and group transformation. The students participated in "Your Story and Mine" classes that guests from Advent House Ministries attended. Using participant observation techniques, they observed several positive effects on project participants, and reported project impacts on institutional and organizational levels that related to capacity building and inter-institutional networking.

In the initial report, David Dilworth, Ju Hyoung Han, and Eric Bailey determined that participants gained new knowledge and awareness through the learning experience, which is reflective of "breakthroughs," or changes in their cognitive state. Participants also developed new insights about family history and historical connections, and made social connections between and among program participants and staff. This allowed for the generation of a feeling of belonging and the freedom to share affection, such as hugging each other.

The graduate students explained that some participants reestablished family connections using enhanced social skills generated through the program. Some received family support in recognition of their quest for positive engagement, and some had the opportunity to rebuild damaged relationships. This provided an additional support structure for the participants to exert greater control over and make positive changes in their personal lives that sometimes precipitated a renewed appreciation for life. Program providers reported on the high levels of motivation displayed by participants, as shown through their punctuality, consistent attendance, and keen participation.

In sharing their findings, one student also told this touching story. One day, Ju Hyoung, who had recently come from Korea to study as a graduate student at Michigan State University, was riding the city bus in Lansing. She herself was feeling rather lonely and isolated in her new surroundings. Several African American participants from the class coincidentally also were riding the same bus that day. Ju Hyoung already had attended many of the "Your Story and Mine" classes, but also had missed a couple of them. The participants ran over to her, hugged her, and told her how much they had missed her at the last class and wondered where she had been. This spontaneous expression of friendship illustrates the trust that Advent House Ministries had established with participants, which had spread not only to museum staff and volunteers but also to the university graduate students. Neither race nor ethnicity inhibited people from interacting with one another.

The students also discussed the program's impacts on the organizers, who learned how to overcome the reluctance of some participants to engage fully in the program. By removing obstacles to participation (e.g., providing rides or bus money to address the lack of transportation to and from events), they demonstrated their sincerity to participants; this, in turn, reinforced a sense of trust among staff, volunteers, and participants. They realized that this population was eager to learn about history and art and to document their personal stories. Some participants demonstrated an advanced grasp of art and/or music. Organizers from Advent House Ministries gained a greater appreciation for oral-history interviewing techniques, and the Michigan Historical Museum organizers gained a greater appreciation of the obstacles facing the homeless population. Both groups gained a greater appreciation for video as a tool for fostering understanding of a particular group of people. Organizers also gained much personal satisfaction from seeing the personal growth of the "Your Story and Mine" participants.

The second group of MSU students—Jayne Goeddeke, Eun Jeong Noh, and Anna Stein—analyzed results of face-to-face interviews conducted by the first group with several of the program participants who had been involved in one or more multi-week programs. Analysis of the interview transcripts reflected self-reported positive impacts of the program consistent with the higher-level stages of the conceptual framework ("personal attitude and behavior change" and "group transformation"). "Personal attitude and behavior change" factors were shown primarily through improved self-esteem (confidence to speak up and various expressions of personal growth) and through creative self-expression. The most frequently reported positive impacts were associated with "group transformation," and were expressed in subcategories of confidence in personal mentorship ability, general relationship building, and opportunities for networking. Students reported that participants valued the staff's kindness, respect, and positive attitudes. They felt confident that they could mentor future participants. The program helped them build positive relationships with their peers in class and empowered them to make positive changes in their lives outside the program.

One participant said, "They were people trying to do something instead of, 'Oh, where we gonna get the next bag of weed?'"

Another said, "I'm not fighting. I'm not carrying guns. I'm not involved with that type of scenery or that type of actions, you know, drugs, or anything like that. So, it's like that's a change there."

MSU students further reported that the participants enjoyed the social activities with the staff and their peers. They liked learning new tools for personal growth, developing self-confidence, and finding their voice to express their own thoughts and feelings.

Additionally, participants identified a variety of program components that particularly excited them. They appreciated the variety of fun, hands-on activities in which they participated. They would like to see additional offerings. External to the formal evaluation, participants also said they developed a sense of belonging with the community; an appreciation for past social challenges as a basis for evaluating current problems and identifying potential solutions; greater independence, self-sufficiency, and understanding of their individual potentials as they transition from homelessness; and a positive outlook on life. Participants were grateful for the opportunities this project gave them.

Impacts of the program extended beyond the participants themselves as their work, in turn, impacted others in communities throughout Michigan. Integrating an art component in the program and mounting a traveling display, incorporating some of the art, highlighted the issue of homelessness and provided this opportunity to impact several Michigan communities. Use of program participants' art, words, and stories in this traveling display further perpetuates the positive reinforcement of the participants' endeavors. Additionally, program participants transitioned from personally showing their work in an enclosed environment to public forums through a variety of activities, including a private show at Perspectitve2 Art Gallery in Lansing's Old Town.

"Your Story and Mine: A Community of Hope" Becomes a World Community Event

Through our endeavors, we realized that "Your Story and Mine: A Community of Hope" has universal appeal, can be adapted to any population, and has the potential to expand. Our team often envisioned sharing the program with other countries, as we knew its benefits were great for those people who struggle with day-to-day challenges of survival wherever they live—but we never imagined in our wildest dreams that it could travel as quickly and as far as it did.

Geneva Wiskemann, founder and secretary of the Michigan Oral History Association and our project advisor for the oral history component, invited me to give a presentation about the project at the Michigan Oral History Conference in Marquette, Michigan, in September 2009. She then encouraged me to give a paper at the International Oral History Association Conference in Prague in the Czech Republic, in July 2010.

While "Googling" homelessness in Prague, I discovered Ilja Hradecký, founder and director of the nongovernmental organization Nadeje ("Hope") in the Czech Republic. His colleague Aftab Hladikova, a social scientist, and I communicated via email for several months and organized a day-long symposium on the homeless that the American Embassy hosted in Prague. Public affairs officer Helena Vagnerova organized the event and arranged for the embassy to fund two translators for the symposium, for which we are all very grateful. She hung photographs of the Lansing participants' artwork on the walls of the American Embassy and photographs by a well-known Czech photographer, Jan Přerovský, who took photographs of the homeless in the Czech Republic. After the symposium, two Nadeje social workers gave my husband, Alan, and me a tour of the shelters in Prague.

Ilja Hradecký and his late wife, Vlastimila Hradecká, were the first people to address the issue of homelessness in the Czech Republic, in 1990, after the Communists left. They began to feed the Roma or gypsies, refugees from Rumania who lived by the railroad station in Prague. As time passed, they also began to feed the hungry

Czech people. Today, Nadeje is a national organization that helps the homeless, the elderly, orphans, and those people with developmental disabilities throughout the Czech Republic. His current wife, Martina, now also works with him.

Through my experiences with "Your Story and Mine: A Community of Hope," I have realized that the homeless may speak different languages whether they live in Lansing, Prague, or anywhere else in the world, but they share similar life experiences—a belief from which this book has developed.

Furthermore, while I have taken the initiative to write this book to preserve these people's stories, it has necessarily been a group venture, involving many mentors and participants. We made this profound journey together through everybody's participation, commitment, and hard work, and we all believed in the importance of sharing "our story" with others.

Those of us who created and implemented the program "Your Story and Mine: A Community of Hope" did not know exactly how the project would evolve, or if it could work. While we were excited, enthusiastic, and positive, deep down inside we were all afraid. We know that we have all changed in ways that we may never be able to understand or articulate—we bonded with one another and with the participants. I believe both mentors and participants have traveled on a sacred journey that we will always honor and treasure.

Outgrowths of the program now include an art workshop that Erika Magers teaches to adults at Advent House Ministries. Chris Dancisak now volunteers as assistant literacy director at Advent House Ministries.

Since I retired from the Michigan Historical Museum, I teach a writing workshop to formerly homeless adults at Advent House Ministries, who continuously inspire me. It complements their GED classes at Advent House Ministries. I had read an article, "Hungry Minds: Tales from a Chelsea Soup Kitchen" (May 28, 2008), by Ian Frazier, a staff writer at the *New Yorker* magazine, about an inspirational writing workshop he has taught for more than fourteen years at a soup kitchen in New York City. His work inspired me to offer a comparable opportunity for people who attended the Advent House Ministries.

In my writing workshop, I provide support to help them develop self-confidence in their GED classes and other spheres of their lives and a greater capacity for self-expression. I have a few rules in the class: they may not criticize themselves, use cell phones, or tap pencils—because it drives me nuts! I have each student share a bit about their week, and then give them a writing prompt that allows for freedom and creativity to empower them and give them a sense of ownership. Those who are willing then read their piece at the end of the class. While I review their stories each week and provide minor editorial written comments, I tell them I will not be judgmental and will not grade them. They also provide supportive, nonjudgmental comments to each other about their writing and life journeys. The beauty of this workshop is that it is not a requirement for anything else. Therefore, people come because they want to come. Is that not the quintessential beauty of learning and motivation? I thank them for coming to class and encourage them to continue to come.

Assignments vary greatly, including such topics as "a place where you used to live," "a favorite person," "a favorite food," "a favorite season," "If," "Hope," "I wonder why," and "If an elderly gentleman or woman walks up to you on the street and asks for help . . ." and "I woke up one night and the moon was shining in my room." I ask them to elaborate as much as possible and to explain the "why" in each choice they make. Sometimes, they choose to write on their own topics, which reveals a greater sense of confidence.

I told them about my high school English teacher who helped me so much when I was floundering and nearly flunking English, and who told me that if I wanted to learn to write well that I needed to read and write a lot. My current students are not part of the original "Your Story and Mine" project. A core group has been coming consistently for a year. Now, new ones come. Some stay for a while and then move on. Their writing is often amazingly thoughtful, refreshing, profound, beautiful, and quite philosophical.

Recently, in class, one of my regular students, Eraclio, handed each of us bookmarks he picked up at the local public library. He also shared with me a book he has been reading of short stories about monsters by famous authors. This was a first for me. While they wrote their stories that day, I read one of the short stories. I was so happy he was expanding my horizons.

One of Eraclio's short essays still haunts me. He is only in his twenties.

When I was walking down the street, I saw a leaf and thought, "Whew, my life is changing." I was a kid then I was a teenager and now I'm a man and my life is great. A lot of hierarchy to it. Next step old man. This time the leaf was brown and dried out. On my part, weakened and grey, I learned that's the way of life but the trail remains. It's up to us which path we choose. No path is a wrong path. It's just a future journey of ourselves.

Another student, Andrew, who has been writing an amazing play, began an essay with "I looked up at the sky, and had a beautiful thought. As I gazed into the dark night sky, it was filled with stars. The air so fresh with its cool breeze. I wondered what the earth may have looked like millions of years ago." He continues, "I imagine in this state of pure solitude a peace. I find I can see clearer, and am totally in tune to the bats and the sound of the wind that normally goes unnoticed. I can hear my breaths, my inner thoughts, sends me to an unchartered distance. I have peace here."

Another student, Krista, wrote: "Life doesn't seem too bad when you can look out and see the sun shining, birds singing, people walking by. Even when it rains, it looks nice."

The late anthropologist Elliot Liebow stressed the importance of understanding other people's lives that are different from ours. He does not believe that those who have a home and family "can see and feel the world" of the homeless. However, he believes that "it is reasonable and useful to try to do so. Trying to put oneself in the place of the other lies at the heart of the social contract and of social life itself" (Liebow 1993, xv).

The participants in this project were all thoughtful and philosophical. They know now that in order to get a good job, they must pass their GED. Many discovered new skills and talents and believe that education is an important key to opening new doors. They are grateful to their mentors who have helped them. Many of them volunteer to help others who have experienced life on the streets with emotional or psychological problems and are still homeless. Their stories tell you where they have been, how they see themselves now, and where they would like to be.

In piecing these stories together, I have not changed their words (except in rare instances for clarity) or the way in which they expressed themselves. I have sequenced their stories in an order that was clearer, organized their thoughts, and deleted repetition. Some talked at greater length and depth than others, depending on the specific questions. *My Eyes Feel They Need to Cry* follows the stories of eight participants—Wynette, Lewis, Robert, David, Jackie, Bill, Dora, and Loren. The focus of the interviews is on their past lives and not on their current lives or the lives of their children, although clearly in many instances they talk about them. In addition to these eight people's stories and art, I also feature several other participants' artwork. Also included are their mentors' thoughts.

Join me now on this special journey and discover these people's stories through words, art, photography, and music.

A Canvas of Homelessness

Aside from extreme poverty and the absence of stable housing, there is no single characteristic that all homeless people share. Some are old men, some are young women, some, indeed, are infants and children. . . .

Amidst the obvious heterogeneity of the homeless, however, three salient and widespread conditions do stand out: first, the extreme level of poverty characteristic of the group; second, the high levels of disabilities of all sorts; and third, the excessive degree of social isolation common to most, if not all.

—James D. Wright, *Address Unknown: The Homeless in America*

Who Are the Homeless?

Homelessness does not discriminate against color, race, size, class, ethnicity, sex, religion, or political affiliation. It affects the young and old—children, parents, and grandparents. Homeless people live all over the world—in rural, urban, and suburban areas, in both heavily populated and isolated areas. As economic resources diminish, the number of homeless people continues to rise. One third of the homeless in the United States are veterans. Typically and stereotypically, a homeless person is someone at risk who grew up in poverty or homelessness with an unsupportive family, with few or no educational or financial opportunities or resources. Some have repeatedly experienced early childhood, adolescent, and adult trauma; physical, emotional, and/ or psychological abuse; and domestic violence. They may be mentally ill and/or addicted to alcohol and/or other drugs, and may have served time in juvenile detention homes, jail, or prison. They have little or no access to medical, dental, or mental health services.

While I worked with other mentors and mentees and now reflect on the issues of poverty and homelessness, recurrent questions revolve in my mind. Why does an individual become homeless? In Michigan? the United States? and all over the world? Why does a safety net not exist to protect individuals, families, and society? While similar themes may ripple through these people's narratives, they each have their own individual story—like theme and variations in a musical symphony.

In *Address Unknown: The Homeless in America*, James D. Wright said, "In painting the picture of homelessness in America today, poverty, inadequate housing, personal disabilities and the like are the pigments, but the destruction of social networks is the brush" (Wright 1989, 90).

Sociologist Peter H. Rossi talks about how easy it is to cross the line between "those with homes and the literally homeless." He writes,

> A life of extreme poverty is one of extreme vulnerability. For most Americans it is easy to roll with all but the major punches life can give; most of us can absorb the shocks of illness and unemployment up to a point. A few months of unemployment or a week in the hospital are serious, but most people have enough financial and psychological reserves to survive either without becoming destitute or deeply depressed. Among the extremely poor, however, the many untoward events that the rest of us absorb can be major shocks catapulting them across the blurred line between having a home and being homeless. For the extremely poor, with no reserves of savings, no safety net of entitlements, and no credit cards, losing a few days' wages or catching a severe cold can mean losing a job, going without adequate food, or getting evicted. Events of this sort can trigger an episode of homelessness. Being homeless is a considerable notch below having a home although being extremely poor. And getting back among the domiciled population is not easy for someone with essentially zero resources. (Rossi 1989, 9)

The canvas of homelessness has many different images and is multidimensional. Toni Townshend and Allyson Bolt, both mentors for this project, talked about three different kinds of homelessness. Most homeless people have grown up in troubled or broken homes with a single parent who was unmarried, divorced, or widowed. They are the *generationally homeless*. Sometimes grandparents, aunts, or adoptive or foster parents raised them. Some lack emotional and physical nurturing and appear to have few inner psychological resources and tools to fend for themselves.

Sometimes, realizing it is unsafe—emotionally or physically—to live with family members, they leave home, drop out of high school, and try to get a job. However, since most have no job skills or jobs, they cannot pay rent for housing. Often they then find illegal jobs. Usually, they suffer from more than one profound difficult or traumatic event in their lives—often repeated traumas in themes and variations.

According to sociologist Christopher Jencks, even when we want to help our mentally ill relatives, somehow, sadly, they do not always let us.

> The mentally ill are most likely to be on the streets. But that does not mean their relatives are more selfish than earlier generations of relatives were. The mentally ill often refuse to live with relatives. Even those who say they are willing to do so are often unwilling or unable to behave in ways that would allow their hosts to live anything remotely like a normal life. That was also the case in the nineteenth century, which was one reason legislation created mental hospitals. (Jencks 1995, 79–80)

They constantly move from one situation to another without stability or the possibility of returning to a home or environment that they can call their own on a short- or long-term basis. They ultimately land on the streets, live in shelters, motels, or Volunteers of America (VOA) facilities.

In the late 1970s, an increasing number of people slept in public places, wandered the streets with their personal items in shopping carts, searched for food in garbage bins, and begged for money. This trend continued in the ensuing decades. "It is a combination of personal vulnerability and political indifference that has left people on the streets" (Jencks 1995, 48).

According to Jencks, the social and political changes that contributed to the increase in homelessness in the 1980s and 1990s were "the virtual abolition of involuntary commitment for the mentally ill, failure to provide alternative housing for many of those we deinstitutionalized, the crack epidemic, increased long-term joblessness among working-age men, the declining frequency of marriage among women with children, reductions in cash welfare benefits, and the destruction of skid row" (Jencks 1995, vi).

More recently, in the first decade of the twenty-first century, because of the recession and tough economic times, homelessness is also hitting middle-class families. These families have suddenly lost their homes because they have lost their jobs and subsequently failed to pay their rent or mortgage, or because of natural disasters such as a volcano, tornado, or earthquake. They are *situational homeless* people. Those individuals who are fortunate enough to live with family or friends are *couch-homeless*.

Toni Townshend said, "Currently, we see new faces of people—middle class people—come into the shelter who have never come before. That's an enlightenment for some people. It's sad to see. They come in and look like the deer in the headlights!"

According to a CBS *60 Minutes* program aired in 2011,

> Unemployment continues to hover around 9 percent and job creation is so slow. It'll be years before we get back the seven and a half million jobs lost in the Great Recession. American families have been falling out of the middle class in record numbers.
>
> The combination of lost jobs and millions of foreclosures means a lot of folks are homeless and hungry for the first time in their lives. One of the consequences of the recession that you don't hear much about is the record number of children descending into poverty. The government considers a family of four to be impoverished if they take in less than $22,000 a year. Based on that standard, and the government projections of unemployment, it is estimated that the poverty rate for kids in this country will soon hit 25 percent. . . . Those children would be the largest American generation to be raised in hard times since the Great Depression. (CBS, *60 Minutes* 2011).

Because of these hard times, increasingly some young adult children have moved back in with their parents. Some are single, some married, and some have children. "A recent survey by the Pew Research Center finds that 13% of parents with grown children say one of their adult sons or daughters has moved back home in the past year. Social scientists call them 'boomerangers'—young adults who move in with parents after living away from home. This recession has produced a bumper crop" (Taylor 2009).

A recent series of stories on National Public Radio (NPR) reported that increasingly, aging parents who were once healthy and self-sufficient are no longer able to take care of themselves when they have mental, physical, and/or financial difficulties. Many are moving in with their middle-aged sons and daughters, and their families provide personal, medical, and financial long-term care for them. More and more families have become multi-generational (Geewax 2012).

The National Coalition for the Homeless (NCH) says that "two trends are largely responsible for the rise in homelessness over the past 20–25 years: a growing shortage of affordable rental housing and a simultaneous increase in poverty. . . . Recently, foreclosures have increased the number of people who experience homelessness"

(NCH 2009a). The NCH also says that homelessness persists because of stagnant or falling incomes, less secure jobs that offer fewer benefits, the declining value and availability of public assistance, limited scale of housing assistance programs, lack of affordable healthcare, domestic violence, mental illnesses, and addiction disorders.

Homelessness and poverty are inextricably linked. Poor people are frequently unable to pay for housing, food, childcare, health care and education. Difficult choices must be made when limited resources cover only some of these necessities. Often, it is housing, which absorbs a high proportion of income that must be dropped. If you are poor, you are essentially an illness, an accident, or a paycheck away from living on the streets.

In 2007, 12.5% of the United States population or 37,300,000 people lived in poverty. Children are overrepresented, composing 35.7% of people in poverty while only being 24.8% of the total population. (NCH 2009a)

Additionally, the NCH says, based on data from the Centers for Disease Control and Prevention (CDC), that

the conditions of homelessness may increase the risk of contracting HIV. A disproportionately large number of homeless people suffer from substance abuse disorders. Many homeless people inject drugs intravenously, and may share or reuse needles. This practice is responsible for 13% of HIV/AIDS diagnoses in the United States. An additional 50% of cases are a result of male-to-male sexual contact, and 33% are due to heterosexual sex. (NCH 2009b)

The increasing number of homeless women and children is another major phenomenon that is transpiring across America. The National Center on Family Homelessness (NCFH)—a nonprofit organization that works to end family homelessness, and that designs, pilots, and evaluates innovative programs and services that provide long-term solutions for family homelessness—completed a recent report, *Homeless Children, America's New Outcasts*. It states that family homelessness is a new social problem:

Except during the Great Depression, women and children have never been on our nation's streets in significant numbers. During the 1980's, cutbacks in benefits coupled with rapidly increasing rents and a dearth of low-income housing jeopardized the stability of all people with reduced or fixed incomes. At the same time, the number of female-headed households dramatically increased. As a result, the nation's population of homeless families swelled from almost negligible numbers to nearly 40% of the overall homeless population today. The United States is unique among industrialized nations in that women and children comprise such a large percentage of our country's homeless. (NCFH n.d.)

Furthermore, the NCFH says that more than one million children are homeless and that family homelessness will only continue to increase. The NCFH also explains that homelessness makes children sick—it is a direct predictor of specific childhood illness. It wounds young children because they confront stressful, traumatic events with the anxiety of not having a place to live and no place to sleep, and so they struggle in school. They believe something bad will happen to their family. Homelessness devastates families.

While various national and state organizations conduct studies of the numbers of homeless people in the United States, they find it very difficult to get precise figures. The NCH reports that some people live on the street, some in emergency housing, some in transitional housing, and others in permanent supportive housing. Most are temporarily homeless. Some live with family and friends. Some are permanently homeless. The homeless population includes single people, families, and unaccompanied minors. The National Law Center on Homelessness and Poverty states: "Each year, more than 3 million people experience homelessness, including 1.3 million children" (NLCPH n.d.).

According to the Children's Defense Fund, which evolved from the Civil Rights Movement under the leadership of Marian Wright Edelman, the first black woman admitted to the Mississippi Bar,

> More than 16.4 million children in America are poor, but they live in working families. A disproportionate number are Black and Latino. Poor children lag behind their peers in many ways beyond income: They are less healthy, trail in emotional and intellectual development, and are less likely to graduate from high school. Poor children also are likely to become the poor parents of the future. Every year that we keep children in poverty costs our nation half a trillion dollars in lost productivity, poorer health and increased crime. (CDF n.d.)

THE IMPORTANCE OF HOUSING

The effects of not having a home are profound. James Wright said, "In a very deep sense, to be homeless is to be without family or friends that can be relied upon in times of crisis or need" (Wright 1989, 87). What does having a home actually mean, whether we rent, pay a mortgage, or own it outright?

According to the United Nation's Universal Declaration of Human Rights, "Everyone has the right to a standard of living, adequate for the health and well-being of himself and of his family, including food, clothing, housing and medical care and necessary social services, and the right to security in the event of unemployment, sickness, disability, widowhood, old age or other lack of livelihood in circumstances beyond his control" (UDHR n.d.).

Ideally, a home is where we live, day and night, with our family of origin, the family we create, extended family—uncles, aunts, and cousins; friends—or by ourselves. We have a roof over our heads to protect us from the raw elements of cold or heat where we can sleep, eat, drink water, bathe in warm water, and use a toilet. If we are sick or tired, we can rest and retreat from the busy world around us. We return home each day after work, school, or recreational activities. If we are lucky enough, we can find quiet and calmness within our minds and peace around us. Ideally, we are safe there—physically, mentally, emotionally, and spiritually.

Some of us have difficulties falling asleep in the comfort of our own beds and homes for a variety of reasons. Maybe we struggle with anxiety, have an overload of issues on our minds, and have a difficult time at the end of the day letting go of our control so we can relax and fall asleep. Perhaps we fear something horrible will happen and do not trust that we will survive the night. Imagine how much more difficult it would be to fall asleep in the outdoor elements with no protection or security—and not because we are camping or on vacation.

Elliot Liebow (1993) says that having our own space creates stability for us and is critical to our well-being. It protects us against predators (criminals, the violent mentally ill), the natural abrasive elements of the weather (extreme cold or heat), and rats and other vermin (4). He also says that homeless women's "greatest need . . . [is] the same as everyone else's: to be assured of a safe warm place to sleep at night, one or more hot meals a day, and the presence, if not the companionship, of fellow human beings (xiv).

Author and educator Jonathan Kozol draws a fine distinction between a home and shelter: "Shelter, if it's warm and safe, may keep a family from dying. Only a home allows a family to flourish and breathe. When breath comes hard, when privacy is scarce, when chaos and crisis are on every side, it is difficult to live at peace, even with someone whom we love" (Kozol 1988, 61).

The participants in "Your Story and Mine: A Community of Hope" all talked about their loss of, or need for, a home. While many are isolated, others communicate with extended family. Many found themselves in situations due to circumstances beyond their control that most of us would find unthinkable. They have no home from which to get their bearings—literally or psychologically. They wander the streets without a compass. They meander emotionally—with little sense of order, structure, or sense of direction in their lives. Depending on the extent of their disabilities, they have greater or lesser control over their lives. They have a difficult time setting and achieving goals, or even recognizing the need to do so. Constant drama and problems overwhelm them daily. They have little internal or external quiet within their lives. They often lack the cognitive tools and skills to cope and problem-solve.

In 2009, I was lucky to hear Steve Lopez, author of *The Soloist*, talk as the featured speaker for "One Book, One Community" in East Lansing, Michigan. In his book, he writes about the night he spent with Nathaniel Ayers on skid row in California to see where Nathaniel sleeps and "what it's like out there" at night (Lopez 2008, 60). He says:

> I try to sleep but can't. I'm thinking about the rat that came up from the drain. Then, when finally I begin to doze, I hear a siren, or footsteps, or a hacking cough. I spy the pavement for cockroaches. Restless, I walk Skid Row for ninety minutes, past hundreds of campers. They're in doorways and boxes, slumped over in wheelchairs. I'm angry about billions spent in Iraq while bomb-rattled vets live like animals on Skid Row. I'm ashamed that in a region of unprecedented wealth, the destitute and the sick have been shoved in this human corral. (71)

Sociologist Christopher Jencks writes,

> Today, any private space intended for sleeping can qualify as a home, so long as those who sleep in it have a legal right to be there and can exclude strangers. The homeless have become those who have no private space of their own, however temporary.
>
> On any given night, the homeless can be divided into two groups: those who sleep in free shelters (the "shelter homeless") and those who sleep in places not intended for human habitation, such as bus stations, subway trains, automobiles, doorways, and abandoned buildings. Those who sleep in outside shelters are generally known as the "street homeless," even though many sleep in abandoned buildings, bus stations, and other indoor locations. (Jencks 1995, 3–4)

At one time or another, participants in "Your Story and Mine: A Community of Hope" had no home of their own with warmth or comfort, but they were all innovative in their search for a safe harbor. They slept in homeless shelters, domestic violence shelters, missions, or motels. They moved frequently, often daily or weekly, from one shelter to another, carrying their few belongings in a grocery cart or knapsacks, never really knowing where they and their families would sleep each night. Some showered in cold water. Some worked to pay for their habits—drugs and alcohol. Sometimes they stayed with relatives. Some lived in cars, campers, or trucks. They used bathrooms in bus and gas stations, or just made them in the out-of-doors. Those we interviewed no longer lived like that.

For those of us who travel for pleasure, we choose to make the trip. We do not travel out of necessity or fear that we will not have a roof over our heads at night to protect us from the elements. While we complain about carrying heavy bags and struggle to put them in the overhead bins and pay extra fees for stowing larger bags in the luggage compartment in airplanes, we are making a choice to travel. Furthermore, we carry a small fraction, not the total, of our belongings. While we must follow airline schedules to get to our vacation destination, we are not on shelter time—which requires us to leave early in the morning and only allows us to enter at a certain time in the early evening if we want to have a bed in which to sleep. Those who live outdoors have even different schedules. They must make sure they have a space.

Liebow (1993) says that, unlike living on the streets, "shelters begin to make physical life possible. But these supports alone are not enough to stave off the devastation and despair of homelessness. For that, the women must finally look to themselves—to their native optimism, their sense of humor, their modest wants, and their faith in God" (15–16).

One participant, Loren, told us that he lived in a car in his mother's garage after she banned him from their home for his inability or unwillingness to comply with the rules of the house. It was freezing cold outside in winter. On one occasion, he slept under the steps of an apartment building. Another participant, Lewis, slept under a bridge by a river for several months. David slept in open fields in Michigan's cold winter. Bill lived in abandoned houses, campers, or laundry rooms in apartment buildings. Robert lived on the streets of California for several years before he returned to Michigan. Sometimes, juvenile detention homes, jails, or prisons became their homes.

The homeless often have no food. As a child, Jackie ate out of a dumpster. Sometimes she and her family ate only one meal a day, sometimes only ate peanut butter for a meal. Sometimes she just went hungry when her family could not find food. Sometimes they waited in line for an hour and a half to eat in shelters, or just bought stale food. Bill "prayed for rain to drink puddle water." David first started playing the guitar because he was hungry. "I play better when I'm hungry. When you feel hollow, you aren't full of stuff that gets in your way."

Allyson Bolt said: "People are worried about where their next meal is coming from, or the fact that they are trying to sleep somewhere else than the shelter. They do not have a concept of what they want three or five years from now. They are not planning for that, particularly people who have been living in generational poverty. Everything is right now, not next week. How will I get through today? How will I pay my bills?"

In one of Lewis's poems, he writes about selling drugs to try to pay for gas for heat: "Robbed for every dollar, begging for extra money to keep the gas paid. / But to try and still get your gas turned off . . . / and we also have a newborn baby." In another poem, he writes, "Young women giving their souls just to see her babies safe and sound," and "another child dead and the other going to sleep with a belly ache."

In addition to the loss of shelter, protection, food, safety, and family, the homeless have often then also lost most of their possessions, the contents and essence of their homes—as they can usually only take what they can carry on their backs in a sack or push in a cart. Furthermore, the significance of the loss is not simply a loss of three-dimensional objects or things or stuff, but is symbolic on many levels. "A home that has grown along with one, however, literally been built around one, is not simply an expression of one's taste; it is the outer edge of one's personality, a part of the self itself. And the loss of that part of the self . . . is akin to the loss of flesh" (Erikson 1976, 176–77). Erikson further reflected that by having to leave home, as the people in the Appalachian flood had to in Buffalo Creek, West Virginia, when the dam broke in 1972, individuals also suffer loss from the community in which they once lived. This can add more stress and layers of complications to their lives as they lose their connection with familiar place and space, family, friends, and community.

CHALLENGES OF THE HOMELESS

The homeless face an endless list of challenges in their lives. They suffer from alcohol and other drug addictions, mental illness, trauma, pain, illiteracy, unemployment, abuse (physical, sexual, emotional, and psychological), and grief. They repeat patterns of unhealthy behaviors of their parents and grandparents if or until something from within or without interrupts the destructive cycle. They often lack an ability to recognize and understand their feelings. They often cannot read or write, which interferes with their ability to find work. They have difficulties dealing with bureaucracies, accessing mental health services, and finding housing. They face prejudice and stigma.

Often these people repeat patterns as adults that they experienced as children. Their parents probably repeated their parents' patterns. Psychoanalyst and world-renowned author Alice Miller watched

> young people who stare dully into space, cigarette in hand, sipping a glass of something alcoholic if they can afford it, and biting their fingernails. Alcohol, cigarettes, nail biting—all serve the same purpose: to prevent feelings from coming to the surface at any cost; as children these people never learned to experience their feelings, to feel comfortable with them, to understand them. They fear feelings like the plague and yet can't live entirely without them; so they pretend to themselves that getting high on drugs in a disco can make up for all they have lost. But it doesn't work. Cheated of their feelings, they begin to steal, to destroy property, and to ignore the feelings and rights of others. They don't know that all this was once done to them: they were robbed of their soul, their feelings were destroyed, their rights disregarded. Others were using them, innocent victims, to compensate for the humiliation they had once suffered for themselves. For there is no way for mistreated children to defend their rights. (Miller 1990, 41)

Substance Abuse and Mental Illness

Toni Townshend reflected on her many years of experience trying to validate these people's thoughts and feelings to empower them on their life journeys. I could almost feel her heart ache as she talked about their profound problems of drug and alcohol addiction, of mental illness, trauma, and grief. Toni believes that alcoholism and mental illness are the two biggest destroyers of life. Eventually, the family often "gives up" on the addict. Furthermore, more than half of all prison and jail inmates have a mental health problem (James and Glaze 2005).

She continued:

> Any kind of addiction is an illness just as much as mental illness is. It is very hard to break the cycle. One barrier often leads to another barrier and another. Some people have more inner resources than others. Homelessness, grief, trauma, and abuse, drugs and alcohol often lead to encounters with the law. They may have a mental illness, start using or abusing a substance; they need money to continue that addiction. Three out of four inmates are functionally illiterate. With a record, it is very difficult to get a job. It is just a vicious cycle and it must be very overwhelming.

The National Coalition for the Homeless states that

A common stereotype of the homeless population is that they are all alcoholics or drug abusers. The truth is that a high percentage of homeless people do struggle with substance abuse, but addictions should be viewed as illnesses and require a great deal of treatment, counseling, and support to overcome. Substance abuse is both a cause and a result of homelessness, often arising after people lose their housing. (NCH 2009c)

The Substance Abuse and Mental Health Services Administration says that

Twenty to 25% of the homeless population in the United States suffers from some form of severe mental illness. In comparison, only 6% of Americans are severely mentally ill. . . .

Serious mental illnesses disrupt people's ability to carry out essential aspects of daily life, such as self care and household management. Mental illnesses may also prevent people from forming and maintaining stable relations or cause people to misinterpret others' guidance and react irrationally. This often results in pushing away caregivers, family, and friends who may be the force keeping that person from becoming homeless. As a result of these factors and the stresses of living with a mental disorder, people with mental illnesses are much more likely to become homeless than the general population. (NCH 2009d)

Allyson shared her perspectives on mental health, the roadblocks to access services and difficulties managing and implementing treatment.

Many of the folks talked about depression as an element of their stories. But, is it situational, chemical, or a little of both, or multi-layers of complex problems in the short and long-term? Then, people get frustrated and there's stigma about mental health illness. We know it. They know it. So, if someone suggests to them that they try talking about depression or anxiety or bipolar or whatever, they're not so eager to do that.

She said these people also have difficulties accessing mental health services and managing their treatment.

Certain health facilities will not take them unless it is a life or death situation, or put them on lengthy waiting lists. They need to go to a doctor who can prescribe some medication. Then they need refills and need to pay for them. They have a difficult time finding consistent mental health services and doctors who are willing to work with them.

You can also advocate for public policy change. The inadequate minimum wage in this country has not grown in the way the country has grown in the last forty years. It does not make sense what we expect people to live off of, if they get SSI [Social Security Income]. That is just unheard of. Then we have clients who say, "I don't know if I can apply for a job because what if they pull my disability and whatever job I am going to get isn't going to be enough to survive? The disability I have means that I can't stand on my feet all day, and those are the only jobs I'm going to get."

Allyson explained that the system does not support self-sufficiency:

It supports maybe being able to survive, but not a thriving system. We do not have free health care in this country so you have to choose between physical or mental health or whether or not you are going to have clothes on your back or eat or whatever. Resolving homelessness is very complex at the system level, the individual level, and the community level. It's certainly more difficult than giving someone a place to live or helping them sustain housing.

Liebow (1993) offers his perspective:

People are not homeless because they are physically disabled, mentally ill, abusers of alcohol or other drugs, or unemployed. However destructive and relevant these conditions may be, they do not explain homelessness; most physically disabled people, most mentally ill people, most alcoholics and drug addicts, and most unemployed persons do have places to live. Moreover, when mentally ill or physically disabled or alcoholic homeless persons do get a place to live, they are no longer homeless but they remain, as they were before, physically or mentally disabled, drug addicts, or whatever. Clearly, then, there is no *necessary* connection between these conditions and homelessness. Homeless people are homeless because they do not have a place to live. (223–24)

Illiteracy and Unemployment

Based on her many years as literacy director at Advent House Ministries, Toni also talked about the difficulties homeless people face trying to find work:

> People cannot fill out an application because they cannot really read or write. They cannot become self-sufficient. They cannot get a janitorial job without a GED because people with bachelor's and master's degrees cannot get a job. Many people who have been homeless for a while would work if they could. Most long for a home—whatever home that might be. Those with severe mental illness who live in tents who will not, cannot, or do not follow any rules are exceptions. They can't be around a lot of people.
>
> Education is one way to help. Three out of four people on welfare are functionally illiterate. Eighty-five percent of unwed mothers are illiterate. The statistics are staggering. It is national. Some states say we have a 45 percent illiteracy rate and that we need a bigger prison budget because these illiterate people will end up in jail or prison. They cannot get a job so they have no money because they are undereducated or illiterate.

However, while these people know that education, having their GED, is the ticket for a job, that in turn is the ticket for a home. Liebow writes, "'A job is the way out of homelessness,' the women often tell one another, just as they are told by service providers, social workers, volunteers, casual passers-by on the street, and everyone else they meet. At any given moment, perhaps half the women are working or looking for work, and even those who cannot work often go through the motions of looking for a job" (Liebow 1993, 52).

Abuse

Erika Magers talked about the challenges women and children have had to face based on their experience with physical, mental, emotional, and sexual abuse. The three women participants—Wynette, Jackie, and Dora—all talked about abusive relationships they had experienced in their lives.

Erika said:

> Sometimes people talk about ending homelessness and ways to end homelessness. When working with people who have been homeless, you realize it is not

about jobs. It is not about houses. It is a component of that, absolutely. But, it is this larger picture, especially people who have been abused as children, who went through traumatic things as children. If we really want to end homelessness, we should work on ending abuse or at least providing better treatment for the abused—better support as a community in general. It does not even have to be in the context of something professional like therapy—other human beings providing support to other people so that those wounds have the opportunity to heal.

According to Allyson,

The person abuses them or their children and destroys educational opportunities and their connections with their family and friends. An abusive partner will take over that person's life. They will not allow them to make phone calls, visit people, or handle money any more, and will make them accountable for their time. They degrade that person, who then experiences low self-esteem. Many other issues accompany domestic violence—posttraumatic stress disorder [PTSD], substance abuse, and other traumas that eat away at the human psyche and at your soul.

A woman will talk about how she ruined her family because she did not remove her children from that situation. She blames herself for what was happening and not the partner who was abusive and violent and destroying the home. That is a typical response to domestic violence. She feels she did not protect her baby and this is her fault. Perhaps the abuser was violent and chipped away at her self-esteem to the point where she does not even know she is in it anymore. Abuse causes you to internalize it—to say, "It's my fault."

If you are a child who has experienced physical, emotional, and/or sexual abuse, you've had to do something to get yourself through it. Often the type of abuse is someone saying you are worthless, you are no good. Alternatively, they give you one set of rules, you follow them, and then they say, "Nope, that wasn't right," and they hit you anyway. After a while, you are going to think you are the cause. Abuse comes inherently with a loss of control. Therefore, I can take some of that back and say, "If I had done this, then this would have happened." It gives you a little piece of control, but it also causes shame and blame because it makes you want to take on responsibility for what is not yours.

Allyson talked about one participant who had experienced generational poverty and watched domestic violence over the years. "She just did anything to get out of that situation and ended up as a fifteen-year-old prostitute. I do not look at the little girl and say, 'Boy, you really made some bad choices.' I say, 'Wow, you did whatever you could to survive.' Some of it is choices and some of it is how our system works and how it holds certain people down and raises up others."

Allyson reflected on the participants' black-and-white thinking, and their belief that the universe is conspiring against them. Most of the people she sees have trust issues. "They are part of a system where they have to watch their backs 24/7. They are living in a shelter system. They are in places that are not always safe. They are not in their own place where they can lock up their personal possessions. They do not have a place of their own. They end up not trusting anyone."

Erika said that to complicate homelessness further,

VOA [Veterans of America] or some of the other shelters can be incredibly stressful places. People are screaming, yelling, doing drugs. Some people are really opposed to personal hygiene. One thing I hear is that the VOA requires people to take showers. Sometimes, people do not. It becomes an extremely stressful environment when you are there and just want to get some sleep and cannot because of something happening. Even if you don't have preexisting mental health challenges, I feel that can lead to anxiety, irritability, and even ulcers.

You may have a mental health diagnosis that inadvertently leads to homelessness because you cannot keep a job and you get kicked out from where you're living. You go to a shelter where your basic needs are met. But, in the end, the stress of that environment aggravates your illness even more.

It's like when you take everyone in our cities who are having a difficult time and you put them in a concentrated area. You can have lots of interesting backgrounds. Just think about that kind of tumultuous energy concentrated in a shelter—maybe a hundred, maybe a couple of hundred people who are all having very stressful times. Then there are gems who crop up, and I'm thinking about some of these people we worked with. And then they say, "Forget about my problems." They then start concentrating on helping others. What's the choice—being stressed out, or I can figure how to help the other people on the ship?

Susan Cancro, director of Advent House Ministries, talked about the need for advocacy and support for the homeless:

If someone has a health problem, whether it's physical or mental, it's important to have someone advocating for you because your health problem is distracting and can impede your ability to take in information and process it for healing. If you are in pain and you are taking drugs for it, it is not easy to sit there and comprehend everything your doctor is telling you about your condition in the hospital. It is nice to have somebody else who is sitting outside it who can hear these things and help you sort it all out when you are not able to do it yourself.

PREJUDICE, STEREOTYPING, AND PROFILING

Prejudice, stereotyping, and profiling are interrelated concepts primarily based on negativity and ignorance. *Prejudice* refers to a dislike for a person, group, or custom based on race, religion, sex, or other factors. An individual who prejudges another individual is prejudiced. When we *stereotype* people, we observe an individual's appearance or behavior and generalize for all people who look or act like that person.

According to the American Civil Liberties Union, "'Racial Profiling' refers to the discriminatory practice by law enforcement officials of targeting individuals for suspicion of crime based on the individual's race, ethnicity, religion or national origin. . . . A new kind of intolerance is creeping into our country—one that shrouds its true identity and uses the law as a means to codify discrimination" (ACLU 2005).

In these three cases, we pass judgment based on appearance, and assume negative things about that person or group of people. We do not ask questions of the individual to understand if our perceptions are accurate or purely negative impressions. Dissipating our prejudices takes time, patience, and effort—and of course, only if we choose to alter our perspective.

Some of us are prejudiced against the poor or other economically depressed people, and in particular the homeless. Many of us believe in the value of helping the poor, yet deep down inside ourselves, no matter what ethnic, racial, or religious groups we come from, we all have prejudices about other people. Such thoughts are the first ones that often pass quickly through our minds.

When walking past homeless people on the street, some of whom beg for money passively or actively, we label them as black, white, Hispanic, poor, uneducated, mentally ill, alcoholic, drug addicted, ex-convict, abused, uneducated, lazy, worthless, unemployed, quadriplegic, paraplegic, crazy, a bum, parasite, pariah, or leech. Do we ever think about the kinds of tragedies they might have experienced that led them to this lifestyle with no assistance to overcome them? Do we ever honestly think about how we might react if we had to face similar situations?

Furthermore, when we enter this world, we have no preconceived ideas of how to think, believe, or feel, nor do we have a concept of others or ourselves. Yet over time, as we experience life, we become educated to one degree or another, formally or informally—through schooling or street smarts. Along the way, we usually develop a variety of both conscious and unintended prejudices toward individuals or groups of people who are different from us. We may or may not even meet or know them. They have different ethnic, religious, political, or sexual orientations; different affiliations; drug addictions or alcoholism; diseases such as AIDS, and long before that, leprosy. Our prejudices may result from our own experiences or the influence of others, including family, friends, and teachers.

We understand now that all people are born untainted, without prejudice, regardless of their race, ethnicity, religion, or social status. Sadly, life then often teaches us to develop prejudices and discriminate. Homelessness, like birth, does not discriminate—people of any background can become homeless for a variety of reasons they never imagined. While birth and homelessness do not discriminate, death also does not discriminate. Eventually, all people become sick and die, or die of old age or trauma.

Several years ago, I gained more understanding of this last universal truth from a nurse who cared for my mother in her last hours of life. When my mother was eighty-eight years old, lying in an unconscious state in the hospital, I was profoundly impressed with her nurse, who was about forty years old. He taught me who the important people are in life. He also taught me that death does not discriminate.

During the wee hours of the morning, I watched how he gently, carefully, and respectfully turned my mother's body to make her more comfortable. After he finished, I began to talk with him. Both he and my mother were immigrants from entirely different parts of the world who had come to America for a better life. He had come from Haiti maybe twenty years before. She had come more than sixty years ago from Bulgaria.

I thanked him for caring for my mother so kindly and thoughtfully. I told him how impressed I was with his respectful approach. He said, "You know, when we come to the hospital, we are all the same. We may be rich or poor, educated or not. But when we are sick, we all need care and eventually, we will all die."

He then asked me, "Do you know who the most important people are who work in the hospital?" I thought about his question but did not know the answer. He continued with his soothing, calm voice. "It's not the doctors or nurses. It is the people who clean the hospital. When you walk into a hospital, you first notice whether it is clean or dirty. You will not want to bring your relative or friend or yourself into a dirty hospital."

In my mother's dying hours and my last moments with her, this man whom I had just met was teaching me about humanity and was bracing me for my mother's impending death. We are all humans and we all must and will die. I began to realize more clearly our primal commonality with one another as human beings. We all must face death—it is just a question of when.

Furthermore, I thought, what if my mother did not have family to help care for her? What if she did not have health insurance? Could she have been on the street? I also realized that in some ways death does discriminate—not in terms of whether or not we die, but under what conditions we die. Once again, sometimes things go awry in life.

When we look at people, how often do we just develop superficial impressions and pass unfair judgments? Do we base our impressions on what they look like and what we think their lives are like, and not on facts or reality? Do we think about what or how they might feel, what they have experienced, what life has given them or taken from them? What are the stories that lie behind their eyes? What stories have created each wrinkle in a person's face and each gray hair? What stories lurk behind their gazes? What happens when we dare to ask? How many opportunities have we passed by not communicating with others? How often do we accept our shallow, superficial definitions and impressions of others without the facts, instead of daring to discover their real stories? How often do we share our thoughts and perpetuate negativity?

Who gives anyone the right to discriminate, persecute, or criticize? Where and how do we develop prejudices and then stereotype and profile others? How does our thinking become flawed or skewed? What happens in our lifetimes that we build walls, negative attitudes, and superiority complexes? What goes awry? We are often self-righteous and blame the poor—thinking we will never experience their life, even though many who never imagined it find themselves in their situation today.

Are we just so profoundly afraid of our ability to survive that we feel better when we can hate and stomp on someone else, when we are greedy and selfish and discriminate? Is it a fight for survival based on a primal fear? Do we think or believe that we will not have enough food and wealth to survive and somehow must take from others, or prevent others from acquiring the essential necessities in life?

The puzzle becomes more convoluted. According to Liebow,

> Fear in all its forms stands out. It seems to take the shape of a giant circle of mutuality: the shelter staff and other providers are afraid of the homeless and the homeless are afraid of the staff; the citizen on the street, the merchants, the householder and whole communities fear the homeless, and the homeless fear the non-homeless citizens. And to complete the circle, the homeless are afraid of the homeless. Thus, everyone is afraid of the homeless, including the homeless themselves, and what is so terrible and intractable about this institution is that everyone is right to be afraid . . .
>
> There is no mistaking the fear and the relative dearth of trust and civility that set the public worlds of the dependent poor apart from others. (Liebow 1993, 116–17)

According to the well-known author and psychiatrist Robert Coles, some people like to travel, observe, witness, and experience other people's worlds for a variety of reasons and motives. Some are conquerors, missionaries, or public school teachers. Some go to teach "the disadvantaged." Some become involved in special programs in this country or overseas to help the poor. Coles writes about authors James Agee, George Orwell, and William Carlos Williams, who decided consciously to live among the poor and/or sick so that they could write about them and share their findings with the world. However, he raises the question as to why they chose to do so. Are they doing it to help the poor or to "enhance" themselves? Furthermore, they have the advantage of knowing they can always leave the world of others and return home (Coles 2010, 33–44).

Throughout our project, Marion Heider, volunteer docent at the Michigan Historical Museum, provided one-on-one support to each participant. She said:

> Unfortunately, we've categorized people into homelessness, and when we do that we have ideas about what it is. It's usually about people who have drug or alcohol issues or dropped out of school or had children too young—like really negative things. I don't like classifying people as homeless because of this image. I would rather think of people who have gotten stuck in bad situations and, like all of us, are somehow trying to work themselves out of it. I do not like the negative image—that the homeless do not want to do anything. Some of the people we worked with admitted that some situations were their fault. However, some of it was a whole lot of bad luck, just one thing after another. And there's just no more inner strength to fight it any more. I hope that's the kind of homelessness that people think about. And not that it is "just their own fault," because it's just not true.

Some of us take for granted shelter, food, clothes, and heat, and then blame, shun, criticize, and condemn the homeless. We feel extremely uncomfortable when passing poor people on the street. We distance ourselves and avoid eye contact with beggars. However, our prejudice comes from fear that perhaps one day we might end up on the street and live in a park, a box, under a bridge, or in a shelter if we do not have a friend or relative who will allow us to live with them, at least temporarily. Sadly, those who live on the street often do not have friends or family who can or will help them. Wright says,

> Many [homeless people] who do have family are so profoundly estranged from them that they in effect have no family at all. Few of the homeless have ever

married; most who have are now either separated, widowed, or divorced. Many of the homeless who have had children do not even know for sure where their children are, having had no contact with them in years. Most of the friends of homeless people are other homeless people with no resources to spare.

In a very deep sense, to be homeless *is* to be without family or friends that can be relied upon in times of crisis or need. (Wright 1989, 87)

According to psychologist George A. Bonanno,

The classic in-group/out-group effect occurs when we blindly favor people we perceive as more like ourselves, that is, the in-group. We are also sometimes blindly unfavorable or unfair to people we perceive as different from ourselves, the out-group. This effect is at the root of much of the prejudice and racism we see in modern life. It is also related to our need to adhere to shared worldviews. The more we define ourselves as part of a specific group or type, the more we can relish a shared reality. (Bonanno 2009, 126)

We are often afraid to accept our negative feelings towards anyone who is different from us, whether they are wealthy, fat, or anorexic, or have a different skin color, religion, ethnic background, or sexual preference. When we see a prostitute, do we ever wonder sympathetically what she has experienced in life that led her to sell her body on the street as a way to earn a living for food and shelter? Do we think at what a young, tender age she might have started this career? When honest, we acknowledge these fleeting thoughts about our contempt for the poor.

Labeling people whom we perceive as extremely different from us due to skin color, religion, ethnicity, income level, does not allow for understanding or compassion. When we meet such an individual, do we look at them straight in the eye? Do we dare shake their hands? Do we keep more physical distance from them than we would with someone whom we perceive as similar to us? However, if we allow ourselves to have a dialogue and then perhaps even develop a relationship with that person, we will necessarily have a harder time maintaining our original prejudice.

Liebow talks more about labeling:

I have tried to avoid labeling any of the women as "mentally ill," "alcoholic," "drug addicted," or any other characterization that is commonly used to describe—or worse, to explain—the homeless person. Judgments such as these are almost always made against a background of homelessness. If the same person were seen in another setting, the judgment might be altogether different. Like you, I know people who drink, people who do drugs, and bosses who have tantrums and treat their subordinates like dirt. They all have good jobs. Were they to become homeless, some of them would surely also become "alcoholics," "addicts," or "mentally ill." Similarly, if some of the homeless women who are now so labeled were to be magically transported to a more usual and acceptable setting, some of them—not all, of course—would shed their labels and take their places with the rest of us somewhere on the spectrum of normality. (Liebow 1993, xii–xiii)

He continues,

I had come to see how inadequate it was to think of them [the homeless] in one-dimensional stereotypical terms such as "mentally ill" or "alcoholics," as incomplete persons deficient in morals or character, or even as "disaffiliated" persons, go-it-alone isolates no longer connected with family or friends. (1)

Furthermore, Liebow says that stereotyping inhibits us from seeing and understanding these people as multidimensional, legitimate human beings with thoughts, feelings, emotions, personalities, and life stories. This does not allow us to understand them in any way; it stops any further inquiry about the person and the process of human interaction. Prejudice, stereotyping, and profiling separate and prevent us from communicating with others to develop a healthy dialogue or relationship with them.

One of the participants, Loren, talked about prejudice. "When you see somebody walking down the street while you're driving your nice car, instead of looking at them like, 'Damn, there goes a homeless person. Look at that person looking in the trash,' 'Why don't they go do this?' or 'Why don't they go do that?'—you don't know what that person's background is like. You don't know that person."

Lopez talks about his mentor, Stella March, who is the force behind "Stigma-Busters," an ever-vigilant service of the National Alliance on Mental Illness. "She taught me Nathaniel is not a mentally ill musician, as I've been referring to him, but a musician with mental illness. It's a subtle but significant difference, recognizing the person before the condition" (Lopez 2008, 81).

The homeless often roam the streets from dawn till dusk. While they may all have a similar, recognizable demeanor, individually they each look different—just like any other group of people. "Bag ladies" carry numerous satchels on their backs and over their shoulders, probably giving them back, neck, shoulder, and arm aches. Oh, how they could benefit from massages, physical therapy, and acupuncture. Their feet are worn and tough with calluses. Oh, how good would a pedicure feel! Homeless men (once referred to as "hobos" or "bums") with unkempt long hair and beards, and women with long, disheveled, wiry hair and many lines on their weathered faces push grocery carts with their total possessions in plastic bags. Maybe they all dream of haircuts, shampoo, and conditioners. Others ride bicycles with front and back baskets and collect pop bottles and beer cans from college campus classrooms, dumpsters, and under porch stoops to cash in for coins. Still others stand or sit by the side of the road holding up handmade signs that say WILL WORK FOR FOOD. Sometimes, those with more severe mental illnesses saunter down the street talking aloud to themselves and gesturing with their hands.

Lopez continues: "Stigma, March says, keeps families from accepting a loved one's illness and seeking treatment for them, and it also marginalizes those who are afflicted. Why else, she asks me, would it be socially acceptable for them to sleep on filthy and dangerous streets? Would anyone tolerate an outdoor dumping ground for victims of cancer, ALS and Parkinson's?" (Lopez 2008, 83).

Furthermore, while more newspaper and Internet stories have appeared that are sympathetic to the plight of the poor and homeless, the mass media often perpetuates the stereotype of them. Daniel Jones, a caseworker at Advent House Ministries who worked with many of these people before, during, and after the "Your Story and Mine: A Community of Hope" project to help them develop jobs skills and life skills, said:

In many ways, I think homelessness itself is glossed over by the general media. It's one of those issues that is not likely to be talked about very often. It raises a level of uncomfortable feelings with people. I think it needs to raise a feeling of understanding, not a feeling of being uncomfortable. I think it comes from the fact that it's a world truth. It's a fact of life. These people may have mental, substance abuse, or alcohol issues. However, in many ways, these are people who also had families, who had careers. Suddenly, they woke up and things went wrong and snowballed, and now they are homeless.

When someone is confronted with that, it's almost like looking in a dark mirror. And confronted with the possibility they may think, this may be me one day, this may be my family some day. And people don't like to see those things. They do not like to see that truth reflected. As a result, no one addresses or talks about the real issues.

Erika Magers said:

Change starts with the community at large being willing to really look at the individuals who are homeless and not judge and push them away because they symbolize a fear that people may have about their own lives, and instead reach out and help them—just in simple ways that they don't lose human dignity. I think something that happens when people are homeless is that the greater community does not want to see them. They do not want to acknowledge that the problem exists or that these people exist who are homeless. Therefore, they just walk by and do not look, or they treat people cruelly. Then, the individuals who are homeless have lower self-esteem and just feel that nobody cares, and it perpetuates the problem even more.

Joel Blau, professor of social policy and director of the PhD program at Stony Brook University, wrote:

If one encounter with a homeless person is awkward, the cumulative effect of many such encounters is discordant. Some people are generous and do not mind occasional requests for money. Too many requests, though, soon exhaust their generosity. Losing their capacity to engage in single charitable acts, they are increasingly inclined to see homelessness as a disfigurement of the landscape, and begging as a personal assault. After a while, public opinion sours, and demands intensify to get the homeless off the street. (Blau 1992, 4)

REFLECTIONS

Even those of us who work hard at trying not to have prejudices still have difficulties with our attitudes. We often delude ourselves and believe we have no prejudices or negative feelings towards those who are different from us. We also may donate to charity—but is that out of guilt or social pressure? Are we giving for the wrong reasons? If we stop and think about our attitudes and are really honest with ourselves, we realize we do have biases. Perhaps that is the first step we need to take to change our attitudes and perceptions. Several experiences in my life revealed my personal shortcomings, thoughtlessness, and initial shallow, negative impressions of people.

As a young twenty-one-year-old married woman, back in the early 1970s, I transferred from Bennington College in Vermont to attend the Haile Selassie I University (now the Addis Ababa University) in Addis Ababa, Ethiopia, where my late husband taught anthropology for two years. I became acutely aware of the many poor, disabled people on the streets. They had no legs or arms—just stubs and stumps, with handmade cleat-like blocks to protect their palms or soles or thighs. Some, driven by a mission, scooted quickly down the streets. Others begged. Some were blind and tapped their tall wooden canes on the pavement. Some with a variety of disabilities worked in special carpet factories, weaving large, beautiful rugs from sheep's wool.

When I returned to Michigan in 1974 with my "newfound" but still naive awareness, I began to notice paraplegics and quadriplegics on the sidewalks in downtown Lansing. As a result of the American Rehabilitation Act in 1973, these people with disabilities had emerged from institutions. They used a variety of prosthetics, wheelchairs, and other devices to help them function in the outside world. Children and adults with disabilities finally had greater opportunities and civil rights in education, employment, and various other settings.

While walking down the street one day, I remember seeing an elderly African American man in a wheelchair—probably a veteran—smoking a cigarette and holding a cup for coins on his lap. He had no legs. I gave him some pocket change. As I turned to continue on my way, I called back to him in a reprimanding tone—"Now, don't buy any more cigarettes with the money!" Years later, his intensely painful expression— almost like a wistful anger—still haunts me. While I had thought I had no prejudice, in retrospect I realize that at the very least, I was arrogant and self-righteous. Who was I to tell someone how to spend those few coins, a supposed gift from a naive, insensitive, sheltered young woman? Was a cigarette a fleeting diversionary moment of relief or satisfaction for him? Was he addicted and could not stop? What had he experienced in his long life? Who was he? And who was I to pass judgment under the guise of a gift?

What happens when we emerge from our own little bubbles with wants, desires, and needs, and reflect on the situation, break the barrier, and engage with another individual? Despite all my efforts to avoid stereotyping, recently while in the airport in Detroit, coming back from a trip to California, I was sadly disappointed with how I passed judgment based on first impressions.

I went up to a counter at a take-out restaurant to get some food for my husband and me. The young African American woman standing behind the counter had a distant gaze on her face as she intensely chewed her fingernails. She appeared sullen, unmotivated, self-absorbed, and profoundly tired. I asked her for a couple of different salads and water. She merely pointed to a refrigerated display case—and said coolly, "There." As a traveler, I am usually pretty communicative and sympathetic to people who work in restaurants. Based on personal experience, I know it is very hard work. Now, I was a tired, hungry traveler wanting someone to be friendly and warm and perhaps even nurturing—very high, unrealistic expectations late at night in an airport.

Her intense mood was profound. Then, I looked at her face more carefully and tried to focus on her fatigue rather than my other negative impressions, to change my attitude. I thought perhaps I could cheer her up at this late hour. While she may have not been motivated, she had good reason.

"When do you get to go home?" I asked her.

"I close at ten," she said. "And I'll be glad to get out of here. I don't really ever want to come back here. I don't think I'll be back here. I don't think I'll ever come back here again."

Baffled, I continued to wrestle with my negative thoughts. I wondered how or why she was so clear that she did not even want to show up the next day to work? Was it that horrible? Then, I thought, Well, she has a job. Doesn't she want to keep it when jobs are so hard to find and keep? What will she do if she just doesn't show up? Doesn't she have any motivation? Doesn't she care about her job in any way? How can she even think of just not showing up with no notice to her employer? Does she have no work ethic or sense of responsibility?

"How long have you been working here?" I asked her.

"Since two this afternoon," she said.

"Well, what I mean is, have you been working for days, months, or years at this job?"

"I've been in the military since I was seventeen. I'm twenty-four now. I just took this job to try to stay focused. I'm a medical assistant and was in Iraq for four years. It's just terrible over there. Just terrible. I've got two children, three and five years old. I'm a single mom, and my mom takes care of them. They hardly know me."

"Will you have to go back again to Iraq?" I asked.

"They could ask me, but I'm not going back. No, I'm not going back. It's just terrible there."

My heart is still very heavy every time I think of this young woman. I wonder if anyone will help her to put her life together after such a traumatic experience. Will she ever heal from all that she has done and seen? Will anyone ever acknowledge and thank her for caring for so many wounded? How many Americans did she tend? How many Iraqis? How many children? Will words do anything to compensate her for all she has contributed with her young life? Will anyone nurture her? What was she like at seventeen? What is her life like now? Will any tenderness she might have ever had be gone forever? Will she become hardened forever? If she does not develop a strong social support system and find sufficient help to get on her feet, might she eventually live on the street like the many thousands of homeless veterans who fought in previous wars in Southeast Asia, and in current wars in the Middle East? My questions are endless. Then, I thought, she was only an adolescent when she entered the service.

"Take care and be good to yourself."

What if I had never taken a second look at this very tired young woman suffering from burnout and presumably PTSD? What if I had never talked to her? Would I have been left only with my tentative, ignorant, inaccurate, negative impression? I can only hope that people will be kind and good to her, and help her as she tries to move forward and reconstruct her life.

In yet another moment, during a recent creative writing class I teach at Advent House Ministries, one young fellow, Eraclio, wrote about an experience he had had in the desert in the Southwestern part of the United States. He was hanging out with friends in the desert, killing scorpions and rattlesnakes for protection, and eating them for a good meal. I initially assumed that he was part of a macho gang and that he and his friends were trying to prove themselves. I continued reading his story. He wrote, "We also ate them if we didn't have anything to eat."

Interestingly, how does the "other," the poor, the vulnerable, at-risk homeless person—often African American—look at those who are white and better off? Toni shared one of her favorite stories from the life-skills class she teaches:

"A young African American man in our project said that he had always had a problem with white women authority figures. He cited a manager at a restaurant he had once worked at.

"'This manager seemed to pick on me and require more from me than the other employees, but then she explained to me at some point that she had pegged me for her management team. So, yes, she did push me,' he said."

Toni then asked, "How do you feel about me, since I am a white authority figure?"

He thought for a moment and then said, "I never think of you as white; you're just Miss Toni to me."

Toni then explained to him that once we really know people and do not judge them by exterior factors, we erase the "color line."

In another instance, I prejudged an individual based on her appearance, demeanor, and profession. I soon learned otherwise. Early one morning, I had a routine medical procedure as an outpatient that required the anesthesiologist to send me into "twilight zone." A warm, lovely nurse who was helping me was confident, communicative, bubbly, and upbeat. She asked me what I did for work. I told her. Then, she asked me if I thought that most homeless people were mentally ill. I looked at her and said with a smile on my face, "I think we are all a little mentally ill!"

Her face then grew very serious and intense. She did not laugh or smile. She looked deep into my eyes and said, "I have a twenty-nine-year-old daughter who is mentally ill and often homeless. I can't tell her what to do, and there's nothing I can do to help her. That's what the staff at the community mental health agency tells me." I said, "I'm so sorry" as I faded under the anesthesia. In retrospect, I realized I had stereotyped this nurse who had been there to help me through my minor, routine ordeal. At first I had thought she was just making conversation early in the morning to distract me from my procedure. Her brief story was the furthest issue from my mind—that she might have such a personally close connection to homelessness. She carried a very heavy burden deep within and needed consoling.

The next chapter will focus on these people's stories about a variety of dimensions of their homelessness. We will also listen to the voices of their mentors.

Their Stories through Words

The use of the unrestrictive term, "the homeless," is in certain ways misleading. It suggests a uniform set of problems and a single category of poor people. The miseries that many of these people undergo are somewhat uniform. The squalor is uniform. The density of living space is uniform. The fear of guards, of drugs, and of irrational bureaucracy is uniform. The uniformity is in their mode of suffering, not in themselves.

—Jonathan Kozol, *Rachel and Her Children*

The Universality of Stories

Everyone has a story. That is unique to all human beings. Regardless of our life experiences, we all carry our stories and memories deep within us. Our stories are not right or wrong. We may temporarily forget or censor them, and others may also try to censor them—but they remain within our memory and souls. No one can take our stories away. We may embellish or downplay their significance. In "The Best of All Possible Worlds" (from the musical *Candide*), when we remember, rediscover, and then share our personal histories, we can better understand them and gain perspective on our past. We can see from where we have come, where we are, and where we might go in the future. We can grieve and laugh, heal from old wounds, and become stronger, more confident individuals. We can let go of some of our emotional and physical burdens and lighten our load, and that allows us to travel more easily on our life's journey in the present and future.

Storytelling fosters positive relationships between people as they share and connect with one another about each other's lives. We can discover other people's stories, gain insight about them, and also reflect on our own stories and better understand ourselves. Storytelling can cultivate empathy as we begin to understand and even respect other people—their experiences, challenges, and journeys that may be so different from our own. Once we understand, then we can become more empathic.

Storytelling is an old phenomenon. Ever since time began, in all cultures all over the world, people have been fascinated with stories—telling their life stories and listening to others'. Before written language, oral storytelling was a way to transmit individual, family, and community history. For years, people have passed on their stories from one generation to the next. They have sat by campfires sharing stories before going to sleep at night. Parents have told family stories, or read them and those of others to their children while putting them to bed. As people get older, they read stories to themselves. To tell one's own story of the day, or of long ago, is perhaps a way of letting go of the day's challenges, adventures, and worries. Reading other people's stories, either true or fictitious—and losing ourselves in those stories—often helps us go to sleep.

Increasingly today, more and more people have become intrigued with telling their stories, documenting them through extensive genealogical research, and sharing them with extended family and friends. Others—oral historians, journalists, anthropologists, film makers—are also providing more and more vehicles to help people share and preserve their stories, for example on NPR's Story Corps, and through books, radio, television, film, and blogs, and other vehicles on the Internet.

A dynamic new program, AncestryDNA, allows people to discover their genetic ethnicity, their family story, "who they were and where they were from." The new test analyzes and compares a massive amount of DNA in over 700,000 locations in the world. By detecting similarities, the test can trace back generations to connect people to the homelands of their ancestors. People have new opportunities to connect to relatives they may never have known, who can provide greater understanding of their family history.

Charles Whitfield, MD, writes: "Telling our story is a powerful act in discovering and healing our Child Within. It is a foundation of recovery. . . . In telling our story, we talk about what is important, meaningful, confusing, conflicting or painful in our life. We risk, share, interact, discover and more. And by so doing we heal ourselves" (Whitfield 1987, 96–97).

During the oral history interviews, the participants told their stories of homelessness in the past through their own words, their own lenses, from their own vantage point—honestly, openly, and willingly. The beauty of their stories is that they are untainted. The people are male and female, in their twenties to fifties. They represent several ethnic groups—African American, Hispanic, and white. Some told stories about growing up in profoundly difficult circumstances beyond their control. Other told stories that were the result of their own poor choices as they grew older. Their stories presented here are not always chronological accounts of their lives, nor are they necessarily complete stories, but are usually short vignettes about different facets of their lives.

They told *their* stories based on their own experiences and perspectives. If asked, their family members might recall events differently or have an alternate perspective. The famous, late oral historian Studs Terkel wrote about the nature of oral histories: "The precise fact or the precise date is of small consequence. This is not a lawyer's brief nor an annotated sociological treatise. It is simply an attempt to get the story" (Terkel 1986, 3).

Sharing their difficult, painful life stories and memories helped them begin to understand their lives in a new light, and to develop self-confidence, self-esteem, self-worth, and social and problem-solving skills as they realized that their lives and those of others are important. Many of these adults continue to have fragmented knowledge of their family history and still need assistance to develop literacy and critical thinking skills, a consciousness of their place in history and community, and tolerance and compassion for others with cultural, ethnic, and socioeconomic differences. Interestingly, when sharing their stories, some realized they were cousins.

They portrayed their worlds from the past *before* accessing services—traumatic events as little children, adolescents, and adults; parental and spousal abuse; struggles with alcohol and drug addiction; prostitution; mental, emotional, and physical illness; living outdoors exposed to the fierce elements and/or spending time behind bars; difficulties completing their education and finding jobs.

After conducting some of the oral history interviews, Allyson Bolt said, "I noticed people's ability to reflect on their lives in new ways. Many of them talked about how they have never really looked at their lives like that before, and how helpful it was. Some noticed how it caused them to think differently by looking at the big picture of their lives so far."

They each willingly accepted our invitation to share their life stories—probably for the first time in their lives—in a nurturing, nonjudgmental, supportive environment. In the past, at different junctures in their lives, they had each been homeless either as children and/or as adults. They struggled to find the basics—food and water, a place to sleep with a roof over their heads, clothes to keep warm, a bathroom, a home—what we all need, desire, and deserve: a place where we can retreat and feel safe from the raw elements at the end of the day. We acknowledged their tough challenges and developed respect for their profoundly complex lives and tenacity.

As mentors, we talked with one another during a roundtable conversation with videographer Peter Frahm, who asked us to reflect on our experiences with the project. We understood that we had all been on a profound journey together and with our interviewees. We had come from different perspectives and backgrounds—professionally and personally. Our ages ranged from our twenties to our seventies. For whatever reasons, we were fortunate that our paths had connected us with one another—mentors and mentees. Our past life experiences complemented each other's.

It was as if we all cooked and ate the most delicious meal together, including appetizers, soup, salads, a main course, and desserts and coffee and tea—a meal of teaching, learning, and listening; writing, poetry and prose, music, and art. We used the most wonderful ingredients—civic engagement, social inclusion, justice, sensitivity, nonjudgment, respect, kindness, thoughtfulness, empathy, love, and open minds—and a love for talking with one another. We all partook of the experience, the feast, with the participants who so generously, courageously, honestly, and willingly shared their life stories and experiences so that we, as well as others, could learn about their lives. They understood we needed their commitment for the duration of the project. They all honored their promise without equivocation.

Toni said:

> As a result of these people's participation in the project, they understood that their lives mattered, that we cared about them, and that others cared about them, too. Sharing their stories was a transformative experience both for them and for us. It helped heal at least some of their past wounds, move them beyond their painful pasts and into the future on their life journeys. This particular stop on their journey not only validated their lives and life stories but also our mission to continue working with them and others who had comparable experiences—those who keep coming and will continue to come to the shelter. . . .
>
> They had thought that no one cared or listened. We validated that it was appropriate for them to share their stories, and we encouraged them to do so. It gave them a wonderful sense of self-confidence.
>
> Sometime after we completed the project, we had people register for a backpack program. I was pitching a new museum program. Wynette happened to be there and I asked her to talk. A year and a half ago, Wynette would not have spoken in public, much less having an open-ended discussion. She volunteered

her story. Her artwork was on the wall. She told the new people how welcoming the staff was at the Michigan Historical Museum and how much fun the program was. She encouraged them all to join. It got to the point where I finally had to say, "That's fine, Wynette, you can sit down now." I think the experience was transformational for some of our clients.

As mentors, we never tried to change the participants, their ideas about themselves or the world. We often wondered what specifically motivated each one to volunteer to tell their stories of homelessness through oral history, art, poetry, and music. Some became involved with all aspects of the project, others only in some areas. While it was important for them to tell their stories for themselves and perhaps their families, it was also additionally valuable for them to share their stories with us as mentors and the community at large—in Lansing, throughout Michigan, and even overseas in the Czech Republic. In that way, others could develop awareness and sensitivity to their lives.

Allyson said, "I was surprised to see how willing they were to be vulnerable and so open and honest. I asked really tough questions in the oral history interviews, and they rarely said, 'No, I don't want to answer that.' They stuck with me. They told me things that others around Michigan would see on film. They were just very honest about their situation and excited about the opportunity to share that with people."

As I slowly became familiar with their stories over time through words and paintings, I began to see them as individuals and realized that each of them had a history and memories, a current life with short- and long-term challenges, and dreams and hopes for the future—just as all human beings do. I no longer thought of them as "one-dimensional stereotypical," as Liebow (1993) has said. They were no longer "black" or "white" or "Hispanic." They were no longer poor, uneducated recovering alcoholics or ex-convicts. They each had their own personalities, attitudes, likes and dislikes, opinions, perspectives, and dreams. Each became a "who," a living human being, and not a "what." They each had their own story. No one had pretense. They had no need to alter their stories for effect or any other reason.

Stereotyping prevents us from seeing or understanding that these people are individuals and not one homogeneous group of people. Steve Lopez has written about Nathaniel Ayre's integrity, which is similar to what I have also discovered about these people:

I deal too often with people who are programmed, or have an agenda or guard their feelings. Nathaniel is a man unmasked, his life a public display. We connect in part because there is nothing false about him, and I come away from every encounter more attuned to my own feelings than I would be after, say, an interview with the mayor or governor. Nathaniel turns my gaze inward. He has me examining what I do for a living and how I relate to the world as a journalist and as a citizen. (Lopez 2008, 196–97)

The essence of these people's stories about who they were, and not what their appearances were, was imprinted on my mind. Jencks refers to David A. Snow's and Leon Anderson's book *Down on Their Luck: A Study of Homeless Street People*, and Elliot Liebow's book *Tell Them Who I Am* when he writes:

Despite all the evidence that mental illness and substance abuse play a big role in homelessness, some knowledgeable people still insist that the homeless are mostly people "just like you and me" who happen to be down on their luck. . . . The homeless are indeed just like you and me in most respects. But so are saints and serial killers. Members of the same species inevitably have a lot in common. We all need food to survive, put on our socks one at a time, remember our childhood with mixed feelings, and worry about dying. But important as such similarities are, our differences are also important. To ignore them when we talk about the homeless is to substitute sentimentality for compassion. (Jencks 1995, 46)

The participants in the program all shared their difficult feelings of loneliness, isolation, fear, anxiety, grief, panic, and lack of emotional support from family. They talked about the challenges coping without the basics in life that many of us take for granted. They talked about their search for food, the lack of warmth in winter or a place to sleep or bathe, the challenges caring for their children. They wanted a place of their own, with their own bed, to which they could return each day. They talked about their physical and mental health issues and their need to protect themselves from their abusers. Interestingly, Jonathan Kozol observed from his experience with those who are homeless, "People in pain move to the heart of things more rapidly than I expect" (Kozol 1988, 39).

Throughout their lives as children and adults, many did not have any direction or know which steps to take or where to go to survive. They lived with tremendous uncertainty and anxiety, without the support of family or friends, for a variety of reasons. They still live with drama, although perhaps not so intense, and through their affiliation with Advent House Ministries and other social-service agencies, they have acquired new, more effective coping skills.

Whitfield believes that they each have individual needs to heal their "Child Within." He says:

The concept of the Child Within has been a part of our world culture for at least two thousand years. . . .

The Child Within refers to that part of each of us which is ultimately alive, energetic, creative and fulfilled; it is our Real Self—who we truly are.

With our parents' unknowing help and society's assistance, most of us deny our Inner Child. When this Child Within is not nurtured or allowed freedom of expression, a false or co-dependent self emerges. We begin to live our lives from a victim stance, and experience difficulties in resolving emotional traumas. The gradual accumulation of unfinished mental and emotional business can lead to chronic anxiety, fear, confusion, emptiness and unhappiness. (Whitfield 1987, 1)

I often wondered how these people survive. I used to think they had few inner resources, but Toni explained to me that homeless people have very strong survival skills—more than most of us have—because of the profoundly difficult challenges they have had to face daily since they were little children. They use these skills to cope with life challenges that most of us have never known or will ever know. Their physical constraints affect them emotionally. Now I realize that they have tremendous inner strength and determination. They are deeply courageous as they meander on their life journeys without really knowing if or when their lives will ever change or stabilize, not knowing if they will ever receive help or if they will be able to help themselves to become self-sufficient.

One day, on my way to teach a weekly creative-writing workshop at Advent House Ministries, I was feeling a bit down about my own personal issues. As always, at the beginning of the class, I asked people to share how their weeks had been. One fellow unknowingly helped me and I thanked him.

He said, "I've had a hard week, but God puts mountains in front of us to climb so we can grow stronger."

While thinking about these people, I wondered if a specific event had put them out on the street. Did they each have a defining moment in their lives that led to their homelessness, or was it the result of many events and circumstances? Had their parents been homeless? Were they repeating their parents' pattern or creating a new one of their own? Do their perception of what happened and what actually happened differ? How do they pass the time each day? What dreams do they have in their waking and sleeping hours? What brings about change in their lives, if any? What is their frustration level? Who were their positive or negative role models? My questions were endless.

I found myself always hoping for the participants to engage as fully as possible in the project so that they would feel better about themselves—or more honestly, perhaps, so I would feel better about myself, our project. I was hungry, greedy. I wanted to feel hopeful and satisfied with our project. Then, I began to wonder if I even had a right to dream for them. Is it a project for them or for us? Or both? As mentors, what were our past and current attitudes? Do we take our homes and lives for granted? Do we criticize those who do not have shelter? Do we forget or not realize that it is possible that one day we or our family or friends might be without shelter, or perhaps might have been in the past?

Talking with Participants

Allyson and I had set up appointments to meet with the participants over the course of a few weeks. One sunny spring morning, I waited for my first two interviewees. Neither one showed up for their appointment. I was sad and disappointed. I discovered that I was feeling secretly competitive with Allyson. I knew her assignees had been showing up for their appointments with her. Did they like her better? Was she more skilled at interviewing than I was? Were my assignees just blowing me off? As a social worker, Allyson loved museums. As a writer, oral historian, and self-trained artist, I loved "psychobabble." By the end of the project, it turned out that we had interviewed the same number of people.

Participants not showing up had nothing to do with either one of us. It was about their own lives: perhaps they had to deal with new daily issues that they were confronting, had overwhelming feelings about other responsibilities, or were afraid of having someone interview them about their very personal life stories. Later, Toni told me that clients often do not show up for appointments at the shelter. They make plans, and then unforeseen, pressing issues come up, which then consume them. They abandon the original scheduled appointment and do not necessarily think to let others know they will not be coming, nor do they necessarily have a way to communicate with others when they need to change their plans.

That afternoon, while I was waiting for Wynette—a soft-spoken, gentle, kind, friendly woman in her fifties—many questions wandered through my mind. Since she no longer lives on the streets, is she still "homeless"? Isn't she really "homeless no more"? I started to realize that I had not been identifying these people's status correctly. They once had been homeless but no longer were. They were formerly homeless in transition.

What was Wynette's family life like? Did she live in one place while growing up?

How did she get into her situation? Had she actually lived on the street, or was she just very, very poor and at risk? What was her life like? What was life like without a home? What does that mean to her? I have heard she has an apartment now. How or why did her situation change? How long has she been there? Will she be able to stay there, and for how long? Does she think she will move again? What is her sense of time? Place? Space? Purpose? Energy to survive? What motivates her? Was there one event or many events in her life that had ultimately put her on the street? A defining moment? Had she been homeless more than once? Was there one event or insight that inspired her to get off the streets? Were her parents homeless? Was she repeating a familiar family pattern? Once she came for the interview, would I even ask her all these questions, or would I get scared or would she get scared? I knew that she volunteers and feeds the homeless at her church, which gives her a lot of pleasure. Where would her interview take me? I was nervous and scared.

On that beautiful, sunny day, I kept waiting and hoping for Wynette to show up. She was usually reliable, but I was disappointed. Did I have a right to be frustrated? Was this project about these people sharing their stories, or about my wanting them to share their stories so I could learn more about them? I found myself not only curious but actually greedy for information. Is that ethical?

I called Toni to see if she could find out what might have happened with Wynette. She said she would get back to me. I wondered if Wynette would get off the next bus. Would she peer around the corner? What is in it for me? For her? What is her frustration level on a regular basis? What brings about negative or positive change? Was I not only sad, but angry that she and the others were not showing up that day?

What about commitment? Did anyone ever make commitments to these people? Did anyone ever follow through with a commitment to them? Did anyone ever help them? Did they ever follow through with commitments they made to others? Who were their role models? What were they like? What kind of medical care—physical, psychological, and/or dental—did they get while growing up? Did they ever get any? And now? What makes them feel good or bad?

After telephoning back and forth to Toni, I learned that Wynette and I had miscommunicated. She had gone to Advent House Ministries, instead of Lansing Community College, for our interview. She would meet me shortly.

Later, I also learned that one of the earlier "no shows" in the morning had also scheduled a medical appointment, and the other had had to go to the Social Security office. Why had neither called? Do they have a phone? A cell phone? If so, had their minutes run out for the month and were they waiting to get their SSI check (Supplemental Security Income) to pay the bill? I had so many assumptions and so little understanding. These interviews were so important to me.

After all, this was not only my work, my passion. The interviews were also important to them, even if not their top priority as their daily challenges of survival were necessarily more important and all consuming. And it was their personal lives we were focusing on—not their work.

While I was disappointed with the no shows, I wondered if these issues were of any concern to them. I tried to imagine any one of their disappointments on a daily basis and realized I had no concept of what even one might be like. How did they manage the instability and unpredictability of their lives? How did they cope with never knowing if their children would have shelter, food, heat, clothing, safety? Today, we have a meal. Tomorrow we might not. Today we have heat. Tomorrow, the landlord might shut it off. Is that an acceptable way of life? Do they have expectations that life ought to or could be better? Does it matter that their actions or lack of action affects others? Are prioritizing responsibilities, getting to places on time, making commitments and following through, understanding that their decisions or nondecisions and choices impact others, even relevant to them?

After each bus stopped in front of me, I looked for Wynette. Finally, I saw her walking towards me. Again, I had made an erroneous assumption. I had thought she would just take the bus from Advent House Ministries to Lansing Community College. Once she arrived, she was beaming. Her face glowed. She said she loves to walk and that it was good for her. We apologized to each other for our confusion and smiled. Many of the questions I had contemplated asking her before our interview were similar to those I had while waiting for the others I would interview.

Feeling Like Nobody

According to Sara Eleoff et al. (2010), "Children who live in kinship care with a relative have more special health care needs, mental health problems such as ADHD and depression, and dental problems compared with children who live with their parents. They are more likely to be black (48% vs. 17%), older than 9 years (59% vs. 48%), have public health insurance (72% vs. 30%) and live in households with incomes at or near the poverty level (31% vs. 18%) . . . their caregivers frequently report having fair or poor overall health or mental health."

Wynette, an African American woman, was extremely thoughtful and articulate. She told me that her father abused her mother. Her Mom gave her to her aunt to raise. As an adult, Wynette, her husband, and her children were evicted from their house and became homeless.

My mother, she liked to gamble. She liked to play cards. My father went over there and drag her down the stairs. She had me early because I was supposed to come in February. I was born in January 30, 1957, in South Bend, Indiana. I was an incubator baby. I weighed only one to two pounds and they thought I wasn't going to live.

My mother was born in Missouri. My mom is still alive. My mother did not want no girls. She wanted her boys and was going to give me to her best friend. My dad wanted me to be a boy and I came a girl so that's how I got the name Wynette. I guess that's how they fit it in with Wyett and I was his first child. Then he got with another lady and had some more kids, but I was his first child.

However, my Aunt Mary, my father's sister, jumped in and raised me and my younger sister. My aunt said, "No, these are my brother's kids so I'm going to take them." So she said, "Whenever you have the baby, let me know." So she came to South Bend, Indiana, from Lansing, Michigan. She brung me home when they let me out. But she always insisted that I stay connected to my biological mother and go to visit her.

My Aunt Mary took me so we knew who our parents and grandparents were. I cried and cried. I wouldn't talk to them. I wouldn't have anything to do with them. One sister didn't like me. I was the oldest. My aunt would force me to meet them.

She said, "You have to get to know your brothers and sisters." Yeah, I grew up with my aunt, but my aunt made sure that I know my mom and my dad. She would take me to Chicago and I just was like, I didn't want to be here. I'd just start crying, cry, cry, cry, and they would put me on a train and send me back to Michigan.

I traveled by myself on the train. I was about five or six years old. And the conductor and all of them would make sure I was okay and I had something to eat and everything, and my aunt would be right there at the stop waiting for me. That was a good experience because I never rode the train, so here was a little girl riding the train all by herself.

A lot of people used to call me all kinds of bad names when I was going to school. So, I kind of felt like I was a "nobody" in life and I just struggled with that. Now, I don't, but I used to. I used to struggle with "no one liked me or cared about me," and I really had a depression. And when I get like that, then I can't be by myself, because then all I do is cry. So I try to be around people so I can have a happy, a happy face instead of a sad face.

In 1988, Jonathan Kozol wrote about the impact of eviction on children:

Mobility is common in America. Families change homes frequently, the move occasioned often by career demands. Their children may be briefly traumatized; most manage the transition in good stride. When a child is torn from his home, when he sees his family's belongings piled on the sidewalk by a landlord or the agent of a bank, when he is left to wait and wither for long months within a series of unhealthy places . . . he may not literally die, but his survival is endangered and his childhood has, to a large degree, been taken from him. He either regresses or is forced to grow up very, very fast. (Kozol 1988, 137)

Wynette continued with her story:

I graduated from high school in Lansing. In 1980, I married Johnny and had seven children: Latoya, LaKashia, Brandy, Precious, Mary, and Johnny and Liza—my twins.

I was homeless a couple of times. I was, geez, I was in my twenties, about twenty-seven, twenty-eight, and a lot of things happened. We were living on Butler Street in Lansing. First of all, the city didn't want to come and fix things, and then they came in and they put a sticker on my house and said to me and my kids we had to move out. After that, we got another apartment. The same thing happened. It was because of the housing and they didn't want to come in and fix stuff. And then my nephews—they sold drugs outside my house. I didn't know. I was pregnant with my kids, and the police came and they ransacked my house and did all that, and then I got put out of there because of that, and my kids got taken away, and my husband, he was drinking and stuff. Then, I lost my kids, but I gained them back.

When they kicked me out of my house, I stayed in a lot of shelters. I stayed with some of my relatives. It was kind of hard on me but I survived. The hard part was dealing with all my kids and trying to make sure that they were safe. Basically, that's what it was. The hard part about being homeless was that you had to make sure that you had a place to go, because in the shelters they get you up at six in the morning and you had to be out at seven. You had to find places to go. You had to make sure that you had meals for your children. If they go to school, you had to make sure your kids got to and from school. That was kind of hard. But I did it.

Then, they took them, and I stayed gone about a year from here. The reason why I came back is because the kids' father got into a car accident and I thought that he wasn't going to live so I came back to support him. I've been here ever since. He's in jail right now, and when he gets out we might get back together. I might marry him and we might move away, because my kids are older now and they have kids of their own, so I don't have to worry about them. Just me.

Wanting a Chance

In 2009, a U.S. Department of Justice study explored the effects of violence on children: "Children's exposure to violence, whether as victims or witnesses, is often associated with long-term physical, psychological, and emotional harm. Children exposed to violence are also at a higher risk of engaging in criminal behavior later in life and becoming part of a cycle of violence" (US DOJ 2009).

Wynette's son-in-law, Lewis, an extremely warm and personable man now in his early thirties, grew up in Chicago, where he spent time on the streets and got into a lot of serious trouble. His father was a drug dealer. At ten, Lewis ended up in a youth detention home in Michigan. As a teenager and adult, he lived for long periods of time in jail, prison, foster homes, under a bridge, and in a car.

In his book *There Are No Children Here*, author Alex Kotlowitz portrays the lives of two African American little brothers, Lafayette and Pharoah Rivers, who grew up in a project in Chicago, not unlike the environment in which Lewis grew up. Ongoing violence, murder, poverty, abuse, drugs, alcohol, and fear surrounded them. This was too much for little children (or any human beings) to digest in so few years living on the earth. Their mother, LaJoe Rivers, said she knows that millions of these children grow old quickly. She described their neighborhood as one that "hungrily devoured its children." LaJoe said, "There are no children here. They've seen too much to be children" (Kotlowitz 1991, 10, 16).

As a little boy, Lewis grew up in a violent atmosphere in Chicago:

My mom had four kids. My daddy had six kids. He wanted to stand up and take a role—a drug dealer. He liked to drink. He toughened us up, making us men selling drugs, and if you didn't listen, he inflicted a lot of fear in people, that old Muslim stuff, Black Panthers. He had a closet full of guns.

My grandmother kept the family together. She took us all in. Grandma use to buy me graham crackers and milk. She played Bingo with us. That's how we learned to count.

I spent the first ten years of growing up in Chicago. It was a real problem getting back and forth to school because of the gangs. They were insane. And I got into a lot of trouble. When I was ten years old, the police picked me up and I went to Starr Commonwealth, a center for troubled youth in Albion, Michigan. Everyone had turned their back on me!

At Starr, we played pool, basketball—stuff that I never got a chance to do. We went camping to Beaver Island, Sleeping Bear Dunes, saw a lot of beautiful things. We used to get dressed up on Sunday to go to the chapel. Maya Angelou came to Starr, but I got into trouble that day and didn't get to hear her poetry. Nadia Komenich, the gymnast, and Jackie Joyce [aka Helicopter Girl], the singer from Scotland, came to talk.

It was nice not to worry about where I got my next meal. I lived there for twenty months and then went into a foster home in the Lansing area. I stayed in Michigan, where the majority of the time I was raised in juvenile detention and foster homes.

Lewis had difficult high school years:

I went to Everett High School. People had good jobs, money, finest cars, BMWs, trucks and everything. These people had money. It became clear to me what I had to do. I started selling drugs, fighting with people. I'm a gangster.

I really loved my foster mom, Ms. Anderson. I lived with her for about a year and a half. Then I moved in with David and Freda Cox. They had a pool, a dog, and doghouse. I went to Sexton and graduated in 1994.

While in high school, I became part of a gang, sold drugs, fought with people, and stole cars. People started calling me "Psycho." This one dude hit me in the face. People kept hitting me in the eye, the same eye. [*Lewis showed me his scars.*] I was arrested for selling cocaine. My foster parents kicked me out at nineteen. When I got out of jail, they let me come back. I been through every system and the Community Mental Health drug treatment program.

The judge said, "We have exhausted our funds."

I told him, "I need a chance."

I had to survive. I bought a car and lived one and a half years in the car, and parked in an unknown location. I walked the streets with my backpack. I stayed in the Back 40s [a vacant lot where homeless camp out in Lansing] and used to sell drugs to the VOA. I lived the definition of homelessness. I stayed with a girl at the river. We had to wipe ourselves with the leaves and bathe in the bus station.

When Problems Snowball

According to the National Coalition for Homeless Veterans, one out of every four or five homeless people are veterans with PTSD and traumatic brain injuries. "Conservatively one out of every three homeless men who is sleeping in a doorway, ally or box in our cities and rural communities has put on a uniform and served this country" (NCHV 2009).

When Robert was a little boy eating dinner at home, his father, who was sitting right across from him, died suddenly. As a teenager, Robert dropped out of high school, left home, and went to work. A white male now in his forties, he had served in the United States military for about six years, worked as a roofer and truck driver, was homeless for six or seven years, and spent time in jail. Eventually, he was in a horrible truck accident and lived in a hospital for a year. His injuries, including a traumatic head injury from the accident, clearly compounded and complicated his previous, ongoing difficulties.

Robert shared his philosophy about life: "I don't think people will ever understand the situation, not until it happens to them. You know the old saying, "You wouldn't want to walk a mile in my shoes"? Trust me, you wouldn't want to walk a mile in my shoes. But I don't think they'll ever understand the situation, not until it actually happens to them. You have to be there and go through it."

Robert experienced childhood trauma:

I grew up in Ferndale just outside of Detroit. I'm the youngest in my family. I have two older brothers and a sister.

It was very sudden. I was eight years old and sitting across the table from my father at dinner when he died from an aneurysm. Well, that's just part of life.

The family broke apart and everybody went their own separate ways. Sometimes, families pull together. Sometime they pull apart. I wasn't close with my Dad. No, not really. I'm sure I was, but at eight years old, I can't really remember all that much. I only remember bits and pieces. It's hard to actually put them into words. There were some good times with my mom before my dad died. I can't really remember all that part either.

I can't really remember the riots going on, but I know it was intense times down in Detroit. I dropped out from school when I was in the ninth grade because I just couldn't handle it at home. I don't know how long it would take to get a GED. I guess it goes by how well you can pick up and retain what you learn, which is somewhat of an issue for me.

Just not having a father there probably is part of my becoming homeless, and my mom—all the things that she went through—dating other guys and trying to pick up her life again. So, I moved out when I was fifteen years old and started working. When I wasn't in school, I was working most of the time. I shouldn't have been working. Actually, I started doing welding and then got into some manufacturing jobs. Any other time was just being on the street and having fun when you're young.

Most parts I remember with my mom are in my teenager years, and a little bit after my dad died. There's good times and also bad. I mean people got to go on with their lives. Not necessarily do you understand that point of view when you're at that age. Hopefully, if you can keep an open mind when you get older, you can try to piece all the pieces together again and understand that people are just people.

As a young adult, Robert struggled in California:

In the 1980s, after I was in the service for a few years, I moved to California and lived there for twenty years. I did a lot of different things in California. I worked, lived on the streets, and spent time in jail. I did roofing, worked at a few different companies, for Honeywell for a while. I was a truck driver—driving from San Diego to Los Angeles every day. I stayed with it for about two and a half years, but that job really wore me out. I then left that company. That was the time of the riots up in Los Angeles. I was driving and actually had to drive the day of the riots.

I was up in Compton [where riots broke out in 1992 after the not-guilty verdicts in the trial of officers accused in the beating of Rodney G. King]. I just left out there to go back down to San Diego. Then I had to go back up there the very next day. They needed some part time in Bell Gardens. So, you could see the fires popping up everywhere and everything. It was kind of scary, but a little bit neat too. Scary that they could have pulled me out of the truck. It was kind of neat just being up there in that part of history at that time.

I was driving a stolen vehicle that I knew was stolen but I didn't actually steal it and I was using it. I wound up getting caught driving it so I went to jail for that. I tend to think it's a lesser crime because I actually didn't go steal it but I knew it was a stolen car and I shouldn't have been driving it.

I've been in jail off and on. I mean probably the longest I've been in there is six, seven months. I don't want to be there again. It's just not nice having your freedom taken away. I don't think anybody deserves to have their freedom taken away.

When I was homeless, I was literally on the streets, mostly in California. I used to sleep outside of a church and wound up helping the people there at St.

Mary's Church in San Diego National City. I was sleeping outside under a little porch that they had out there and wound up getting to know the director of the maintenance department and helping him do a lot of projects, and he got me into the building for a while. But it's a lot different out in San Diego than it is here. The warmth. It doesn't get as freezing cold, so it's easier to be out in the streets there. It kind of has to do with my attitude towards things, too.

I just like having that free spirit, not having to be tied down to one place and paying rent to people. I don't think it should be like that. I got a weird mindset. I'm more like a Native American, so you can call me a great white Indian if you want to.

Being out in the streets and out on your own. I think that's what happens to a lot of people that were in the military. You're out in the woods and all you got is your tent. That's the best way I can put it—is that you're just out there in the middle of nowhere. I was actually homeless in California probably six, seven years.

I don't think anybody's story is even close to being the next thing as the other one. I think everybody's story is totally different. There's all sorts of reasons why people are out there doing what they do, their beliefs and things that happen to them. When I was on the streets in California there were people I knew who were abused when they were younger, and just all sorts of things happened. Drug abuse is a big part of it. I think some of it is mental stress from people that have been in the service and everything like that.

While out in California, I began working for myself for a while and then got into a real bad truck accident. I swerved to avoid a head-on collision. I got the worst out of it. The other guy just kept on going. I ran into the ditch and the truck caught on fire. When I came to, I was being burned, and I went to the hospital and that's it. This was just before I came to Lansing in 2006.

I was in a coma for a few months. And it took me about a year to get out of the hospital. That was in California, in San Diego. It was just one of the hardest things I've ever been through, and I was in there by myself in the hospital, didn't have anyone come to see me or anything, having to learn to walk again. Just all the pain you go through. Some people say I'm a walking miracle, but I don't think so. Well, just God's not done with me yet. Whatever it is I still gotta do.

The constant day-to-day pain that I'm in wears me down and everything and it's just hard. It's still pretty fresh. I'm forty-four right now. I had compressed vertebrae in the neck. Burned, I think they call it 26 percent burn on my arm and part of my face, skin grafting, head trauma. I was on a respirator for the whole time I was in the ICU for, I think, a good four or five months. I think they told me I died twice.

I remember that when I was in the coma I was in a different world altogether. I was trying to find out more about that. I couldn't find anything else on what other people had been through when they were in comas, but to me it was just in a different world. It was hard to separate reality from where I was when I first started coming around so it was pretty traumatic to sit back and realize you weren't out doing the things you were doing when your brain goes out like that. I had out-of-body experiences and just different realities, I guess, in my brain, just a weird thing to go through actually.

It's hard to put it into words but it was—I don't know if you believe in extreme theory or whatever where you walk different universes, or different parts of the things, but my mind went someplace where it was living lifetimes. I was in a coma. I mean I went to these different places, different worlds. Just a lot of things that were just really hard to separate from what was real from not being real and I still sit here trying to think about what it could have been. I'm not a brain surgeon so I couldn't tell you. I think it was just the brain's way of taking the body away from all the pain that it's in.

I never thought it would get better. I wish I would have died, and I started to come to. That was my first thought after the accident. Don't want to be here, don't want to be in the pain, don't want to have to go through all this stuff, just better off being dead, but came around to the point where you're not dying so you got to turn around and get better. So just got to put that one foot in front of the other one and go through all the pain.

At least it taught me something about how far you can reach down inside yourself and come back, how much you can actually take, as far as being on the verge of being dead and coming back again to life.

Being Hungry

Frederic Diblasio and John Belcher (1993) have written that "The sense of failure and stress caused by the inability to secure basic needs and sometimes safety and by the isolation and alienation of homelessness . . . can lead to low self-esteem. The feeling of worthlessness that low self-esteem generates can prevent individuals from successful functioning in their occupational, social, and leisure activities. . . . In homeless people, it can block motivation to find gainful employment, housing, and other essential needs. Failure to secure needs often leads to despair and worsens an already poor view of self."

David, a white male now in his early fifties, grew up in Grand Rapids and attended special education classes. Some people criticized him and made fun of him and his artistic talents. At eighteen, he married, had three children, and then divorced. He then traveled for many years with his brother around the country—much of the time, they were homeless. During his travels, he and his brother wrote songs and played them on his guitar on the streets. "I first started playing the guitar 'cause I was hungry. I play better when I'm hungry. When you feel hollow, you aren't full of stuff that gets in your way. While growing up, I believe my family was trying to put a damper on my gift of music. Too many people told me I don't have talent."

However, David remembers a fairly happy childhood.

My dad was a buffer for Keeler Brass, a car parts place. My mother sold baby clothes at Baby Bliss. I have six brothers and two sisters. I went to Special Ed and they went to Caledonia High School. But the house was filled with love. Ma would have a big pot on the stove for everybody to eat. I had a pretty good life. She cooked chicken and dumplings, I'm at a loss for words. I didn't like it very much. Chili was my favorite, I guess.

I grew up in a big farmhouse on 68th Street. Kalamazoo was up the road. But Dad didn't keep heat upstairs, because he wanted to save money. If you wanted to get warm, you came downstairs, but we also had lots of blankets so it didn't hurt us much.

My parents bought a lake. It's called Angel Lake in Grand Rapids. It's west of Sand Lake—going up towards Muskegon. My brother and I, we'd go fishing. I'd get up in the morning at five o'clock to go fishing. When the steam was still on the lake and the sun not even coming up yet, just throw my line in there and watch the bass hit it. I guess those are the good times. I could see the mist on the lake. I'd get maybe ten bass, maybe.

I enjoyed growing up with my brothers, and sometimes I miss not going through some of the stuff they did 'cause they would . . . I don't really want to talk about it, but they would go out to the tavern and raise heck. Sometimes I would tell them, "I want to be like you guys, to do what you guys did," but they told me, "You don't want that life." They said it was no fun doing the stuff that they did.

Later, after David divorced, he traveled with his brother.

My brother took me and we went to Arizona and Idaho. So I did a lot of traveling. And that's where I picked up the guitar and started playing. I liked the traveling 'cause I needed to clear my head after my divorce. My three kids are young adults now, in their twenties. They live in Grand Rapids, Camelot Trailer Park.

I'm close with this one brother, but it's because I traveled with him for a while. I was in Idaho for like nine years. Idaho was peaceful there. It's like they have the same climate here except the cold is a little different cold here. It's like not a damp cold. You just don't have all the wetness of the cold. And right now, it's warming up out there. It's in like the sixties and seventies compared to our weather here. I miss Idaho quite a bit. Before I left to come up here, I was fishing for rainbow trout up in the mountains with my brother. I took them home and cooked them. I fried them.

David returned to Michigan and was homeless.

Eventually, I decided to move back to Michigan, but had no resources to try to begin my life anew on my own. When I got off the bus from Idaho I didn't know where I was going to go. I went and slept in a field there for a while, but it was March and it was real cold, and so I stayed out there for maybe three or four days. It was kind of cold but it was about the same time as it is now, but it was almost the end of March so it was in the forties. I had to get up in the morning because it would be quite brisk and walk so I could get the warmth back in my legs and my feet, but then somebody told me, "You need to go to the mission 'cause you're going to freeze." So I took that advice and went to the mission. And I was there for six months.

I write songs a little bit, and I was playing the guitar on the street corner for a while just to make some money in Lansing. I didn't do too bad, I guess. I went out and got a license, otherwise you're panhandling. So I paid $5 for a license to play.

Childhood and Domestic Violence

According to the National Children's Alliance, "In 2010, an estimated 1,560 children died from abuse and neglect in the United States. In the same year, Children's Advocacy Centers around the country served over 266,000 child victims of abuse, providing victim advocacy and support to these children and their families. In 2011, this number was over 279,000" (NCA n.d.). The U.S. Department of Health and Human Services Administration for Children and Families states that of all children who were in foster care during the year 2009, an estimated 0.05–2.04 percent were the subject of substantiated or indicated maltreatment by a foster parent or facility staff member.

When Jackie was a year old, she moved in with foster parents who abused her physically, mentally, and emotionally for several years. Her biological dad had also abused her older siblings but died before Jackie returned to live with her mom and stepdad. Who put Jackie in a foster-care home where the parents abused her? Is there any screening or careful follow-up of these families? What were the criteria for an individual to become a foster parent? How could the abuse go on for so long and no one notice? Are people who work in the social welfare system too few and overworked and burned out? While the percentage of cases of foster-care abuse may be statistically relatively small, it is still too big; certainly it is unacceptable for even one child to fall through the cracks.

When Jackie returned to her biological family, they bounced around from state to state and were homeless—living in her parents' car, motels, and shelters. Tired of constantly moving, she left home at fourteen, dropped out of school, and went to work.

A white woman now in her early thirties, Jackie had had multiple exposures to abuse. Her foster-care dad abused her. Her biological dad abused her siblings. We do not know if he abused Jackie, as she moved into a foster-care home by age one. Later, her husband, originally from Honduras and the father of her two daughters, abused her. Her daughters witnessed this abuse. Ultimately, Jackie and her daughters became homeless.

According to the National Coalition for the Homeless, "Battered women who live in poverty are often forced to choose between abusive relationships and homelessness. . . . Approximately half of all women and children experiencing homelessness are fleeing domestic violence" (NCH 2009c).

Jackie remembered the foster home from her early years:

I remember when I was two. I remember really young. I actually was in a foster home. I lived in San Bernardino, California. I was five, almost six years old when I finally was able to come home. I know there are a lot of good foster homes out there, but I was actually in a bad one. I was abused and actually went to school. I had bruises all over me.

I think the biggest impact in my life, though, has been in the foster home because it was such a bad experience. I guess I had a lot of common sense even then. I remember they used to have these bushes outside their driveway where I would sit. I'm like three years old and I would hide from them, and just sit and think about where I was and not wanting to be there. It was just luck, I guess, that the foster mother had went on some business trip. The foster father had sent me to school and the principal had seen bruises on my arm where my shirt wasn't covering it.

They had Child Protective Services check me out. I told them. I was honest. I said, "Well, they beat me with coat hangers. They beat me with sticks. I was whupped because I didn't want what they ate. They'd send me to my room all the time without food. I go nights with no dinner. I mean for a little kid, that's bad, and I used to tell 'em. I remember hoarding food in my room because I was always hungry. They had like a hall closet and I would go in there. I don't know why, but this man would keep these energy bars, or something to that effect. This is in the early eighties so I'm not sure what it was. I would get up in the middle of the night because I was hungry because they didn't let me eat that night and I would eat those. They would count them the next day, and they knew, and I would get beat for it.

It was just a bad cycle. I was sexually abused there, so I went through a lot of things. I had a bad view of guys when I came out. I remember my stepdad—I didn't go and sit next to him, talk to him for two years. I couldn't be around older men. It scared me and so I guess it's learn, live, or die—you gotta change your life even when you're young. You gotta realize the things that happen to you then, what kind of person did it, and move on. That was a big part in my life, remembering that, and it's changed my life for the better because I realized what bad people were really early, which most kids don't. Their mother might tell them, you know, "stranger danger," but you don't really know until you've witnessed it firsthand.

Jackie recounted how she returned to her own family.

The school stepped in, and then the state stepped in and they allowed me to go stay with my grandmother. She actually had custody of me, but she was too sick and her husband was dying of cancer. She was already taking care of my sister. By then, I'm five years old, so she gave me the option to go and live with my mother or go back into another foster home. Since I had already experienced a bad foster home, I decided to go and live with my mom. I moved back in with the family that I didn't even really remember.

I'm the fifth child. Yeah, so my mom couldn't even really afford the children she had, and the foster parents I had lived with would move around so my mom couldn't see me, because they were hoping on adopting me.

It all worked out though. I ended up going home. They were living in San Bernardino and we just bounced around from place to place. I think they were living at the Circle 8 Motel, and there was six, seven people there, because my mom had remarried another man and he's been my stepdad since I was one.

When my biological dad was alive, he was just a really bad man. He had done a lot of bad things. My mom at that time was working in a meat factory. She was doing the paperwork for 'em. My biological father and my mother's brother stole blank checks from the work, and my mom actually went to prison for forty days until she was exonerated from it because she had nothing to do with it. My uncle went to jail for like five years for it and my father got off scot-free.

My biological father was very abusive to the children. This man had sexually molested people in my family—other girls that were in my family. He used to poke my brother in the hand with a fork because my brother was left-handed and he wanted him to be right-handed. He'd make him sit on a toilet for three hours to potty-train him and would scare him, keep him in the dark because he would wet his pants. He beat my older brother with a two by four, and then he hurt my other two sisters sexually. I was under one year old when it happened, but I hear all the stories about it afterwards from siblings, from everybody.

My family, a lot of times, seems to have really bad luck. When you do have a choice in life, and it takes you down one road, they just maybe seem to make the wrong choice. So, it seems like every time we turned around, if you get one step forward, we were like four steps back, financially. They say money's not everything, but it actually is, because if you don't have enough money to have a roof over your head, to feed your children, it's just, it's a very scary thing.

Moving back in with my own mom and stepdad was intimidating. I didn't know these people and had to learn who they were and figure out where I fit in there. My mom was on public assistance from different places. Every once in a while she'd get a job—usually it was at like a convenience store doing management stuff. She did some college work, but never went all the way through. She had done bookkeeping. But she had made not so many great choices and financially didn't have a lot of money.

I remember my stepdad used to go "mattress hunting." He would find just old beat-up mattresses around on the street or by people's dumpsters. He would attach them onto his car and go take them to some mattress place. You'd get like a dollar or two for every mattress you brought in. So he'd make, like, extra money that way. It was interesting, I mean different.

When I was around eight, me and my younger brother used to get different things from the dumpsters. We would find clothing, toys, electronics, all different things people had just thrown away. My stepdad's pretty good at tinkering with things, fixin' stuff, and we'd put it out there, when we did have a home, and we'd sell it for yard sales. I used to do like the little lemonade stands, making extra money.

Over the next few years, Jackie's family moved a lot:

We bounced around a lot—something would happen. My Mom would lose her job and then next, we would have to go, and my stepdad always had like a big car, like a big ole Lincoln, so we'd all fit in there. Many times I remember me and my brother being in the back of the car. My oldest sister, I think she moved out when she was seventeen and did her own thing and started having children. My oldest brother, he had some mental problems so he was institutionalized off and on. He was bipolar and they didn't realize he was then, because they didn't diagnose that then.

Mainly it was just my mom and two kids and my stepdad, but sometimes it was fun. You're young and camping, being in the back of the car. He'd find a little TV or something and we'd play little games back there or be able to plug it into the AC/DC plug.

I remember we moved to Nevada for a while. We had to stay at the mission. We would be out at six in the morning—me and my brother having to wait a couple hours for the bus to pick us up in the snow. Usually we'd wander off because we didn't even know where we were going at first. We were staying at parks, feeding the ducks in the morning and the afternoon, waiting to go back to the mission while they were out looking for a job. They just weren't able to find nothing up there so we ended up having to move from there.

We went to Utah for a while. That was my real, big first taste of snow because we were there during the wintertime. We had a house for a while there. But it seemed like when we did get a house we always had other people living with us. When we very first moved there, we moved into this mission. There were these little trailers like everybody lived in and you had to go outside and you'd have to cook, and people did like community cooking outside with big ole pots and soups. Some things were bad there, because there was this trailer that had the showers in it. It was weird, yeah, and cold. Half the time you didn't have hot water, and sometimes you just wished you had a nice warm house to live in.

I think I was like twelve years old then, and got the idea, you know, "Oh we're poor." We didn't half the time have the right clothes to wear to school. My mom liked to gamble, so that wasn't really great. Las Vegas had this place called St. Vincent's. You could go there for the afternoon and get something to eat, but you have to wait in line for like an hour and a half to get in there. We would just sleep in the car, eat. I remember eating out of a jar of peanut butter because that's all we had. One other time in California, me and my brother would go behind this one grocery store and we would get their day-old goods, like their baked goods and stuff. I think about it now and I can't believe I did that, but that was our means of survival. Thank God we never got sick doing it.

I think it was the last trailer park we had lived at. I was just getting ready to turn fourteen and my mom had taken money from her job. I guess the boss had found out and it really caused a lot of problems in the family—everybody arguing and fighting—and then everybody kind of went their separate ways and my mom and stepdad separated. So he left me and my mom only there, and knowing that we weren't going to be able to pay the rent.

Finally, Jackie left home:

At fourteen years old, I moved out. I guess I was getting tired of it. Luckily, the same day I found a nanny job for these Filipinos. I babysat their kids at night so I had a roof over my head. I worked in a factory, the Freeman factory, illegally, because you're not supposed to work there until you're sixteen. They did shampoos and lotions and hairsprays. I worked there in the morning and babysat at night. I did that for close to a year.

When her husband—he was in the Philippines—came home he was kind of lecherous. Yeah, and I'm fourteen years old, and he wasn't a very nice guy. So I knew I was going to have to find another avenue to get out. I found another family that needed a nanny. So I was a nanny for them until I was—I think it was two months before my seventeenth birthday. I worked at Jack in the Box in the morning and I was a nanny for them at night.

Well, it was getting old, too. Finally, I needed, I guess, a change. Also, it got to a point where they weren't paying me no more so that was just like I was babysitting so I could have a roof over my head and working a lot more hours than what I needed. I went and came back to live with my mom for a couple months.

Jackie then moved to Tennessee:

I had my oldest brother living in Tennessee—and he had called me, wanting me to come up. He said, "Well the jobs are better up here. Come on up here. I'll pay for your ticket if you go." So I hee-hawed him about it for a while because I really wasn't sure—that's a long way to go! Finally, I just decided, "Okay, you pay for my bus ticket up and I'll go." So, I ended up in Pigeon Forge, Tennessee, in, I think it was October of '94.

I got a job the next day working at Sagebrush and worked there for eight years. I started out being a busgirl. When I left there, I was kitchen manager, so I ended up doing everything there. They sold that company and they had other little restaurants—a Beach House and Mel's Diner—a fifties kind of diner. My family started migrating, one by one, because they were going through a lot of different things. Every one of my siblings were having children. I was the only one that didn't have any.

My one brother was doing crystal meth and he had two boys and just had a baby girl. I just made him realize that what he was doing wasn't the greatest thing. It took him awhile. I guess that's a pretty bad thing to be on, but he cleared himself up. He's got a good family, takes care of his kids.

I was working a lot of hours and I felt a little bad for them. I had my little apartment and we ended up getting a house. I had extremely good credit then, and it went down because I did bad choices. I should have just thought of myself and got myself together. I didn't, because I was thinking about them.

Jackie married, had two little girls, and became homeless again:

I wanted a family. I'm twenty-six years old, have no children. Well, I made bad choices myself in 2003 when I was living in Tennessee. I met my children's dad and I didn't realize I had a rough life, but I was never in a lot of domestic violence, except for when I was a little kid in a foster home. It's a lot different when you're a child and it's an adult and when you're an adult to another adult. I married someone that was violent and an alcoholic. I don't do drugs. I don't drink. I think my crutch is that I smoke cigarettes.

My homelessness in Tennessee was I ended up having to leave my husband to go to a domestic violence shelter. It was really hard because I had two little girls, and I decided I had to make some changes in my life for myself and for them because I didn't want them to go through what I had already went through as a child.

I learned from everybody else's mistakes. I'm going to get out of this abusive situation. When he was sober, he was such a good guy, but when he was drinking, he was such a bad guy. I mean I woke up.

I guess I didn't really look deep enough into the person that I picked for. Well I didn't really pick. We ended up sort of dating and I found out two months later that whoop! I was pregnant and so I was like, "Okay, this means something" and started realizing he wasn't such a great guy. He's from Honduras, so he had a lot of issues. I have little Spanish girls. They're very beautiful girls, but he had immigration, alcohol, and violent issues.

I was like, "Well, we can work through these, if we love each other enough, we can work through 'em" and I loved enough, but he didn't. He was like Dr.

Jekyll and Mr. Hyde. I woke up many a times with butcher knives being next to my bed. One time I woke up and the headlights of my vehicle were—his family had painted 'em black.

Okay, I'm living in this townhouse, eight and a half months pregnant, and he's out. One night, he's supposed to be coming home from work. He comes home with some guy. I've never even seen the fella before and he swears it's his brother, but it's not. It's some drunk he's done found, or a cousin, who knows? And I have my sister living with me. I have her younger daughter staying there. Then my mom and stepdad are actually staying there because they lost their place. My stepdad got really sick and at that time we didn't know what it was, but it was like the prelude to intestinal blockage and rupture. He's went through like ten surgeries, but he's still alive.

My husband and this guy come home, and I open the door and they're both soused. The first thing I know, okay, let's get my husband upstairs to bed and if he can go to sleep, he'll be fine. But, no, he's aggravated because I guess he starts arguing with this fella and I'm trying to get the one fella out of the house while getting him upstairs. They start brawling and fighting and next my husband puts it on me. He beats the living crap out of me and takes off.

I have to go to the hospital that night to check to make sure I was fine, and they gave me shots to calm me down. I ended up having my daughter two weeks early because of it. I let our doctor know everything about what had happened because I was worried because he had hit me in the stomach. I was worried that the baby was hurt or something. They thought she was fine, but it ended up inducing my labor early.

But, the thing that was funny was, I come back home, it's like three in the morning. I'm tired, bruised up, and here comes the sheriff's office calling me, saying that my husband was on some back road with like four or five other drunk people and that they did a test on him and said he was sober. I knew he was soused when he left three or four hours before, and they wanted me to come pick him up because he didn't have a driver's license.

And I was like, "You're crazy. I just got out of the hospital for him beating the living tar out of me. I will not pick him up." And they said, "Well they took everybody else that was in the car to jail." Well, they didn't really want him driving because he was drunk, but because they had some break-ins at some of the rental cabins that they decided to let him drive. So, he ended up driving over to the house and sat in the car and he went on a three-day binge. He would hound me and hound me until I couldn't take it. I brought him back because I guess I had my own issues.

I didn't realize that my immune system had attacked my thyroid, and that that's where this depression was coming from. I thought I was having some bad baby blues or something and I just didn't think I could do it without him. I went through a lot of crazy feelings like that, and then I realized actually I could and that I didn't need him. But he made me feel all the time that I needed him—that I couldn't do it without him—and I didn't realize that was half of his ploy. I think it was in my last six months with him I found out other people that he had dated before me and how they had got pregnant and lost their babies, and it made me realize, and wonder if it was due to him that they lost them. And he beat them.

He would work under the table pretty much wherever he could get, because he wasn't legal, so that was a really big issue with us and with me being pregnant. When you get farther along, it's harder to get another job and take care of the guys, and half the time what money he was making, he was gambling with his friends, or it was going to alcohol, or "My family needs this or that." Our family needs never came first.

Another time, he ended up threatening our lives and almost killed us one night and finally—I'd had enough. I mean I woke up. Well, when he was drunk, he was drunk, and he had a bad habit of wanting to drive when he was drunk. I had went to my mom's house to do laundry and he was supposed to pick me up. When he got there I didn't realize he had been drinking and we had gotten in the car. There was a really big ravine. It's called the Pigeon River on the Spur and Gatlin between Gatlinburg and Pigeon Forge. Many people have wrecked, and if you go down there, there's a good chance you're gonna die. You can seriously get hurt. He kept trying to turn the car into the river to go down the cliff and he was scaring us. The girls were crying. I was crying. I was trying to get him to calm down. He's hitting me as he's going.

I'm begging him to stop the car just so we can get out, and he finally pulled over to stop the car. I'm halfway out of the car—I have one leg out of the car, my back end out of the car—and he decides to take off and I almost got hit by another vehicle. When we finally got to the house—he wouldn't let me get out. He just kept us in the house and was standing at the door.

I didn't see what was before me, but when I had my youngest child, it kind of helped. She saved me. I kind of got my brain back together and realized what was going on and what other people were seeing that I wasn't seeing. So I knew I had to do—whatever I had to do—after I had her, to get on my own, have my own transportation and get away from him, so I did what I could to do it.

I was very outgoing, and the day I left him I could put on one hand all the people that I used to know that I used to do things with and converse with, and then what I had now. I had my family because I wouldn't let him get rid of them, and I had my children. In a way, it helped because it limited opportunities or things.

If I had all these friends, and all these things, then maybe I would have stayed in Tennessee, but when I left, I had my children, my family—my outer family, my mom and them—so it was like, "Well, where do I go from here?" I had to make a plan, a goal, to make a better life for us. I had to get a job, get a place.

He didn't even want me talking to his family. He spoke English and Spanish, but you know, I never learned Spanish, because that was his avenue of always keeping things from me.

The friend I have up here in Michigan that has my nephew, she just kept calling. She wanted me to leave him and make a better life for me and my girls. I hee-hawed about it because I didn't think my life was so bad then, but I realized after I had Angelina, my youngest, yeah, it was that bad. I mean I got to the point where I cried every night and I felt like I was backed up into a corner. That was probably the worst feeling I've ever had. My marriage to him at the end was very low, and when you're there at the bottom, there's only one way to go is up. Sometimes it takes a while.

You gotta get over the sadness; everybody goes through the "Oh, it was my fault. Maybe I should've done this. Maybe I should've done that." It took me a while to get over that, and make a better plan for me and my girls, and realize that you know it was him, not me, and move on from there.

But with my marriage, he cheated on me a lot, but he kept it to himself. Everybody in town knew about it and this is, I mean, a small town, but kind of big, and it was a tourist town. A lot of people knew me and they knew what he was doing, and some people told me, "Hey, look, he's here and doing this," or "He's out at this bar doing this." He would swear he wasn't and then we'd fight because I accused him. Then he would accuse me of doing something and, like, I was always at home so that wasn't happening. Then, he beat me.

Well, I used to "recycle my problems." I did do that. I did that in my marriage. My interpretation of recycling is that you see what's before you. You're seeing it. You're getting the data, you know this is wrong, this is wrong, this is wrong. This is not going right, and you just grind it up and keep on going in that same life. I got to the point where I knew things were wrong. I didn't want this marriage anymore. Being pregnant with Angelina, my second daughter, having her, that just made things so much clearer.

And I'm like, "Oh my God, look at what you're going through." I mean, "Look at what you're putting your daughter through." I thought my biggest reason for staying there was to give my oldest daughter, her name's Tatiana, was to give her a father. I wanted her to have a father. I guess that was a big issue for me. I realized, "You know what, Jackie? She doesn't need a father, not if it's a man like this, she doesn't. You know she's better off without one because you're making her life worse, and you're wanting to make it better but you're actually making it worse," and that was really a douse of water. I don't think most people realize what they're putting their family through when they go through something like that, so they just have that moment of clarity. They see what's before them and realize what it's costing them.

And it costed my daughter, but she's okay. If I go into a grocery store 'til today, you'll see bottles of wine, little six-packs of beers. My daughter will say, "Oh my, I hate beer, that's yucky." She'll go on and she'll tell anybody about how her daddy drinks beer, and "He's mean when he drinks beer." My daughter remembers this. She's seen him beat on me. She doesn't like arguing. She doesn't like fighting. I just couldn't believe that she's four years old and now already knows she can't stand people that drink, which I guess is a good thing to a point.

But I feel like I've done that to her, because she's my daughter and I should have got her out of it before I did. So, I have a lot of regrets, and my best way of amending them is to try and give her the best life that I can. I'm sad about it at times. I try not to cry about it. I guess it's helpful now when you're sad about it. You let the feelings out and stuff, but sometimes when you do it, you're left stuck in the same rut because what is it—the self-loathing of "what did I do?" "how did I do it?" and I have a bad habit of doing that. I analyze myself—why I did this, why I did that.

I moved to a domestic violence shelter with my two daughters and within a year moved to Michigan.

Family Estrangement

According to the National Institute on Alcohol Abuse and Alcoholism,

> The relationship of alcohol and drug use to homelessness is interactive and iterative in that it is both a cause and an effect of homelessness. . . . It is difficult for an individual with limited financial resources to remain in stable housing. When significant proportions of those financial resources are spent on alcohol or other substances, maintaining stable housing becomes even more difficult. However, it is difficult for an individual to focus on substance abuse treatment when basic survival needs for food and shelter are precariously and unreliably met. The stress

and danger associated with homelessness also may feed back into the cycle of relying on alcohol or other substances as a coping strategy. (NIAAA n.d.)

Bill was making seventy to eighty thousand dollars a year—but all his earnings went for drugs and alcohol. A white male now in his forties, he worked hard but was in and out of jail and prison. Finally, one day his wife kicked him out of the house and he lived in his truck, abandoned houses, campers, and laundry rooms of apartment buildings.

Allyson Bolt wrote about her conversations and interview with Bill:

He talked of times he would pray for rain, so he could drink the puddle water. . . . It was particularly interesting to hear Bill's story because he is in recovery from the addictions. So, he was able to talk candidly about how he got the low points, what he is concerned with now, and who he wants to help. He is one participant who is already functioning in many ways in the mentor role. When I got home tonight, the image of drinking water from the puddle stayed with me. It always will.

Bill told us the story today about living for a while between a washer and dryer in an apartment building. He was passing a house the other day and he could smell Bounce dryer sheets. He said it reminded him of those nights in the laundry room. Bill has severe and chronic neck pain, but is in fairly good spirits.

When I interviewed Bill, I was quite nervous, wanting to make sure I did a good job, asked the right questions, and stay out of the way as much as I could. I realized that though I only had a few basic questions in my head about the interview, I subconsciously had a plan for how it would go—What was his childhood experience? His family experience? Where did he go after he was out of his parents' home? Where did things start going "wrong?" What was the lower point? What gave him hope? What has he done since getting out of that situation? What does he want others to know who have never experienced homelessness? It basically functions as a timeline of a person's life. I was excited to get his perspective because he has shared some very low moments with me, but also is in a place now where he believes that is behind him. So, to get that angle will add another perspective to homelessness.

Bill began his life in Canada:

I was born in Argentia, Newfoundland, in Canada, and lived there for six years. My dad died when I was six. My mom remarried right away. I remember playing in Newfoundland. It was wonderful. I played—my playground was a castle which was the first transatlantic tower, they called it. That and St. John's Harbor. I was playing around with fishermen who used to go out and net fish by hand.

My stepdad was in the Navy. So, we moved around a lot. We stayed on the naval base. Well, half my time I spent with my grandfather. He worked on the ocean liners, the freighters that carried coal. My uncle was the governor of St. Johns. My mom was just a housewife. My mom has never worked in her life. I have a younger sister, one year younger. I had an older brother. He was killed on an oil-rig accident. I was about twenty years old when that happened. But he was raised by my grandfather, so I didn't see him that much. I don't know why he wasn't raised by my mother. He just wanted to stay with grandfather. He wanted to stay there and we traveled so much.

When I was six, I went to Midway Island by Hawaii, then California and then Tennessee. My favorite place was Midway Island. No cars, all bikes. That was neat. I was there for two years. I've always been an adaptable person. I adapt to environments around me. I fit in easy. I guess I have that personality.

So, I never had no trouble with school kids or nothing like that until I got a little bit older, because I have a thumb missing and so I got teased a lot. I was born with a thumb but no bone. At three years old, they cut it off, so it wouldn't just flop around. But when I got to first and second grade, I was the teased kid. And I held some resentments and anger.

I tried to block out getting picked on to not deal with it. I tried to joke about it to hide the hurt, telling kids that I slammed it in the door and it fell off, or I had it in a hot dog bun and I ate it. Then they used to put the Muscular Dystrophy boxes on my desk in school. They'd come by and donate money. Well, the kids are cruel, but I always had a pocketful of candy. I'd take the money and go buy candy and bubblegum. You just try to hide the hurt by joking about it. Sometimes it's the only thing you can do, just laugh, so that nobody notices. I had a hard time when there's other kids getting picked on. I used to really stick up for 'em. I didn't want anybody to go through what I went through. So, we had one of them kids in school that had one of them kidney bags, and they used to snap towels at him in gym class. It angered me, and that was anger more from what I felt, probably, not him.

So, I was raised by mom and stepdad. He's real strict and I feared him. He was loud. Wasn't abusive physically to my mom, but verbally he was. He had a fear about him. That's why I don't like to argue with people. I used to hear my dad yell at my mom. I have a deep voice and it bothers me. I try to talk low so that I don't sound like I am yelling at somebody. But, I couldn't stand it. I used to cover my head up with the pillow when they argued. I walk away instead of dealing with confrontation. There was some make-up, but we were just so thankful that the yelling stopped. It's like, "Man, I can't wait 'til it stops." It was a long, quiet time—a couple days of not talking. But I couldn't stand it. I hated it. I know walking away isn't the best way to deal with it, but, if I can't talk normal to somebody, then it's not worth me getting into that battle, because there are too many memories. There's no resolution by yelling 'cause we end up saying things that hurt people when we don't mean it. And the tongue is awful sharp.

My stepdad was in the military. And we moved to Lansing. He's a plasterer and drywaller. And my mom continued to stay at home. They're both still alive. My relationship with them is pretty good. I don't talk to 'em very much. My dad's retired and they pretty much do their own thing. I don't have a whole lot going on and they don't. Their big thing is going to Wal-Mart, literally, or walking the mall. And I don't need my mom to call me every day and say, "Hey, we walked the mall today." But my sister talks to 'em every day. And she has a closer relationship than I do.

My stepdad basically said when I was eighteen, it's time to get out of the house or start paying rent. He said, "If you want anything, you gotta work for it." I started working in the bar when I was fifteen. I was a dishwasher at the Blinker Light in Potterville. My dad was, "You want anything, you go get a job." And I been working ever since. Except for the last few years, but I've always worked one or two jobs.

Bill believes his troubles began at eighteen:

When I was eighteen, I started paying rent a little bit, and I went to start at college. I got in a little trouble, so I kinda left. I got sent to prison when I was nineteen years old. Alcohol was a factor that made me make a poor choice. There's consequences. Cost me two and a half years of my life. I got out, got a job couple days later. I did the best I could while I was locked up to improve myself. I took some classes that teach you how to do building trades, plumbing and drywall stuff. I took some college classes, some business classes, and tried to do what I could to improve myself. The only thing I didn't do, which they didn't offer—well, they did, wasn't required to go—was AA. That's what caused me to be in trouble. I wish they would have. Every time you get in trouble, what's the biggest factor? And it was alcohol. And they never addressed it. And if they would have, they probably would have stopped my criminal career then. When I got out, I continued to drink and make poor choices and I would get in trouble more.

I did a couple of li'l stints in the county jail and then I went back to prison. I got out in '84 and then went back in 1990. Drinking and using caused me to make another poor choice and I went back for fourteen months. This time they required me to go to AA. I didn't take it serious, and when I got out again, I got a job the next day where I worked for two years. Alcohol cost me that job, and a couple of weeks later I got another job that I stayed at for nine years as a mechanic. But, I dealt with alcohol and drugs, and my employer never knew I had a substance abuse problem.

I had to work to support my habit. I liked to work. I knew I had to work. I kept it together between eight and five. Never went to work high or drunk. In that period, I had gotten married and had a son. But I had worked a limousine job right after I got out of prison the first time. That triggered my drug addiction quite heavy. It introduced me to cocaine. Peer pressure. You want to be accepted, so you do what you have to fit in with the crowd.

I had a son and I was spending a lot of time hanging out and not doing the fatherly things. One thing led to another. Went to prison, got out, and continued bad behavior. Got a job at the dealership and I was making $17 an hour and taking home $500 a week, and plus I had my own scrap-metal business where I was making money. I was making probably seventy to eighty thousand dollars a year and I had nothing to show for it. Nothin'. It all went to drugs and alcohol.

My wife said, "I don't want you around the house. You are not responsible." And that's what started my homelessness. I started living out of my truck. She kicked me out of the house for almost nine months one time. I stayed in my truck—almost two years.

At times, I've lived in abandoned houses and campers that are on the back of trucks. I bought one of them and just shoved it into the driveway of a house that was abandoned. I've laid my head down in laundry rooms of apartment buildings before. I'd pray for rain water so that when I'd be so thirsty I'd get out and would drink water out of a puddle in the parking lot. The majority of the time I was in a vehicle. They didn't even know I was homeless. They would let people off work early. Well, when everybody left, when it got dark, I would go back to the dealership and park in the parking lot, 'cause that was a safe place, and just curl up in the front seat of the truck. Either had so much in me to drink, or ran out of money for drugs. I wouldn't even put money in my gas tank. So, I had to make sure I could at least get back to work.

I'm living in a truck. If it wouldn't have been for the uniforms they provided, I wouldn't have had clothes, 'cause I wouldn't waste money on laundry. I would stop at a Shell gas station and wash my hair in the sink. And try and do the birdbath wash in the sink before I went to work. I mean, nobody at work knew. The only friends I had were the ones that I got my drugs from. They were doing the same thing. And the cocaine. I basically isolated myself 'cause I was ashamed.

My family knew I was doing something that wasn't right, and I just cut myself off from them because I was ashamed of what was going on. My son knew I was doing something. He knew I was doing something that his mom didn't like, that she would ask me to leave. And, after a while, he caught on to what was going on. I missed a lot of his growing up. Anytime there was school events, I was there. And I was sober and I wasn't high, but other than that—in and out of his life. I missed it. I was either in a drunken stupor or high. One minute he was six or seven years old and the next minute he's sixteen or seventeen years old and he's getting his license. And where did all that time go? But, I was in such a fog that I didn't even realize it was passing me. It is tough on our relationship.

At one point, he tried to find me. Well, his mother knew that I was staying in an abandoned house. He used to come up on the porch of the house and knock on the door. And holler, "Dad!" I would be on the other side of the door, less than two feet from him. I'd have my alcohol and my drug paraphernalia and I wouldn't move 'cause I didn't want him to hear me. I'd just be cryin'. There's times that I'd just stay in my vehicle at a rideshare. Sometimes he'd come up and be beatin' on the window of the car. Sometimes I would get up. It all depends on what condition I was in. Sometimes I wouldn't. You know, pretty soon, he just said, "Screw it." He basically said, after a while, he called me his "sperm donor." But in the last four or five years that I have been clean we've been doing real well. We have a real good relationship. He calls me "Dad" now.

But it was a very bad time. And for me to ignore that feeling and them emotions, I just kept using so I wouldn't have to deal with it. You know how bad I felt about the relationship with my son. And in order to not deal with it, I just kept using drugs. I was doing three hundred to four hundred dollars a day of cocaine. I was capable of making that kind of money a day, legally, by working and by hauling scrap metal—not by robbing stores or stealing. I am that creative.

That job ended in 2000. No driver's license. I didn't have a driver's license for a lot of years, but the addiction was getting so carried away that I was using so much. I was exhausted from having to hustle to make that money, so that at five o'clock I kinda slam down a few beers and then get off and running doing the drugs. I was physically exhausted from trying to figure out, how am I gonna do it? There was too many years of doing it constantly.

I had this sort of balance almost, of control and no control. And I didn't do it during the workday. And I didn't do it on Sundays. But as soon as those set hours were in place, it was like I had business hours from nine to five. When businesses or people were out moving around, I was capable of making money—either working on cars, hauling scrap metal. I mean 'cause I worked at an oil-change place and they only provided oil changes, but if I seen something else is wrong with the car, I would offer to do that work. And say, "Look, I get outta work at noon from the oil-change place. Meet me at AutoZone. For $60, I'll put a water pump in your car instead of you spending $300. And it would take me twenty minutes and there was $60. And if I did two or three of them in an afternoon, that's a couple of hundred bucks. And that's easy money."

So, now it's 2000 and I don't have this job anymore, but I still have the scrap metal. I also went to work at an oil-change place in East Lansing. We were doing sixty cars a day, seventy cars a day. They are college students. That was another gold mine. You got college students that want repairs done to their car. I could do brakes quick, for $40 or $50. They saved a lot of money. Mom and Dad were happy that somebody would do it on the side. Wouldn't have a $300 bill. And when you are dealing with that many cars and customers, they don't have a clue that I have an addiction problem.

It finally got too much. I got pulled over one night. And I had cocaine on me and I went to jail. I did good. I was on a tether. I did real well. I was clean for a couple years while I was on probation. And as soon as that tether was off, I still had it under control. I was going to cognitive-behavioral-thinking classes trying to identify what triggered my use. You know if I ever got the itch, I used to carry a basketball around with me and I'd pull over and just start shooting baskets until I got it out of my system. Then all of a sudden, I got that itch. Then, I started using again.

I didn't reach out to anybody. But you know, I'm stubborn. I think that if I made the problem I can fix the problem. And I wasn't qualified to fix it. I was off on another run again until I got caught. My car broke down one night. A policeman seen me walking and gave me a ride. I thought the car was out of oil. And he said, "That car's not registered to you," so they impounded it. And I had just bought it. When I opened the door, he said let me search through the car. And there is cocaine in the car again, so I went to jail again. I just kept repeating the same cycle. I wouldn't follow what needed to be done to stay clean.

I was determined to do it. And for the last five years I've been clean. Not by sponsors. . . . I got tired of it. I got tired of the same thing over and over.

No, it actually frustrates me 'cause I try to tell 'em what I've been through, and I'm sure there's a ton of people telling me and I wouldn't listen. And I'm sure they're not going to listen until they feel they've had enough. Until they've hit their bottom. But all I can do is just keep saying, "It's not gonna get you nowhere. I'm livin' proof." But it all comes on their own time. When it's gonna affect 'em, like it did me, when I said, "That was it." I went to jail for the last time, for a year for substance abuse, and I said, "That's it. I don't wanna do it. I'm too old to be sittin' in jail. And there's a purpose, I mean, for my life."

For people who have never experienced homelessness or poverty, don't try to identify what you see on TV as that's the way it is. It isn't people just laying in the curbs or just walking around with a paper sack, wine bottle, or nothin' like that. Homelessness can be defined in so many different ways. There's people that are homeless that have education. If you think you're gonna be homeless, the thing is, try to be willing to change, to adapt. You might not be in a six- or eight-hundred-dollar apartment, and you might have to take a job at $7 an hour. Minimum wage. If you lose your job and you find yourself homeless, you gotta be able to adapt. You gotta be able to make sacrifices until you can build yourself back up. But if you're not willin' to make sacrifices, and you're gonna try living that lifestyle, wear them designer clothes, you gotta humble yourself. If it means shopping at Volunteers of America for second-hand clothes, you gotta be willing to adapt. If you're not, your struggles are going to be tough. Emotionally and mentally it's gonna drag your butt down, if you're not willing to adapt. Instead of Fire Mountain, you gotta go to Rally's and eat 99-cent burgers. Instead of regular ground beef, you gotta eat ground turkey, you know? You gotta be willing to adapt and make sacrifices.

Sexual Exploitation

According to the National Alliance to End Homelessness, "It is commonly estimated that 100,000 children are victims of commercial sexual exploitation (CSEC) each year. Further, there is evidence that the number of children being exploited is increasing. The U.S. Department of Justice (DOJ) reports there is an increase in the online solicitation and 'grooming' of children for CSEC, the incidence and violence of online pornography involving children, and only advertisements of children available for prostitution" (NAEH n.d.).

Author R. Barri Flowers wrote in his book *Runaway Kids and Teenage Prostitution* that runaway kids who lack food, shelter, and other fundamental necessities often turn to prostitution. Some become addicted to, or abuse drugs and alcohol. Others move on to "drug dealing, petty theft, and violent criminal activities to support drug habits and make ends meet" (xiii). According to Flowers, approximately 74 percent of runaway kids are white, 20 percent are black, 4 percent are Hispanic and 2 percent are of another race or ethnicity (10).

Dora grew up in Texas. Her father was an alcoholic and abused her mother. Dora, her mother, and siblings moved to Michigan to live with extended family. At fifteen, Dora ran away from home, became a prostitute, and used drugs and alcohol. Eventually, she returned to her family, but as an adult married a man who abused her. Thus, the family pattern repeated itself.

Allyson wrote in her journal:

It was a difficult time for Dora to be interviewing after she had to go to court regarding an assailant, but she wanted to continue with it. She was able to notice the patterns within her family, noting that her dad had been abusive to her mother. She said that her Dad never hurt the kids, but was verbally abusive to her mom. Dora noted that her brothers do not treat women well, and that she has been in many abusive relationships. She seems to be struggling with periods of wanting to be alone, vs. finding herself in toxic relationships. Dora mentioned that she likes being around positive, happy people. She is definitely that way when she comes to programs at Advent House Ministries. I always see her with a smile on her face. I see the patterns, often in women, of learned silence around mistreatment. Many women internalize the anger and do not show it to others, whereas the men—those who are abusive—often express their emotions through hurting a partner or something or someone she cares about. I believe Dora fits into this pattern. She is often highly anxious and depressed and I think it is in part because of this learned silence.

Dora began her life in Texas:

I'm originally from Laredo, Texas. While growing up in Texas, my father drank alcohol excessively, went out with other women, fought a lot with my mother, and abused and beat her. When living in Texas with my dad, it was more like my mom and dad fight all the time and my dad would beat on her when he would come home and he would be drunk. He would go out with other women, and my mom would sit at home and cook his dinner 'cause my mom had to work as well. We had a maid that took care of us and so it wasn't really a good family situation.

The abuse spilled over to us 'cause some of us take abuse from other people. As far as us, the girls, we think that being abused sometimes is okay. And my brothers are abusive to their girlfriends. All three of them are abusive to their girlfriends, and I've been in a few relationships where I've been abused.

Dora, her siblings, and mom moved to Lansing:

Anyway, my mom decided to move with me to Michigan to get away from him. I've been here in Lansing since I was eleven years old. We struggled a lot when we first moved here because we had to live with my mom's family, her brothers, and like, we could only eat when they wanted, when they would let us eat. There's six of us, but one sister lives in Texas, and so the other five of us, we all had to sleep in the same room with my mom. We had to do a lot of chores, and put up with a lot of stuff from her family. My mom used to cry all the time 'cause we didn't have enough food. We didn't have enough money.

One day, she just happened to be looking through her purse and found a $100 bill. So we got to eat really good that day. We ate Kentucky Fried Chicken. I remember that so clearly. It was really like God had put that there for her cause. That's how she felt, and like, she started crying when she found that $100 in her purse. After that day, my mom promised we would never have to live with family again and be hungry or anything like that, that she would always take care of us. The reason we were in the situation was because my father was abusive to her.

In Michigan, I went to Mt. Hope Elementary. I didn't know a bit of English when I first came here and that was really, really hard, to not know English 'cause we came from a whole different world. It's like going into space and the aliens are up there speaking their language and we speak English.

I started going to school and I hated school because the kids used to pick on me. Then I learned to speak English very well. By the time I went to the seventh grade, I didn't like school anymore. I dropped out—my mom was really strict, and in a Mexican family you're not supposed to have friends, or have friends come over, you're not supposed to go to their house. You're not supposed to have phone calls. And I wanted friends, and I wanted to talk to my friends on the phone.

At fifteen, Dora ran away:

Running away caused me a lot of pain and misery because I ended up with a few people that meant no good for me on the streets and prostituting myself, taking drugs, and drinking alcohol for a year or two. I describe this as self-abuse. My mom reported me as a runaway and then the police took me home. I didn't want to be there so I left again. That was the only way I knew how to make money, because I was fifteen. I was a kid, and so I have grown up a lot from that to what I am today. It's like me abusing myself, like me allowing them to do whatever for the money in order to eat and have somewhere to live.

I stayed in a house full of people—girls and guys—and the girls all did the same thing and so I got tired of that, too. I used to get high, smoke weed, and drink a lot, and pop pills and everything. I didn't like that life style. It wasn't for me. And I did it for two years and I left it alone. I did go home finally.

At seventeen, Dora married and then divorced.

I just got up one day and decided I don't want to be there with him because it was abusive and he wouldn't let me see my family or talk to my family. So, I just got up one day and I just left. I didn't take no clothes, no anything, and I filed for the divorce myself, and then I didn't know how to pay bills or rent because he always took care of that. He took care of me because I wasn't allowed to get a job because he didn't trust me. That's part of the abuse, the control. So, when I left, I hated that I had to go to my mother's house to live with her, but I stayed with her only a little bit, over five months. Then, I got my own place. It felt good to have my own place and pay my own bills.

So I was married seventeen years and lived in Lansing that whole time. He wouldn't let me work. My days were like hell, because every day I had to clean, cook, do laundry, iron, and make sure everything is perfect. Today I am still the same person. Have you ever seen *Sleeping with the Enemy*? It's kind of like that at home. Everything had to be perfect. I got out of that relationship. And things are still like that with me. I know it's crazy. I should want my stuff all messed up and everything, but I don't, I have to have everything like Sleeping-with-the-Enemy Guy. He used to want all the labels a certain way and the towels a certain way. I'm still like that.

If things are messy or all over the place, anxiety comes up. I don't like it. If they move something, or if there are kids around, they like to touch things. I just go right behind them and put everything right back. I'm following them like running behind them so they don't touch my things or move them from the way I had them. My friends and my boyfriend say I'm bipolar, but I don't know, 'cause one minute I'm really, really happy. Then, next minute, I could just be crying for nothing and sometimes, so they say that I'm bipolar. I'm like, okay, whatever that might be, but who cares.

The anxiety started when I lost my baby in 2000. I've been on anxiety medication and depression medication . . . since 2000, and it's 2009. For nine years I've been on medication because I get really depressed. Being alone, sometimes it's good in the daytime, its good, but when nighttime hits, it's really hard.

Loneliness

Substance abuse is a serious problem among the homeless. "Although obtaining an accurate, recent count is difficult, the Substance Abuse and Mental Health Services Administration (2003) estimates, 38% of homeless people were dependent on alcohol and 26% abused other drugs. Alcohol abuse is more common in older generations, while drug abuse is more common in homeless youth and young adults. . . . Substance abuse is much more common among homeless people than in the general population" (NCH 2009c). Also, according to the National Coalition for the Homeless, 42 percent of the homeless population is African American (NCH 2009d).

In an interview, Loren shared the difficulties and feelings he had struggling with his mother, who evicted him to the garage. He also talked about his issues with alcoholism, trying to keep a job, living out in the cold, and his inability to comply with rules. Loren said, "Staying at the shelters, it's really . . . no, it's not rough. It's a lonely feeling, because the streets are rough."

Loren grew up in a loving home:

I went to Wood Creek Elementary School and then Dwight Rich Middle School and eventually to Sexton High School. I liked growing up with my friends and enjoyed playing basketball. My parents adopted me. I have two younger brothers.

As a child, my family and I took trips to Charlevoix and had a trailer in Sandy Pines. My parents eventually separated, and my mother worked hard to support me and my brothers.

I had a lot of love growing up. My family took care of me. I really appreciated that. My father taught me to be a man and the responsibilities that come with being a man, watch him as I was growing up and seeing how he lived his life. It made me in some ways want to model my life after him because I got a lot of things that I should have paid more attention to that I'm going through now. I wish I was more like my Dad. He's taught me a lot.

Loren got tough love in the garage:

My mom been there with a lot of love and she gave me that mom tough love. Well, she put me out of the house, the times when growing up and you do things. We'd argue and we'd do different things to make mom mad. A lot of times I deserved it. I used to have my friends over a lot and that sort of thing, and I used to want to do it my way. So, my mom, I don't blame her for any of this. She did what she had to do and she was strict with me. She wanted me to learn what it would be like if eventually, I'm out there on my own having to deal with everything for myself. So, she put me in situations where she was always there if I really needed something. I could always go back to her, but she wanted me to be an adult and learn what it would be like if she wasn't around, and the things that you do. Why do I keep going through this?

Man! I used to stay in my garage, the garage! And these were one of these hard times. I had a car in the garage. My dad bought me a car and I never got it running, so I used to sleep in that car a lot of nights at my mom's place in the garage. I had to do that and that wasn't easy, 'cause it was cold outside a lot of nights. It was wintertime and I had to deal with the elements of the cold. I was thinking about getting back inside to get warm and thinking about what did I do to get into this mess, and how can I stop doing what I'm doing so I can do what's right? Why do I keep going through this?

The main thing was I worried about why me and my mom keep going through this, because my brothers had their situations with my mom but they never got put out. Yeah, why me? So I never really understood that, but it taught me a lot. It made me strong. And I found that I can deal with the weather. Both my brothers were smarter than I was in that aspect. I was into a lot of different things.

I didn't want to continue to live like this, so, at the time, actually it all works out for themselves these kinds of situations. I still like to drink my beer. I love my beer, but it was a time that I wasn't drinking to excess to where you just drinking to drown out your sorrows and you just drink a lot. Things look more alive to me. I see my family. I was around my daughter. I was working my job and I had somewhere to go, so it was all right. So, I slowed that down a lot and it was just nice to finally live right.

Me and Mom, we just get along better, and she knows I got my apartment and everything. Looking back on this now I'm thanking her for what she did do, because it helps me understand more about surviving and depending on yourself. And straightening up because life works one way, and I liked to do a lot of swerving.

To me, it's business. You get up in the morning. It's a routine. It's a way to conduct yourself in society, in life, and I didn't see it then. I still got to focus on it and it's still really hard for me to realize now, but I'm on the right track. Go to work, you come home, you pay your bills, you take care of your family. Family is where it's at. You have a little dinner, watch a little TV with your husband or your boyfriend and what not. You wake up the next morning and you go back to work and you start the day all over again. You take care of your business. If you don't take care of your business, you will be hurting some kind of way. That was one of my biggest things and I'm still going through that.

Life's no room for all that side stuff which I love to do, with the partying and stuff and ignoring what you're supposed to do business-wise and shoving it off to the side. You can't do that no more. I realize situations that I've been in and what I'm going through now, and having my place and everything, and sitting down and talking with people about leases and that sort of thing. And paying bills now—that's where it's at. To me, that's life, that's the way it works.

Less swerves, right? That's right, a lot less swerves. So, in 1999, I lived with my girlfriend for two years. Well, me and her eventually moved on. I stayed with my brother out in Spartan Village. He's a graduate from Michigan State, so I stayed with him. My ex found another guy, so she still let me come around and be there and still see the kids, of course, but I had to come at certain times. They eventually got married and he moved in, and then that put me in a tough spot because I had to leave and that wasn't easy.

Loren became homeless:

The lowest point for me probably, during that stretch of time would be, I slept under some steps out there in East Lansing in this apartment complex. At that time, I have to say I wasn't working. That would be my lowest point, because I was homeless. I had no job, I had nowhere to go. And I'm sleeping under some steps. That'll be something that I will never forget.

I had my duffel bag who I used to call Lucille. It was really nice. A lot of people didn't have this bag. My mom, she got it for me for Christmas, and she must of ordered it somewhere or something because the way it was made and everything, it was just a nice bag, and no one else had that bag. Right, yah, my special bag. Lucille always had everything. I kept all my clothes, all my special personal items, my hygiene items. That bag was always with me wherever I went. So we'd always be out there. I put it on my back. We'd be out there.

There were spider webs on the side of the steps. It was cold out. It was wintertime. And I'm hearing people walk around, going in and out of their apartments, yah, having fun. College kids, yah, it's Friday or Saturday. The lowest point, I have no food, I have no money, just living. And on top of this, I'm trying to stay warm. I'm tired. I've been out living that lifestyle. And, you know, I startled the lady. She seen me. So I spent outside in a bus shelter in case the cops come. That has to be the lowest point.

Well, the shelter was in Lansing and it was like eleven or twelve o'clock at night. It was late, and I would have had to walk a long ways. Yes, it would have been worth making that walk, I suppose, fo' sho', looking back on it now, but it's a lot of politics and stuff too. Some of the people at some of the shelters, they'll take care of you for the emergencies, when it's cold, but sometimes, you get put in a situation and I believe I might have been on a bar or something like that from the mission. Nothing major. I could come back, but I couldn't spend the night, that sort of thing.

Well, there's a guy there. He'll use his job against you, so you need him. He has this power over you. I didn't make my bed. It was wrong. I didn't hurt anybody. I didn't put my top sheet over it and then, my blanket over the top. To me that doesn't solidify the fact why do you have to bar somebody who needs a place to eat and sleep for a silly reason like that. So that means, you hungry, you out there and you homeless and you have no food and you can't come 'cause of something silly like that. To me, that's just a power trip. You're losing sight of what you're doing and why this place is in existence, and why it's there. But those are the rules. You got to basically suck up to these people just to survive, and to me that's wrong. You got to act a certain way, just so you can sleep or eat. It's like walking on eggshells, and to me that's just not cool.

Reflections

The next step for these individuals is to break up their negative life cycles. They will need to recognize and understand their sad pasts and destructive behaviors, and to make changes in their lives as they abandon old, unhealthy habits and move on to become more constructive and self-sufficient human beings.

A Change in Direction

Education empowers you. You never lose the knowledge once you have the knowledge. No one can take that away from you. It's yours for life. You had all these other things taken from you, but they cannot take education away from you.

—Toni Townshend, Advent House Ministries

HOMELESS NO MORE!

Not everyone who has lived on the streets remains there. Some find a way to leave this way of life—perhaps it is even a response to their lifelong feelings of abandonment. They are now in charge of redirecting their lives. How and why do some find the courage, strength, motivation, and inspiration to change and move their lives forward? How do they discover how to access, examine, and confront their profound core issues? How do they develop the capacity to begin to realize they must abandon destructive habits and get an education so they can find a job to become self-sufficient? These questions will not leave me alone. Sadly, because of the severity of their mental illness, some are not even able to begin to conceptualize a way to get off the streets.

Leaving a life of homelessness and finding a home is a profound endeavor. Cultivating one's personal inner resources and developing new concrete skills involves finding meaning or purpose, becoming literate, developing trust, having a mentor, accessing human social services, and finding work—and not necessarily in any set order. Each individual's journey is different. The challenge requires repeated efforts, often with small successes and many failures—one step at a time. People need tremendous hope and faith to travel such a profoundly difficult road. They may be the only family member who takes this route.

Elliot Liebow (1993) talks about women who take the step to leave the streets and access shelters:

> Most homeless women . . . look to shelters to provide that minimum security, nourishment and sociability that begin to make life possible. It is there that the women put together the physical basis for life in a city: food, protection from (human) predators and weather, safe sleep, clean water for washing oneself and ones' clothes, toilets, and a few creature comforts as well. Shelters also serve as a home base for women who have no homes, and provide a pool of persons from which they may choose acquaintances, associates, comrades, and friends. (4)

Liebow continues:

> For homeless women on the street, the struggle for subsistence begins at the animal level—for food, water, shelter, security, and safe sleep. In contrast, homeless women in shelters usually have these things; their struggle begins at the level of human rather than animal needs—protection of one's property, health care, and avoidance of boredom. The struggle then moves rapidly to the search for companionship, modest measures of independence, dignity, and self-respect, and some hope and faith for the future. These needs are not particularly sequential or hierarchical. One can just as easily be immobilized by hopelessness and despair as by hunger and cold. Body and soul are equally in need of nurture and the women must grab whatever they can get when they can get it. (26–27)

BREAKING THE CYCLE

Change is a gradual process involving major and minor transitions; it takes time and patience. Having problems is difficult. Confronting and acknowledging them is even more difficult. Chris Dancisak, former director of community relations at the Michigan

Historical Museum, has said that making necessary change is the greatest challenge we have as human beings—particularly when it relates to survival issues. The older we get, the harder it is to change. However, when change occurs, it can be very sweet.

Mental-health professionals often talk about how individuals repeat family patterns unless they discover a way to interrupt the cycle—usually with the help of others. In a famous article, "Ghosts in the Nursery," Selma Fraiberg (a professor of child psychoanalysis) and her colleagues Edna Adelson and Vivian Shapiro wrote:

> In every nursery there are ghosts. They are the visitors from the unremembered past of the parents, the uninvited guests at the christening. Under all favorable circumstances, the unfriendly and unbidden spirits are banished from the nursery and return to their subterranean dwelling place. The baby makes his own imperative claim upon parental love and, in strict analogy with the fairy tales, the bonds of love protect the child and his parents against the intruders, the malevolent ghosts. (Fraiberg et al. 1975, 387)

The people who participated in "Your Story and Mine: A Community of Hope" grappled with numerous difficult dilemmas as they tried to rid themselves of the ghosts that haunt them. Perhaps they grew tired of their pain. They worked to break up the destructive patterns that they learned from their parents and grandparents, who had inherited them from their ancestors. They left what was familiar and comfortable—although counterproductive—to become more functioning, self-sufficient human beings. Usually, a combination of factors led them to make positive change. In any event, they are now pioneers in a world they and their families never imagined, considered, or experienced. They are weaving new patterns in their families' life tapestries.

In his book *Healing the Child Within* (1987, 125), Charles Whitfield includes a poem by Portia Nelson, who talks about the journey many of us take down the same road, repeatedly making the same mistakes until we find a way to break up unhealthy cycles in our lives.

AUTOBIOGRAPHY IN FIVE SHORT CHAPTERS

(1) I walk down the street.
There is a deep hole in the sidewalk.
I fall in.
I am lost ... I am hopeless.
It isn't my fault.
It takes forever to find a way out.

(2) I walk down the same street.
There is a deep hole in the sidewalk.
I pretend I don't see it.
I fall in again.
I can't believe I am in the same place.
But, it isn't my fault.
It still takes a long time to get out.

(3) I walk down the same street.
There is a deep hole in the sidewalk.
I see it is there.
I still fall in . . . it's a habit.
My eyes are open.
I know where I am.
It is my fault.
I get out immediately.

(4) I walk down the same street.
There is a deep hole in the sidewalk.
I walk around it.

(5) I walk down another street.

INGREDIENTS FOR CHANGE

Susan Cancro, executive director of Advent House Ministries, has talked about how change involves numerous ingredients, often both sweet and bitter. As people discover their inner resources and find meaning and purpose, motivation, trust, literacy, mentors, and more, they must also abandon old friendships and activities that they once enjoyed. As they make new choices and leave a world of living on the streets with drugs and alcohol, or spending time in jail or prison, they often experience much confusion about how and with whom to spend their time. A variety of both abstract and concrete strategies, patience, and tenacity are usually necessary for their new journey in uncharted territory. They must also learn to be kind and forgiving to themselves.

Toni Townshend, literacy director at AHM, introduced me to the work of educator Ruby Payne, who offers some ideas as to why and how people leave poverty: "Typically, poverty is thought of in terms of financial resources only. However, the reality is that financial resources, while extremely important, do not explain the differences in the success with which individuals leave poverty nor the reasons that many stay in poverty. The ability to leave poverty is more dependent upon other resources than it is upon financial resources" (Payne 1998, 16–17).

Payne said that these resources—emotional, mental, spiritual, and physical—include a support system, relationships, role models, and knowledge of hidden rules.

> Emotional resources provide the stamina to withstand difficult and uncomfortable emotional situations and feelings . . . and are the most important of all resources because, when present, they allow the individual not to return to old habit patterns. In order to move from poverty to middle class or middle class to wealth, an individual must suspend his/her "emotional memory bank" because the situations and hidden rules are so unlike what he/she expressed previously. Therefore, a certain level of persistence and an ability to stay with the situation until it can be learned (and therefore feel comfortable) are necessary. This persistence (i.e., staying with the situation) is proof that emotional resources are present. Emotional resources come, at least in part, from role models." (Payne 1998, 17)

Meaning and Purpose

Erika Magers, artist and art therapist, has talked about the writings of Viktor E. Frankl, a psychiatrist who survived four concentration camps, including Auschwitz, in the Holocaust in Europe. Erika said that one day she found Frankl's book *Man's Search for Meaning* (1959). "I took it. It was free. If I find a book in the garbage, that's how I know it's a book I need to read. I read it on a train."

She continued: "Frankl believes that those who can find meaning and purpose during times of profound difficulty are more likely to survive. He became curious why some people survived and others did not. In doing so, he gave himself a purpose. If man has a reason to survive, he can survive anything. I get chills. He kept picturing his wife. He did not know that she had already died. Writing this book gave him a reason to continue even after his wife had died."

Frankl wrote: "Forces beyond your control can take away everything you possess except one thing, your freedom to choose how you will respond to the situation. You cannot control what happens to you in life, but you can always control what you will feel and do about what happens to you" (Frankl 1959, x).

Literacy

Literacy is the ultimate major factor that helps break the cycle of poverty for these people. The National Coalition for Literacy states that literacy helps adults to "get, retain or advance in a job; get off public assistance and earn a family-sustaining income; complete high school or obtain a GED certificate; transfer to a community college or training program; help their children succeed in school; manage their family's healthcare; or learn English, understand U.S. culture, to become an informed citizen" (NCL n.d.).

Toni believes that her job as literacy director is to help these people become as self-sufficient as possible. Some are pursuing an education—including life-skills classes, GED classes, and job-skills classes. They understand now that literacy is their key to moving their lives forward.

> Most of our clients have self-esteem issues stemming from endless different events in their lives. While teaching the GED classes that are basically academic, we try to take a very holistic attitude towards the students because we know they are grappling with so many different issues. It is a wonder that they are in the classroom at all. They come in here feeling they are academic failures. School was a bad experience for most of them, so there was a reason they dropped out. We try to help them overcome these issues.
>
> Literacy is the most important, valuable key to helping them break the cycle and [get on] the path to become self-sufficient. Some states even base their prison budgets on literacy rates. . . .
>
> Most of the students that I work with now come to me with almost nothing physical that they can claim as their own, and their lives are very unpredictable. Once you become educated, you reach a point where you begin to like learning instead of dreading it, and then you want to know more and more and more. You always have yourself as a good resource when you have knowledge. When you learn to do something like solve an equation in algebra, no one can take that away from you. You will always know how to do it. If you have not done it in twenty years, you might have to review it a little bit, but it comes back.
>
> According to Chris Dancisak, "It does not matter what your economic or educational status is, you can take advantage of the things around you and move to higher levels of success or you can turn opportunities into disasters. I suppose a lot of it also has to do with love and nourishment where there's somebody who is willing to push you in the right direction rather than let you go in the wrong

direction with your life. Now, I tell my students that getting their GED as an adult is the hardest thing they'll ever do."

Susan Cancro says that poor communication is one of the biggest problems that stems from a lack of education and possibly extensive use of drugs and alcohol.

Together they make it much worse and reduce the person's ability to communicate effectively. What I see many times is someone who is smart but does not have the vocabulary or the trained ability to analyze that comes from just learning. They cannot evaluate their own issues or communicate well, which results in anger and frustration. Not having the words to express yourself, or the ability to pick up on the nuance, can be an extremely frustrating experience, particularly when asking someone for help to communicate with a social service or government agency.

Trust

Trust is another key ingredient for making changes in life, finding meaning and purpose, and becoming literate. The participants in "Your Story and Mine" often lacked this element in their earlier relationships with family and friends. The trust that Advent House Ministries staff established was a critical ingredient in the success of the participants' engagement that empowered volunteers and museum staff to work closely with them. Without it, we could never have launched and built the program.

Chris Dancisak has said that "Trust is probably the biggest factor to create a successful learning environment in the classroom or any circumstance with a mentor/teacher role. Without establishing and maintaining that trust and confidence, probably little educational experience will take place, because you never otherwise get beyond that point. Trusting people around them helps these folks turn opportunities to experience and move forward with life rather than looking backward."

Daniel Jones, a caseworker who helps clients with jobs and life skills at Advent House Ministries, said: "One of the biggest obstacles I faced in the beginning of my work at Advent House Ministries was basic trust. Many people have come to me with so much hesitancy because so many others have made promises to them in the past who have not kept those promises. There's a trust issue, plus nobody knew me in that community. Once they saw me in the community and once I had that trust as someone [who] could be depended upon, an initial trust began."

Recently, while my husband and I vacationed in northern California, we hiked through a redwood forest where we met another couple from Iowa who were both physician assistants. They had worked in a soup kitchen for a couple of years, providing medical services to the homeless migrants who spent their summers there and went south in the winter. Each year, the couple gave one hundred dollars to a local pharmacy to purchase over-the-counter medications and other basic medical supplies for the homeless. The pharmacist donated far more than one hundred dollars' worth of goods. The woman told me that the hardest challenge she and her husband had trying to work with these people was establishing trust. One day, she said, she punctured someone's boil at lunchtime. The homeless people were amazed and ever since then have trusted them and accepted their help.

Marion Heider, a docent at the Michigan Historical Museum, worked intensively one-on-one with the project participants while they talked about their lives and painted their stories. "I would just try to have them tell me in a nonthreatening environment how and what they're doing on any given day. Eventually, little by little, they would tell their story about their lives—not the total thing—little things here and little things there. It was just our nonjudgmental approach. 'This was your life and that was a very sad situation. We're really glad you're here. How can we help you express what you want to express?'"

Mentors

Many have written about the importance of mentors. Some children who grew up in poverty were lucky to have had a mentor—a family friend, relative, teacher, counselor—who helped them weather life's difficult hurdles. Others did not. Having once had a mentor often helps these people navigate their current journeys through adulthood. Having mentors as adults is also profoundly helpful. To become literate, an individual needs sensitive, supportive mentors.

Psychologist George A. Bonanno wrote:

> People confronted with the pain of loss need comfort. We see this same need in just about anyone faced with aversive circumstances. Children who survive poverty or abuse, for example, usually have someone in their life they can talk to, someone to lean on, someone they know will be there even when everything else seems to be falling apart. This person might be a close friend or confidant, or perhaps a positive adult figure. The availability of a disadvantaged child of a caring and supportive helper has such a salubrious effect, in fact, that it may

even cancel out a genetic risk for depression. The same is true of adults exposed to potentially devastating events like war, assault or natural disaster. They consistently fare better when they have other people to turn to. (Bonanno 2009, 72)

Allyson Bolt, director of the employment program, also talked about the importance of people having a mentor while growing up.

There's research that says that if you have had one adult you can count on regardless of who that person is, who is a constant, always in your corner, you have an increased likelihood of resilience—maybe a cool teacher or Sunday school teacher or coach. . . . Furthermore, as adults, some people will use support groups and some will not. Some will reach out to others. Some will keep it all in. This depends on our personalities, gender issues, cultural issues, or family issues—views about reaching out, using the system, and accessing the system.

Accessing Services

People who participated in "Your Story and Mine: A Community of Hope" once lived on the street. They floundered and were directionless for years. They are now in transition and have a relatively stable living situation in a shelter or an apartment. For a variety of reasons, they decided to take that giant step and access human services so they could positively change the direction of their lives to become self-sufficient. Somehow, they found personal motivation—each with their own reasons and explanations.

They accessed Advent House Ministries, which became an umbrella for all the essential ingredients necessary for positive change. In their interviews, they each talked about leaving the streets. Somehow, they realized that literacy and education were the keys to open doors to find a job. Some developed an appreciation of religion and spirituality. Many made amends with family members—many of whom they had not seen in years. Some left abusive relationships. Many stopped abusing themselves. They all continue to work very hard on their personal issues and realize this is a lifelong commitment and venture.

While these people traveled without a compass in the past, they discovered Advent House Ministries—their new compass. This nurturing environment is a profound resource—like an oasis in an urban desert—with a cadre of mentors with many skills from a variety of professional and personal backgrounds. Each mentor was positive, supportive, validating, and nonjudgmental. They help their guests discover a new, healthier life through education, literacy, job-skills and life-skills classes, substance-abuse treatment, medical assistance for physical and mental health problems, dental health assistance, spirituality, and religion. Their efforts reinforce the participants' desires to "break the cycle."

Those who accessed Advent House Ministries have begun to develop self-confidence and growth in ways they might have never imagined. As adults, they now have mentors, which they may or may not have had while growing up. Their mentors try to help them break a cycle of destructive patterns and identify resources to help them with work; education; mental, emotional, physical, and dental health; child rearing; and legal services. Over time, they develop new perspectives on their lives and gain greater insight into themselves. They have begun to respect and value themselves and their struggles, to realize they made poor choices in the past, but they also did not have the right tools to cope with the inordinately difficult challenges they faced early on. They are kinder to themselves. Coming to Advent House Ministries parallels the last line of Paula Nelson's poem I quoted earlier: "I walk down another street."

Susan Cancro talked about the challenges, change, and loss these people face each day as they try to break out of the cycle of poverty and homelessness.

> I don't think we can comprehend the level of personal strength, integrity, and intelligence that they bring to making these changes in their lives. We sit here and help with referrals and advocacy, but we are pushing that person to jump off that cliff with a parachute and hope that they land [safely]. We hope we have given them good equipment, but they are the ones who have to take it and do that. When they do land, they traverse that terrain themselves. Nobody can do it for them.
>
> These people are doing something actively to solve their problems. It is a huge change for someone to make from being chronically poor to having stability—working a regular job, maybe owning their own home. They lose friends and family—those supportive connections. They no longer have things in common with the people who have walked this far in their lives. Suddenly, it becomes a personal loss and criticism to that friend or family member. They have to try to make new relationships—a huge stress, an almost impossible task, because they cannot develop the rootedness in those new relationships that they had in their old relationships. Making this step to stability or normalcy is lonely. We're helping people and we're asking people to give up so much. Change does not happen quickly for human beings. These are dramatic life changes, when we change our life patterns, particularly when we exorcise our relationships. To make those changes takes a lot of support.

photo essay

Erika Magers directed the art component of "Your Story and Mine: A Community of Hope" and guided the individuals and the group as they painted vignettes of their life stories of homelessness and self-portraits. Some individuals painted pictures but were not interviewed at length. Their art is included here. Others participated in the oral history component but did not paint any pictures.

Wynette painted a picture of her husband and seven kids outside one of her homes when it was condemned. Here she is laying out her family photographs as she plans another picture. She also painted a self-portrait.

When Lewis came to the art classes, he asked for a piece of paper and a pen to write a poem. One day, after we talked, he decided to paint a picture, and he included a poem he had just written in it.

LaKashia, one of Wynette's daughters, is married to Lewis. Here she shares her painting "My Book of Life" and the "VOA." She works now as a home health caregiver.

Initially, Robert was resistant to painting and said he was not an artist. Then, he decided to paint symbols of his hard life—the chains, death, a broken heart, and the military.

David brought some of his paintings to the first art class. His art flourished during the program. With a new job, he no longer needs to sell his blood to buy paints, brushes, and paper.

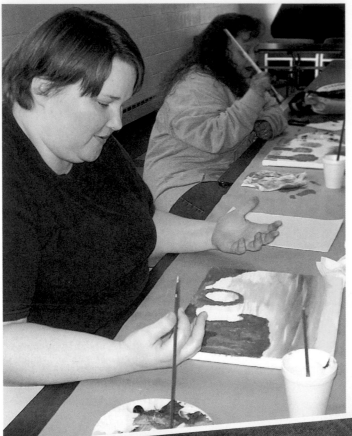

Jackie said, "Well, there's so much homelessness in my life that I could have been painting for a couple years on it."

Dora said that this painting reveals the changes in her mother over time, and the new feelings of hope after she found a $100 bill in her purse, bought her children a dinner at Kentucky Fried Chicken, and promised them they would never go hungry again.

Robin, another participant, said, "What gives me strength each day is just always thinking positive. Now I'm starting to speak up. That's the big change. I'd just sit like a bump on a log, don't say nothing. But then I realized, I was like, 'Oops, nah, it's time to start speaking up.' I graduated from Sexton High School. Having that diploma means a lot to me. I rather see my kids do the same as I did."

Brandy, one of Wynette's daughters, loves triangles and wants to see the Eiffel Tower. Erika cut a canvas into a triangle for Brandy. When Erika was in high school, she also painted on a triangular canvas. Brandy painted a picture of herself playing the drums. A music savant, she plays seven instruments and performs at her church on Sundays.

LaKeya, Wynette's niece, is a cousin of Brandy and LaKashia. LaKeya was one of the original courageous participants in the pilot project "Your Story and Mine." LaKeya painted this picture, "Green House—Not Safe."

OTHER OUTGROWTHS OF CHANGE

Over time, as I got to know these people better, listened to their stories, saw their art, and read their poems, I developed profound respect and admiration for them and their struggles. Contrary to what I had imagined, they each have a tremendous reservoir of inner resources, resilience, and courage.

However, I do not wish to create an idyllic image of these people and their current lives. They still struggle as we all do in our own ways. Clearly, however, they have questioned the choices and decisions they made in the past and those of their ancestors, and have taken giant steps with tremendous courage, patience, fortitude, and stamina to find new ways to manage the bumpy, often treacherous, rocky new paths.

They changed for a variety of reasons. Some made conscious decisions. Some had new dreams they could have never imagined that they wanted to fulfill. Some wanted to realize old dreams they had had before they encountered numerous roadblocks—both internal and external—on their journeys through life. Some tired of old patterns and habits. They were inspired to make changes for themselves and create opportunities for their children so they would have a better life than they did.

Jackie finished her GED and now goes to Lansing Community College. She said, "I just want to give my children a better chance so that maybe, they can afford to go to college and just whatever I do will impact them. That's what I'm hoping for."

Lewis is grateful to his children, his wife, and mother-in-law. He said, "Our children make us bloom. I blame [La]Kashia, for turning around my life," he said. "I fell in love with Kashia and my mother-in-law, Wynette."

Many reconnected with family members, made amends, or tried to repair family relationships. They created opportunities for their family members and themselves to heal from old wounds, lack of connection, and poor communications. Some have found joy and happiness in these renewed family relationships. Others still struggle with them, and their ties remain fragile and fragmented—but at least they took the first step to try.

While Wynette's aunt raised her, she made sure that Wynette and her sister stayed in touch with their mom, even if it meant traveling by train alone as a child from Lansing, Michigan, to Chicago. At some point, Wynette lost touch with her mother.

Now, Wynette says, "I stay in touch with my mother after many years. . . . At first I didn't understand, but now I do."

Robert explained his reason for returning to Michigan from California: "I came back to Michigan because my family was here. I had a dream in my head after my truck accident that I could at least try to unite the family." The relationships did not work out as well as he had hoped they would.

While growing up, Bill's son tried repeatedly to connect with his father, who was addicted to alcohol and drugs, but became profoundly frustrated. As time passed and Bill improved his life situation, he was able to respond and connect with his son.

"My relationship with my son is now quite good," Bill said. "He's seen my clean time. He sees what I do out in the streets helping homeless people. . . . Now I am there to give him some life skills, try to make him think about decisions and consequences."

As a teenager, Dora had run away from her family and become a prostitute. She left that way of life and now, as an adult, she talks to her mom every day for half an hour. "When I first ran away and I dropped out of school we were not close. I hated her." She now also talks to her dad once a month.

Toni says that in this process of change, some people have also discovered religion or spirituality.

> Even in the face of horrible events in their past or present lives, they think that God loves them and God's presence is in their life, and they say a prayer. Anything good happened to them, then praise God. "I got all this good food from the pantry" and they praise God. They tend not to praise or give credit to themselves. When something happens to people in poverty that is good, they tend to say it was good luck. It was God, pure luck. But, if something bad happens, it's their fault, and they can't make that distinction. People with low self-esteem tend to do that all the time.

For example, Wynette said, "I asked the Lord to help me through a lot." David said, "I came here to start over with a spiritual beginning and not to be afraid to use my talent, because people get a lot of joy out of my singing."

Some talked about how much they just really like to volunteer and help others who are even needier than they are—even though at times it can be to their detriment when they focus on helping others rather than themselves. Wynette said, "I enjoy feeding the homeless."

Over the years, Robert, who was unusually philosophical and thoughtful, had worked, spent time in jail, and ended up living on the streets of California for several years. He also survived a traumatic truck accident. He said, "Well, people come into the world with nothing and they're going to go out with nothing, so while we're here, all we have to give is just of ourselves."

Sometimes, life traumas propelled them into new, healthy directions. Some avoid negative behaviors. Some have stopped using drugs and/or alcohol. Some left abusive relationships. Others stopped abusing themselves. They now realize they do not need to tolerate abuse from others or themselves. As Dora said, "I'm just tired of the abuse thing and I want to be happy even if that means being by myself. I don't care, because I'm happy."

Some of the participants have now developed hope. Bill said, "If I could tell the homeless people I work with one thing, it would be 'Don't give up hope. It's never hopeless. When you get to bottom and you can't go no farther down, the only way is up. There's always hope.'"

These formerly homeless people grapple with basic human issues just as we all do—but it is, perhaps, a matter of degree of need and extremes. In their stories about homelessness, we learned about the choices and decisions that put them on the streets. When we further explored their lives, we discovered the profound changes they each had made. Now, they told us about the giant steps they had taken to get off the streets and access services to help themselves. For a variety of reasons, they acknowledged they had made poor choices. Now, they make better choices. Some still waffle between newfound behaviors and old ones. Even with our own individual personalities, we have more in common with them than we are willing to realize or acknowledge.

Robert said, "We have faces, we're real people, and no two stories are exactly the same. Some of us ended up here because of misfortune. We're trying to get our lives back together. . . . I think everybody's story is totally different. There's all sorts of reasons why people are out there doing what they do, their beliefs and things that happen to them."

Here are some of their stories about breaking the cycle of homelessness—through accessing help, changing direction in their lives, giving up drugs and alcohol, leaving abusive relationships, reconnecting with their families, valuing religion and spirituality, attending literacy classes, and seeking jobs. As they tell their stories, remember that they are not always complete, but are usually vignettes from different eras of their lives.

New Choices

When I first met Wynette, she squinted a lot and had bad headaches from problems with her eyes. Over the course of the program, she developed more confidence in herself. She finally agreed to have eye surgery, then got glasses and had fewer headaches. She was so happy and relieved with the results. Over the years, she has become a stronger individual. She talked about the importance of Advent House Ministries, reconnecting with her biological mother, the importance of family and religion, and volunteering to help the homeless.

Wynette accessed services:

When living at a night-shelter, what I had to do was to make sure that all my kids got their baths, make sure that they had their school clothes on. We would either catch the bus or get a ride and then I would send them to school. I would go to work at the Advent House in the bake shop. So I did that mostly.

I used to hang out at the Advent House all the time with my kids. They had a shelter home there way, way back. Me, my kids, and my husband, my cousins, all stayed in that one house together that Advent House owned. It was right across the way from Advent House where the park is. They would let people come in there and stay. The only thing that we had to do was to save our money, because they would provide everything for us. We slept there. It was an overnight shelter. We did everything: cooked there, uh, we had to buy our own food but we survived it. I mean it was really nice.

Pam Fulton was the one in charge. I remember Pam. She was a very good lady. She helped everybody and my kids loved her to death. Pam was the most sweetest lady that I know. We went to her house. She lived in Lansing, right across from the church on that one little street by the Sparrow Hospital. And her husband was sweet, and when the holidays come she would help everybody. She would leave no one out, because she said that that was very important and she wanted to make sure that everybody had something even if it was just one thing. Everybody got helped. I'm going to miss her.

Me and my kids, we used to go grocery shopping. We would take the cart from the store and wheel it down the street and bring it home. We did the laundry the same way, just get the cart and get all of our clothes together, take it to the Laundromat and wash them and bring them back. It was on Willow Street. Yeah. It was fun.

I love to walk and we walked all over. When I was homeless, my friend stayed in Dewitt and I used to walk from Dewitt to Lansing. It would take a couple of hours but I did it. You know it wasn't that hard to do.

Chris, the lady that used to run the bake shop at the Advent House, taught me that we couldn't do nothing from boxes. We had to do everything from scratch. So, that was kind of hard, but we did it, and we catered. We made a luncheon for the mayor of Lansing a long time ago. We fed over 150-something people, but the mayor really liked it so he gave us a bonus for doing a good job. I had fun doing that.

I think Susan Cancro and the others at Advent House are really, really great. They're my friends throughout everything. I can say that Susan, Ms. Toni, all of them, have been there for me. I praise God that they're still in my life because I think if I didn't have them, I don't know where I would be or what I would be doing today. I would really probably be home sad, and they make me happy, you know, they make me want to keep going and not try to stop, so I'm really glad for them.

Wynette reconnected with her mother:

I'm in touch with my mother now after many years. Well, you know, at first I didn't understand, but now I do. She always say, "You loved your aunt way more than you loved me," and I said, "No, that's not it." So I forgave her. My aunt always told us, "No matter what your mom did, that's still your mom and you need to love her."

My aunt believed in making sure me and my sister know who our parents was. That was something that she instilled in me. She said, "No matter how your family treats you, you always love them," so I was brought up that way and she kept us in church and everything. You have to forgive sometimes. If I could change one thing in my life, I'd spend more time with my mom, but I can't change that.

My aunt passed away a long time ago. And my sister passed away too. I've had a lot of loss. I try to give back to my children and the community.

Wynette's children and grandchildren are very important to her.

My kids and grandkids are the most meaningful to me because I love them all. I write letters to my ex-husband because he's in prison, and I send him cards and do stuff like that. I can go and see him, but I don't like to go to jails and prisons, so I don't go, but I do write him. He writes me all the time. And he sends me Mother's Day cards and stuff like that. He's been there about five years and has four more years to go.

My grandkids have a lot of meaning for me. Maquan, he's twelve and he just had a birthday, and Monet . . . Demetrius, he's ten, and Toot-Toot is seven, and Dennis is eight, and let me see . . . Trapice, she's one and Mary's baby is one. They're all ages, but they're a joy to me so I just like to be around them a little bit, and I watch them.

Religion and feeding the homeless are a big part of Wynette's life:

Religion is very important to me. There was a lady down there at the Advent House that was doing these crosses. Lewis, my son-in-law, told me, "I want you to wear this cross," and so I've been wearing this ever since. I don't go nowhere without this. He loves me and he just gave it to me and he told me that I was the most wonderful mother-in-law that he could ever have.

I asked the Lord to help me through a lot, but by me not being with my mom and dad when I was a baby and living with my aunt, she showed me a lot of things and always told me that no matter what, I can do anything that is possible within God's hands. I can do whatever that I wanted to be.

I enjoy feeding the homeless. On Mondays, Tuesdays, Wednesdays I work at Mt. Hope Church in Lansing. It's on the corner of Genesee and Walnut. It's by the park right across the street, the little red church right there. The pastor's name is . . . I'm at a blank now. But anyways, Pastor Elmer Cox. He's a really nice man.

I've been working there for a while and what we do is the lady cooks there and sometimes I help her cook, but I just do all the desserts. I cut up the desserts and I do the punch and the water. I roll up forks. I make Kool-Aid. We get desserts from Kroger's so I hand them out. They have really good meals down there. I do it Wednesday night from six to seven. We have chicken, mashed potatoes, corn, rolls. Yesterday, I bring in my special seasoning for the chicken.

It's all different kinds of homeless people down there. Right now we're dealing with this one man that has emotional problems. We have to keep our creamer and all that on the top because he'll take it and he'll dump it all and no one gets none, so we have to do all that.

They have a clothing bank where the people can come in and get clothes. We do have a little bit of personal needs there for the people. They're getting ready to do the Christmas services. It's going to help them get clothes and more stuff, but it's a nice little church and the people's all nice down there.

I've been working at the church for about ten or eleven years. I wanted to do this because I think, out of all my life, I've been teased a lot, and I just feel like I needed to try to help somebody that was disabled, didn't have a lot. So, I try to help everybody when I can.

The Importance of Family

Lewis is indebted to his wife, LaKashia, who helped him transform his life. He talked about religion, his involvement with Advent House Ministries, and the importance of his children as a source of inspiration for making his life worth living.

Lewis is grateful for his wife, children, and mother-in-law, Wynette.

When I was last in prison in Ionia for two and a half years, I began doing Bible studies. I kept sending my poems back to my wife, Kashia. Now, I got my minister license. I'm thinking about the family.

I blame Kashia for turning around my life. Years ago the doctor told me, I won't have kids, that I pop a willy, popped my jewels, that I never have kids. When she got pregnant, I thought she got pregnant with someone else. She's crazy about me. I fell in love with Kashia and my mother-in-law, Wynette. I now have three of my own children with Kashia.

Our children make us bloom. Our children make us want to do better. It's like, "Wow, now I get a chance to have people hear me."

Lewis discovered religion and Advent House Ministries.

Since I got my minister license, I'm finally getting a chance. I don't know how I'm going to get the money but I'm going to come up with something like four hundred dollars to try to get my driver's license back 'for I can be on the road for me and my wife and kids. See, I'm thinking again about my family. Now, I'm thinking about trying to get us some wheels to ride around. There again, I'm thinking again about the family. I want to start my own church and keep doing my poetry.

When I got out of jail, I wanted to do the other courses. I wanted to finish up my Bible studies. I didn't know there was such a thing. And if you get 'em all right, you get a gold seal. Finally, I finished them up. They gave me a Bible with my name on it. I was trying to figure out how to become a minister. I was just reading about ordained ministries online. Oh, my, "Wow, I thought this was fake! This is fake." It was talking about—they're going to send my ministry license? I was ordained on September 28. I was like, "Wow, it finally came." I already knew that it was in me.

I come down to the Advent House and stuff. I did my little prayer thing. I ain't totally evil in life. I want my goodness to shine. I don't want to tell about all the sad things in my life, the bad things anymore. I want to tell people about how I've changed my life—the good things in my life. And what I'm going to do to affect the community and these kids. They grow up too fast. They need somebody out here to hear that. They need to hear that. I know that God is calling imperfect me, imperfect men like me and you, men and women, to preach a perfect gospel meaning, to tell the kids about our experiences.

I felt like I'm just even blessed to breathe this air. And it's like God is saying, "Hey, I'm giving you chances. I'm giving you chances to make an impression on somebody." Even you, like right now, you're making an impression on me. And I'm able to express myself instead of yelling at my wife and she's sitting there like a wall, not even listening.

Advent House is a real inspiration to me. I am very grateful to them for their programs. Dr. Johnson [Joan Jackson Johnson, a former member of the Advent House Ministries board] took us to the City Hall, introduced us to the mayor—Virg Benero!! The mayor know me by name. Can you imagine that? Seriously, and I only met the mayor one time on Christmas, a year and a half ago. The mayor was up in there washing dishes with me, when I was working on weekends, washing dishes. So, finally, Dr. Johnson introduced me to the mayor while she was doing the segment. I think that the mayor will remember me again.

So, one day, me and my friend, we are walking on the east side. And they cleaning up some gang graffiti. And he said, "Ah, wait a minute." And he just stopped right in the middle while he's doing what he's doing. And he say, "Hold on." And say, turn the camera on me. And they should turn the camera on the mayor. And he's giving me my share. And he says, "This is Lewis and he writes poetry." And wow, he remember my name. Oh, wow! A lot of people don't like Virg, but I love him. He's working on the community. So, of course I was going to vote for him. And I'm glad he's still the mayor.

Reconnecting

After living in California for twenty years, Robert returned to Michigan to reconnect with his family. He talked about the critical truck accident he was in that profoundly affected his life, the importance of religion and spirituality, his philosophy on life, and helping other people. He attended life-skills classes at Advent House Ministries.

I came back to Michigan because my family was here. I had a dream in my head after my truck accident that I could at least try to unite the family, but so far it hasn't worked. Yeah, I'm in touch with two brothers actually. One's still living in Detroit and it's kind of hard to get down and see him right now. I took a bus down there, the Greyhound. My brother helped pay for a bus ticket from California.

My mom is in a bad state right now, so at least I got to see her. She's in the hospital. She's got bad emphysema and stuff. I've made some inroads. Well it's part of my mission—why I wanted to come back here was at least to touch bases with the family.

But, it's not working out with my siblings, at least the way I envisioned it—that we'd all get together and just hopefully start having family reunions or something like that, but maybe that can still come out down the road. I haven't heard from my sister, Maria. I don't know what she does. She knows I'm here but chooses not to get in touch with me—at least not at the present time. After my father died, we just went our own ways and we grew apart. My oldest brother is going to college right now at Lansing Community College. He's going for welding. My other brother is just working down in Detroit. My middle brother and my sister have children. I never married and never had children—just pretty much single, living in sin.

I was glad to finally hear from my brother because I tried for the longest time to find him through the Internet. It wasn't a question of him not answering. It was just through a friend that we grew up with. I left a message on an Internet site and luckily I didn't delete it out of my email. It was twenty-something years that we weren't in touch. A whole lifetime. Yeah. A whole lifetime.

It was more melancholy. I think he was glad to see me and stuff like that, but he has a hard time showing emotions too, like me. But I did run into a friend of mine that I hadn't seen in twenty years and that was more of an emotional greeting, but I guess that was because we lived our younger lives, we did the same things. We lived together when we were sixteen, seventeen years old, so that's probably why.

The accident put me in a situation that I didn't want to be in, but I'm dealing with it the best I can. All the problems have been since the accident and it's hard to do anything. If I had not been injured that bad, I don't know if I would have come back to Michigan. I believe in destiny. I also believe in God, and God moves us to places where we're supposed to be. When I got in touch with my brothers I was like doing that little soul-searching part and saying, "Is this the right thing to do or not?" So I figured it was worth a shot. In a sense, He moved me here for whatever reason.

Right now, I'm living at a place called the Barnabas House run by a church down the street from Lansing Community College. They let you stay there for six months and then review what you're doing and how things are going. If they want you, they can let you extend it another six months. I was planning on going to the VOA [Volunteers of America] and then my brother, he's the director of the Barnabas House, got me into the house where he's at right now.

Well, I'm living off of the food card. You've got to go down to the Department of Human Services and apply. You have to meet their level income or just basically no income whatsoever. Then they'll issue you a card for six months or a year, and they expect you to live off of $176 a month, which is doable, not very good. We got a kitchen and a microwave with an oven. You're supposed to clean up after yourselves. It doesn't always work as good as it should. Well, I'm in my room by myself but there will be someone else coming.

Robert loves to help people.

My motivation is just try to do unto others as you like done unto you, to be a good person and help people out when you can. I went out and worked for my meals. I go around collecting cans and bottles to make money.

Well, people come into the world with nothing, and they're going to go out with nothing, so while we're here, all we have to do is, all we have to give, is just of ourselves. It's hard to find people that will take that. I mean a lot of people will use it and abuse it, and it's hard to find people that really just appreciate that that's the gift we really have to each other. It's just the time that we're here.

I'll do anything to help people—get up on a roof. I'll start painting. If they're out working on their car, I'll go over and help them work on their car. If somebody's broke down on a side of a road and needed a jump and if I have the time, I'll stop to give the jump and give out a little bit of advice. If you see someone else that's on the side of the road broke down, stop and help them. It's too many people that's bustling around and not paying attention to each other. I've felt good helping people out when they really need help. That always makes you feel good, and when you see someone else in trouble and you can lend a hand or an ear, just a couple of kind words or something. Always nice.

Being Patient

David moved to Lansing to try to figure out what he was going to do with his life. He came to study the Bible and find work. He quit drinking alcohol. He talked about the importance of playing the guitar and having faith. He also talked about people making fun of him and his creative abilities while he was growing up. David lacked confidence in his younger years and said that he did not receive encouragement for his artistic and musical endeavors. Sometimes, people even made fun of him—but he realizes now that they did not understand him.

When David signed up for "Your Story and Mine: A Community of Hope," he had been looking for a job for about a year and felt little hope of finding one. I happened to be at the session he attended when Toni was promoting the program. He talked to me after the class about the artwork that he had done over the years. He was thrilled about this opportunity. I was ecstatic about his wanting to participate. This program was ideal for him.

Several weeks into the program, David was glowing. Something had changed. His tutor from the Capital Area Literacy Coalition (CALC) had taken him to the dentist, who had pulled an infected tooth pro bono and has committed to continue to do more dental work for him at no cost! His mentor, Daniel Jones, had also helped find him a job at L&L bagging groceries for nine hours a week. His tutor took him to get some new clothes! David had been so motivated at his job that his boss upped his schedule to twenty-seven hours a week. When the L&L grocery stores closed in the Lansing area, David got a job at the Radisson Hotel.

Interestingly, art therapist and author Cathy Malchiodi has written:

The problem is how to remain an artist once one grows up. A look back at what happened to the young artist you once were can review your sense of self-exploration and restore authentic expression. Sometimes there is a lingering memory of a particular person who ridiculed your art, misunderstood what you were trying to communicate, or gave you a poor grade in art class. Taking a mental inventory of memories, events, experiences, and attitudes about art that you developed during childhood is often helpful." (Malchiodi 2002, 40)

David had returned to Michigan to complete his Bible studies.

I first came to Lansing when I was forty-two, like in 2001–2002. I worked for Denny's on South Cedar. It's now out of business. I then went back to Idaho.

I came back to Michigan from Idaho this second time 'cause my brother asked me what I was supposed to do with my life. I said I'm supposed to go back to Michigan and to finish the Bible course I started in 2000. When I get done I can get a diploma and be clergy 'cause I haven't had anything in my life that means anything to me, but this would mean something to me. I got to pursue it and go all the way through it.

David talked about his family problems:

My father died in 2004. He got colon cancer, or something in his colon, and he lasted about two weeks and passed on. He was eighty-nine, so he lived a good life.

My mom is eighty-five years old. I talk to my mother on the phone once in a while, but I come here to Lansing to get some work and then talk to her one-on-one about what she wants, because she's supposed to will some property to me. I didn't know how to take that with all the strife that's going on in the house, 'cause I think everybody would like the property for themselves. And there are nine siblings altogether.

This time I was trying to get away from a situation. They're sort of fighting over a will, so I came back here to clear my head and go to Bible school in March 28, 2007. Faith Tech Bible School, just a private school to study the Bible, has been helping me and giving me strength in a spiritual way.

My three kids are young adults now in their twenties. They live with their mother in the same trailer park, Camelot Trailer Park, in Grand Rapids. Yeah, I went back about three years ago to see them. They don't really want anything to do with me 'cause they all got their own lives, so that's why I come back to Lansing to explore my options for myself—not that I'm cutting them out of the picture, but I need to know what my talent is for myself.

The reason I won't go back home to Grand Rapids is things get heated between me and my mother about the way I believe, because when I came here I believe something that she doesn't believe—that I got filled with what they call the Baptism, the Holy Spirit. She said either that I got filled with nothing or that I got filled with the devil, and I didn't. But she wanted me to go back to her church and denounce what I got. I wanted to come here and get a job.

David discovered Advent House Ministries:

While at the mission, I got hooked up with Advent House through the transition house when I called the Alcoholics Anonymous before winter came so I would have a place to stay. I told them I had a drinking problem, and they put me up over by the Advent House, and they sent me to Daniel Jones to look for work.

My stomach was bothering me so I quit drinking before I even went there. I had a rip lining in my stomach so I quit drinking long before that, but I would still drink. I don't want to kid myself. I still wanted some beers now and then, but my mind is sharper without it.

I've lived in Lansing about a year and a half. I've been looking for work since June of last year. And all winter long. Just general labor like at a store, or McDonald's or Burger King. I live at the transition house at Oakland and Martin Luther King. It's like a family house. Five men stay there and all share the kitchen, bathroom, and stuff. So, it's like a family-oriented place. It's familiar to me, since I grew up with so many kids in the house.

These are difficult times right now because I can't find a job, but I just pray about it and try to snap out of it with music and all this talking to God. Trying, 'cause I can't do nothing about it. Eventually a door will open. I just got to have the faith that it will. I've learned to have faith and am still learning to have faith with my Bible classes.

David finally believes in his music:

The only reason I wouldn't play the guitar in front of my family, it's like they're jealous because I have a talent. "Oh we've heard you. Get out of here." I'd rather pursue it. I don't care if they find out about it. I don't know why people are like that 'cause they can't play an instrument. They act like they're jealous, and that's almost kept me from wanting to play.

Maybe it's my outlet. Maybe it's the way that I need to get to do something 'cause I did pray about it and I asked God what to do, and he showed me midsummer. Sent this guy by me once, and then another guy came by with the same company and said, "You need to call us. This may be your way to get off the street." But I listened to too many other people. Too many said, "You don't got talent. You ain't got no voice."

But other people told me I did. I got to believe in myself and not other people. Just because I grew up with them all my life doesn't mean they know me and who I am. I stopped talking to them because I believe they are trying to put a damper on my gift of music. I wanted to put my guitar down and not play.

Well, I came here to start over with a spiritual beginning and not to be afraid to use my talent, because people get a lot of joy out of my singing. And if they don't, I guess I don't need to play for them. I think I got "a calling," but maybe I need to pursue this field and play my music and let the spirit move me into to do what I need to do. Yah, it makes me feel good too.

David reflected on his fears:

Yah, I think I just got to relax more. I could probably write if I just put my mind to it and do it. I just have to rely on some people who want to help me. There's a big difference between people who want to help and people that are critical.

Yah, I think I had a fear of budding, you know, of budding, and coming to bring my gift out, but I know I got to pursue and do it because I think I was held back long enough. I shouldn't let anything stand in my way. This is what I'm supposed to do. I don't believe in dreams but I believe in miracles, though, so I might as well pursue this thing and do it.

Taking Advantage of Opportunities

Jackie left her abusive husband, moved with her two daughters to Michigan with help from the Veterans of Foreign Wars, discovered Advent House Ministries, took in her niece to live with her, earned her GED, and began to attend Lansing Community College.

Jackie described her move to Michigan:

After leaving my husband and going to the shelter with my two daughters in Tennessee, eventually, I got together with the VFW [Veterans of Foreign Wars] National Home for Children in Michigan. I started the process for coming up here to live to change my life. I had someone in the program that I knew. Her youngest child is my nephew, so that was a big help. So I have a little family here.

The VFW gives you the opportunity to live here up to three years and go back to school, or further your career. They provide a roof over your head. I'm lucky enough they provided me with a car to be able to go to school to get my GED, which I'm almost done with—all I have to do is my math, which is a struggle for me. That's my Achilles heel. When I quit school years ago, I didn't even finish the eighth grade.

I'm pretty excited and happy that it's taken me one year living in Michigan and I'm actually going to start college.

I had to really decide if what I wanted was to make this big change, because it's not easy. It's hard, but it's been very rewarding. The weather out here in Michigan is a little interesting, but I'm getting used to that. A lot of good things have come to us since we moved out here. My girls are happy because they have a daycare. The VFW has so many different opportunities for the children and parents to succeed that I'm just trying to grab everything I can to do it.

I also took in my eleven-year-old niece, my sister's daughter, to live with us because she comes from the same background. Hers is actually worse, because her mother probably should never have been a mother, and so she just went through a lot of trauma. I didn't want her to go to a foster home. She's very, very active. She also was abused, which we come to find out. We don't know where, who, or how, but she needs a lot of therapeutic intervention so she can hopefully succeed. I thank God. I might not have great school skills, but I have a lot of common sense, so that's what's helped me in my life. I'm stubborn. Now my niece gonna start seeing a psychologist and a therapist. She has gained twenty pounds since she's lived with me. This is somebody that was eleven years old and weighing fifty pounds, so I'm excited. She's almost eighty pounds now. She's happy.

I knew that if I didn't start doing something to change my life, where's my kids going to be? I always wanted children. They are expensive. They require things, especially as school starts. I just want to give them a better chance so that maybe, they can afford to go to college, and just whatever I do good will impact them. That's what I'm hoping for.

I knew I needed a better career. One year I worked fifteen hours a day or more. I made $17,000 that year. When you have children, that doesn't cut it. You can't flip your rent, your electric, your water, your lights, your phone, your car, your insurance, you just can't. So I'm like, "Well, financially, you either limit your expenses or acquire more money, so I knew I had to go back to school."

Jackie found Advent House Ministries:

Well, I found Advent House because when we came to Michigan in the summertime there was no other schooling open to acquire your GED. I went down there and started doing my GED classes.

A year ago, I would have laughed if somebody told me that I was going to school now. The prospect of that many years is daunting. When I stepped out of Michigan State University and taken that GED test, and, whew, ahhh! It's a nice feeling because I'm like, "It wasn't as bad as I thought it was gonna be."

When I got my results, I got extremely high scores on them, and with my science I got top sixteen in the nation. Then for my social studies I got, like, top ten, so I was like, "How did that happen? I don't know." I went then for my reading and writing and I did really well on those.

Advent House has been a really big help. One of the teachers there helped me and let me know that if you don't have your GED, but you're close to it, and you want to start taking classes at Lansing Community College (LCC), there's a waiver you can take that enables you to get in under at a little bit lower score.

I'm actually starting Intro to Psychology and am beginning Typing because I'm a two-finger typer. There are so many broad ideas, and I don't want to just say, "This is what I'm gonna do." I'd like to leave it open because I might change my mind and see what fits me better. After my first few semesters, I'll have a better idea on how I enjoy this or that. I hope in the fall I'm gonna take some art classes, so I might add them together and see how it goes. It's a new journey. It's a little scary. I'm nervous, but I'm excited too.

Jackie is grateful to the VFW and her Grandpa:

I've gotta thank VFW because they have helped me more than they even know. They have helped a lot of families. The reason how I got into the VFW—my mother's father, my grandpa, he was a fighter pilot in World War II, so he was a war hero. He had a lot of medals. He was shot down and injured by shrapnel, but he became a post-office worker for the rest of his life. I never knew him. He died of cancer before I was born. My oldest sister did know him—that was "his little girl." He loved her to death, but it's neat because through him—even though he's passed away, he's actually helping his grandchildren and great-grandchildren.

He was in active wartime. When he quit the military, he left under your DD214, with medals under good conditions. That's your paperwork you get when you get out of the military. It gives you all the information on what they did. I don't know if they sent him home after the shrapnel or if he ended up going all the way through, but it's interesting because he's actually German. He didn't really talk much about it, my mom said. But he was a fighter pilot, and he actually got to go to Germany and rescue a lot of the Jewish people from the camps. It was really hard for him, so when he came back he never told anyone else he was German because it was such a bad thing. He was liberating Jews.

My mom didn't even know that he was a fighter pilot. He always told her that he was a gunner. It was kind of neat for her going through this, because she's going through the Women's Auxiliary part of the VFW, which is in Newport, Tennessee, twenty minutes away from where we lived. They actually broke it to her and let her know, and she cried and cried and cried. She learned something new about her dad that day—that he had done so many good things. He had the Purple Heart and everything. She never knew, so that was neat.

He couldn't talk about it because he actually witnessed what the Germans did. He'd seen it, and it was just so horrific to him that he didn't want to be a part of it. I don't know when he immigrated or his family immigrated to America, but he was full-blooded German. When he seen what they had done to the Jewish people it was just really hard on him. He had come over beforehand and was serving in the American military. I learned something new about my family. They can even do it from the grave, you never know! It'll be nice if I can ever help somebody else out.

I mean, there's a long way to go, but I'm happy every day. I get stressed because I have a very big agenda usually. The results are showing. I just take one step at a time, one day at a time, and go from there. My confidence has gone up. At the end of my marriage I couldn't do anything because I was in a corner. Everything I did was wrong. If God ever set a boundary thing for people saying, "Okay, this is how you're doing the wrong thing, or this is how you know you're going down the wrong road in life," I was there, because everything I touched seemed like wrong. Even our vehicles would never stay running. I cried all the time. I'm like, "This sucks."

Jackie reflected on her life.

I talk to all my family. My stepdad—which I call him my dad because he's just, he's always been there—he's an alcoholic also, but he's not violent, he's just strange. That's something that I have hoped that he would change. The one big thing that I learned was "You never get nothing for free. You have to do it on your own." And so I've set my own boundaries and realize I can't always help them when they need it, because I have my own family now and I have to think of them first. Hopefully, he'll quit.

I think a lot. I mean it's trial by error. It doesn't matter if you're in school or not. It's everyday life, and you can have your PhD or whatever and everything else, but if you don't have a good grasp on everyday life and what's going on, you're gonna struggle. That's kind of like what I've learned. I learn from my own mistakes, but I learn from everybody else's too. Sometimes I learn things the hard way. Sometimes I think that's the best way to learn because you're not gonna do it again. I used to say I gave my own self my own therapy. You have to heal yourself. You can hear it from a lot of other people, but if you can't start it yourself, you're not gonna change.

Jackie is happy she came to Michigan:

Since I've stepped into Michigan, more opportunities have popped up! Things I'm doing actually—I'm fulfilling them. I'm getting them done and it just feels right, where everything in Tennessee just felt so wrong. When they said, "Give me an idea of how your weather, your own personal weather is like therapeutically there in Tennessee," it was dark. There was no sunshine. There was no light. At least sometimes you have an idea of a path and everybody sort of follows along on that, be it spiritually or educationally or emotionally. There's some word to guide them with what they're doing with their life and I had none.

It was just an extremely bleak time in our lives, and then, I had an avenue. There was that little, little shot of "Well, if you take this chance, which it might not work out, it might be a really bad idea going there, it might turn out bad. That's a long way to go from your family and you've never been to Michigan before. It could be awful." I thought all those things and then I thought, "Well, you know, I'm gonna take this chance. I'm gonna do it." I was scared. I was nervous.

I remember I got into Ann Arbor. My stepdad actually came with me just so I wouldn't be in the car with my girls alone. We stepped out and took a big breath of the air. I was like, "Oh my God, it's so clean." The air was so crisp and so clean. We get a lot of pollution and stuff over there in Tennessee because there's some big plants not far from where we live. So, actually, they do talk about the pollution up there and there's a big difference—not as much humidity neither.

I was like, "Ahh, I remember that day." I'll probably remember it for the rest of my life because, you know, just little moments that stay with you. I was like fresh, it just felt like a fresh start. So, since we've been here, that's the way it's been. And I've had so many people that have helped me to achieve, so it's not been just me. I've taken every opportunity that's come to get the help I need to get to where I need to be. I'm so thankful for these because I had none of those back there. None of the opportunities, and none of the people there to say, "If you need somebody to cry on your shoulder or if you need somebody to say, 'You can do it!'"

Taking the Initiative

Bill is an extremely personable man. He talked about his choices in life. He regrets his past decision to drink and use drugs. Finally, he decided to quit and made amends with his family. Now, he has a good relationship with his son. He accessed a shelter and sought psychological help. He volunteers to help the homeless, surrounds himself with positive people, and finds strength in religion. Currently, he volunteers many hours a week at Advent House Ministries and sits on its board of directors.

Bill worked on rebuilding his relationship with his son:

The toughest choice that I made that I regret was choosing alcohol and drugs over my family. I hung out with the guys after work for an hour or so, drank beers, and chose them over my family. None of them guys at work used cocaine, but I drank for a little bit. That was the cool thing to do. Then, I was doing the cocaine, and they never knew. But, I chose that lifestyle. I chose to be homeless, instead of my family. They were supportive and everything like that. And there was a roof over my head. And there's consequences. And that was a big regret.

My relationship with my son is now quite good. He's seen my clean time. He sees what I do out in the streets helping homeless people. He knows it's positive, it's not negative. As a dad, I am there for him as far as making suggestions. Before, I wasn't. Now I am there to give him some life skills, try to make him think about decisions that he makes, and the consequences of them. I have enough life experience that I can tell you what's gonna happen if you do that. It's up to him to put to use what I give him—how he processes it and applies it to his choices.

I've sat him down and told him about being so high and sleepin' in the backseat of my car. And I was afraid to get out of my car, so I would just pee right on the seat, or into a pop bottle. Stuff like that. I've shared that with him, so he understands it. It's good because if one thing I've taught him, is that that's not the lifestyle, of drinking and drugs, that you want. He's seen where it goes, and he doesn't use, and I'm thankful.

Bill said, "You gotta pull yourself outta that pit!"

Yeah, I finally stayed in a shelter 'cause I tried to commit suicide in 2004. I got frustrated and cut my arm. It was just a cry for help. I knew I didn't do no damage. But, a friend of mine from counseling said, "I got a brother that runs a shelter." And, I went there and got on some antidepressants and started helping the people.

Communication is a big thing. You have to communicate with your case-worker. Caseworkers have to communicate with their clients. I was open-minded and I was patient. I knew that if I didn't identify what I needed and let somebody know that, it wasn't gonna get done. And I was gonna stay swimmin' in that pit. It takes some of your own doing. You have to wanna pull yourself outta that pit. Nobody owes it to ya. You have to take the initiative. If you don't have the motivation or incentive to keep going, you're not gonna get better.

I try to take care of myself along the way. I go through my periods where

I get depressed and I wanna isolate myself. When I do that, then I know that I'm not focusing on me. Because having a lot of people that are having negative things going around you, can suck the life out of ya. I just need to have positive people around me to talk to, like the people from church, people that are doing well, that honestly care about me, that know what I am going through. They are there to help.

Church has been a positive thing for me. It's been there. I've been in a lot a car accidents and I know that there's a higher power that's looked out for me over the years. Since I've been dealing with the homeless, I've got confirmation that that's what I should be doing. Because if he, God, was done with me, the first time I hit that tree at sixty miles an hour and rolled my car, and smashed my head on the steering wheel and broke it in half, I'd have been done a long time ago. And it's just taken quite a few bumps on the head and stuff like that for me to figure out what he has in store for me.

For five years, I've volunteered full-time to help people, and there are needs that I need that can't be met. I have a cell phone that I need to be able to pay for. I've been blessed that some people been helping me with it. I've been volunteering rather than getting a paid job. The time wasn't right. God will put something in my life that'll provide pay for me. He's provided all my needs. I learned to appreciate them things more now because I can lose it all and not have nothing. I keep my needs to a minimum, and I'm happy. I don't need the flat-screen TV, the newer cars, or nothing like that. I'm blessed that I can walk to wherever I gotta go. I have places I can eat. I don't need to eat steak and potatoes. I am perfectly content with spaghetti, or Kraft macaroni and cheese, or fried bologna.

I can plant that seed and I can harvest nice things for myself. Nice things to me now can mean a brand new $10 pair of jeans at Max 10. I have a hard time with that because when I get something new, instead of appreciating the blessing that comes to me, I tend to look around and see if somebody needs it worse than I do. So, I have a hard time sometimes because I think, "Ok, I'm all right. Who needs this worse than I do?" And I have to look at blessings and take them instead of turning them away, because they are just things that God's providing for me from the seeds that I plant. I gotta stop trying to play God sometimes and just let him do the driving. And not let me be in control 'cause I can. I'll run the car off the road. I'll be in the ditch again.

I've been in a ton of accidents, and how I lived, I don't know. But, I think there's a purpose. And I think it's helping people that are needy and homeless. Because I had everything. I made good money, and I was just never happy. I'm happy now. Yeah. I've had to humble myself and learn how to be grateful for what you have 'cause it can all be taken away. Helping people that are less fortunate than me makes me happy now. When I finally went to a shelter, I could relate, understand what they were going through. Unless you've lived it, it's hard for you to relate to somebody. I know what it's like to stand in front of a store and beg for a loaf of bread. I know what it's like to do a bird bath, gas-station bathroom.

I've been an advocate out in the streets all the time. I'm in touch with them. I can relate to what they're going through. When I know somebody has a need, I try to make it happen right away instead of waitin' for the red tape, the politics of it. Just—somebody needs clothes. I've always had good relations with different people around Lansing through all the businesses I ran. So, I have people that I reach out to. I didn't burn a lot a bridges. They know what I do now. They know I'm clean. They know I'm sober. They know my heart is in the right place.

If I could tell the homeless people one thing, it would be "Don't give up hope. It's never hopeless. It never is. When you get to bottom and you can't go no farther down, the only way is up. There is always hope." Just try to set small goals for yourself. Don't say to yourself that in a week, I'm going to have a job that pays $30,000 a year 'cause if you don't obtain that goal, then you get depressed. And then you give up. You have to start small.

The New Me

Dora left her abusive husband, lives alone, and manages her own finances. She has reconnected with her mom and dad, discovered Advent House Ministries, and tries to surround herself with positive, nonabusive people.

Now, I got my own place and it felt good to have my own place and pay my own bills. I learned how to pay my bills and speak for myself, because when I was with my husband, I wasn't allowed to say too many things and I wasn't outspoken. I was always really quiet and wouldn't really talk. Since I've been alone, I'm very outspoken. So, I got to know me again. And I like the new me, because now, I pay my bills. I promised myself I would never be homeless or be with somebody that's gonna abuse me or use me.

My mom, too, became a really strong woman after she left my dad and came here. She did what she had to do to take care of us. Up until this day, she still makes sure we are okay. And we do the same for her. So, basically, it's like I learned from her. She was taking the abuse at first, then she left and became the strong woman that she is today. I want to be that. And she doesn't need a man to make her happy 'cause she hasn't had one—well she has had one. She says her grandkids and us kids make her happy so that's all she needs. So, that's what I want to be when I grow up. I'm not grown up yet.

Of course, I'm strong now. I'm kind of a crybaby. I'm very sensitive, so I cry about everything. If I get bad news in a letter I'm gonna cry. If I get a card that's a happy card, I'm still gonna cry, or if I even hear my sister's voice from Texas, I'll cry. So I'm very sensitive. I'm very, very in touch with my emotions.

I have worked since I left my husband. I learned how to develop pictures because I worked at Rite Pharmacy, not Rite Aid Pharmacy—Rite Aid store, not the pharmacy. I learned how to develop pictures and be a cashier. There was a lot of things I didn't know how to do. I didn't know how to fill out an application, get a job. I didn't know any of those things, and I learned on my own. When I got my first job, it was only five dollars, five dollars and twenty-five cents an hour, I remember, and I was so happy. No, it was five dollars and twenty cents. I just wanted to be somewhere. I wanted to be out. I wanted to be seen. I wanted to do something, I wanted somebody to depend on me, you know?

Getting my first paycheck felt really good. I wanted to work all the time. I wanted everyone to get fired so I could get their hours so I could get their money. Yeah, so it was really good to earn a paycheck on my own and know how to manage my own money without having to give it to someone else or have restrictions on what you can and can't buy. So, it was really good.

Today, me being single is really, really good because I have my own place the way I want to. It's cute. It's like my kitchen. It's all red with Betty Boop stuff. My living room is Betty Boop, and everything is perfect to me. To some other people, well you need new stuff. Well no, this is mine. This is what I like and I don't care what other people think or what they say. I'm just happy to be alone and do what I want whenever I want. It feels good to not have somebody tell you what to do, be scared to talk or be scared to do anything. You can just get up and do whatever you feel like. Come in when you feel like. But I don't go out at night, so it doesn't really matter whether I want to come in at three or four in the morning because I won't do it. All the things that I wanted to do, I did when I was younger, so now I'm more like, if I don't have to leave the house then I won't, because of my anxiety.

I have a lot of nieces. They mean a lot. It's like I'm their mom. I'm the oldest of the girls, so my nieces and nephews all depend on me. Sometimes it gets really stressful, but I can handle it because I've always wanted someone to call me Mom and they call me Auntie, and that's okay. If they need money, if they're hungry, whatever they want, I'll do. If they come over, "Auntie, I want some corn bread," I'll make it. You want some cake too? I'm the good auntie they all run to.

I knew my father's mother and father. They were pretty nice and my father was an only child, so I don't understand why he was abusive to my mother. I got to meet my grandmother on my mother's side, but not my grandfather, because he died in the war. They were all from Texas. My grandmother is still alive and she's going through the Alzheimer thing. She's in a group home, an old folks home. Sometimes she remembers things and sometimes doesn't. She's over ninety.

I talk to my mom every day for like half an hour. We talk a lot. When I first ran away and I dropped out of school, we were not close. I hated her because I was a teenager, and all teenagers hate their parents like they do these days. And when I grown up I learned the meaning of her—how she wanted to be strict with me because it was right for me, but I didn't see that. I thought it was her just not wanting me to have any friends or any fun or anything, but it wasn't. She wanted good for me, to have a good life, but I ended up going the wrong route.

I talk to my dad like maybe once a month. He moved here like ten years ago, so he's been here with us. He and my mom communicate better now that that they are not together, and sometimes my mom has a boyfriend, of course. My father lives with my older brother. Sometimes my father will bring my mom flowers, sometimes candy and stuff.

"Why didn't you do all those things when you were younger and with her and with us?" I ask him.

He says, "I was stupid. I was an alcoholic," and I was this, I was that.

I'm like, "That's not an excuse."

He has said he's sorry. I forgive him because I'm not in that situation anymore where I'm being abused and think it's okay, because my mom taught me otherwise when she left him. My dad never hit us. My mom used to spank us. He yelled at her, not at us. So, he was a good dad except for the part of hitting my mom and verbally abusing her, but us seeing and hearing it was scary. But, he never took it out on us or yelled at us.

I know Jesus wasn't perfect. I'm not a spiritual person, but I know he wasn't perfect. People give me hope to get through the day. I've met a few people that I really, really like—and nice people, not people that scream and yell or are abusive. I try to put myself in different situations because I'm not used to it. Fifteen years ago I wouldn't have cared what type of person they were, and today I do 'cause I feel like my friends are going to be a reflection of me and I'm gonna be a reflection of them. So if I hang out with bad people, I feel bad.

I like it at Advent House. I love Ms. Toni. She's a really great person. I've never met anyone like her before. I've had really serious talks with her. She's an understanding person. You know not everyone is perfect. Advent House is a really nice place because they help you with a lot of things, not just schooling. There's a lot of programs there. There's not a lot of funds, but other than that, it's a really nice place to be, to learn. I wouldn't want to be getting my GED anywhere else but there. I like the people there.

My anxiety gets really bad where I don't want to go to school. I don't want to do anything. I've called Ms. Toni and tell her, "I'm not going to school today." I never tell her, "It's my anxiety." I always tell her something else. It's usually my anxiety. It won't let me leave the house. I get really sick and start throwing up, start shaking and getting nervous. Even with my medication, it doesn't work.

I have been to a therapist before. I don't feel comfortable telling a stranger my business. See, you're not a stranger, Ally. I've seen you before. I've talked to you. I've been around you and I know you're a happy person. I see you happy and smiley all the time and I feel comfortable talking to you. I'm sure happy people have anxiety issues, too. Not everybody can see it, and not everybody knows what kind of issues we all have. We all have something. We're not perfect.

I'm just tired of the abuse thing, and I want to be happy even if that means being by myself. I don't care, because I'm happy.

Overcoming Mistakes

Loren accessed shelters and Advent House Ministries. He acknowledges he needs help—a first step—and continues to work on his personal challenges, maintains a positive attitude, and believes he can overcome his mistakes even though he often waffles.

The missions and stuff like that, you have a low self-esteem and they are there to help. And that's a good thing, but your mindset is you're homeless and you got to look to these people to help you. So, in that aspect, that's rough, mentally rough, to admit you need help. You out there by yourself, homeless, you have nowhere to go. You need somewhere, food, bed, to eat, but you know you step out into the streets and you're out there by yourself, no one to turn to. It's a very, very lonely feeling. You're there with other people that are in the same situation, and it's just a very, very lonely feeling and that's what I mean by rough, it's lonely. And it's hard in this world, and you get the feeling that no one cares.

There are people out there that do care, and I thank God that they are there in my life now. But a lot of people don't really know what it's like to be alone, homeless, not having nothing, no foundation to stand on. You make these mistakes throughout your life and no one has caused these for you. I realized that the situation that I was in, I created for myself. It was all on me. My parents and my brothers—they helped me while they could, and my ex, but eventually even though I created this, it still got to be a certain level of what people don't understand. It's hard. Everyone needs love. Everyone needs a chance, no matter what kind of mistakes you made in your life. You can still overcome those mistakes.

I had no place to go, so I went to the shelters after that. I stayed at the mission on and off. I'd have to say 2001–2002 all the way up to last year. On and off, mission, day to day. That's rough, you know, but then I got blessed. Staying at the shelters, it's really . . . no, it's not rough. It's a lonely feeling, because the streets are rough. Being on the streets are rough. I know people that stay in the woods and that sort of thing, and that's rough.

People need to see this as a crisis—people outside sleeping under bridges, out in the woods sleeping. I see them. They drink. That's their friend. That's their family. In their mind, it's easy to turn to alcohol like that and drugs, so I thank God for the missions and stuff and Loaves and Fishes.

I wouldn't say I made friends, true friends, but I made a lot of good acquaintances there. It did help the loneliness. We all look at, "we're in this boat together." You understand me and I understand you. We are going through this day together, and I just met this person, but we have a lot in common—more in common than with people I've known all my life.

With the drinking and drugs, I was alone. I mean I had friends and stuff and we did it together, but mainly I did a lot of it by myself. I was in the shelter for about seven years almost, just about, on and off. The lowest point for me was being in the shelters.

One good thing I like is the people at the mission. They bring their kids in and they help serve food, and their family members, or even if it's all adults, people are in touch, they see what it's like out there. They see it and they're helping, and it reminds them that these people out here need help. But also, what it's like on the other side, and the fact that you don't want to be on that other side, because it's cold outside, and it's a cold world. It's tough. It's tough. So I would just say my advice to anybody that got it, don't lose it. Be willing to understand the other side of life and the people that aren't as fortunate as you. Stay in touch, that way you know. Let your kids serve somebody that's homeless for two reasons: one, they're helping and they're giving back. They're seeing how you can help society out and that's a good thing. Then, for adults and especially for teenagers, how you can . . . your life can slip from you, quick.

I was in high school, and I never thought I'd have to go through none of this. And just the simple mistake that you make. Keep 'em in touch with the fact that these are all still people out here and your life can slip.

There was a gap in time between when I left the shelter and when I got this apartment that I have now. Fortunately, I stayed with some people who were my in-laws at the time; my dad's wife's sister and her husband took me in and I stayed with them for a year. During that period, they carried me over and I owe them a lot. They've done a lot for me. We still have our quarrels and whatnot, but they were that bridge to where I'm at now. I did household work and that sort of thing, yard work. During that time, it took me off the street and it really got my mind transitioned from living in the streets—then, boom, into an apartment and living wild, like you were in the streets. It got me used to living in a structured environment with people, and taking care of business in the home, and what you can and cannot . . . you know, structure, foundation. So, it helped me when I moved into my apartment because I was able to continue that way of life.

I wasn't sober there. I was still drinking my beer; a lot of the drugs and stuff I don't do anymore, but I still drink my beer. It's that too. I don't have to do it to the extreme and the extent that I was on the streets. 'Cause on the street, you figure, you know, "Hey, I'm out here anyway, I'm gonna do this. I got a few dollars I'm a do this, I'm a do that." When you live in a home, we have our moments, we partied and whatnot. We did what we did, but it wasn't nowhere near the extent to what I did when I was actually homeless, so I thank them for that. They helped me out a lot.

And then I used to stand in front of those doors and panhandle out for loose change. And it was funny 'cause I was just in a store—Mike's M9, down there on MLK. They asked me 'cause I used to stand in front of this door all the time, panhandle for change when I was homeless and stuff, you know, hustlin' and whatever, get the drink or whatever drug I was using. I go in the store and he's like, "Are you standing out in front of my store?" And it's raining, and to me, now, it's funny because I don't do that anymore. You know, I'm glad. I'm proud of myself, and it's partly . . . mainly to do with them taking me out of that situation and then mainly with myself as well not desiring. I've learned how to do this, and as I got away from that, I realized that's good I don't have to do that.

It was funny to me because he was like, "You standin' in front of my store?"

"Nah, I'm not standin' in front of your store. I don't even live over here no more." You know what I'm saying? And he's like, "Oh, where do you live at now?" and I told him and he was like, "You got a job?" and I said, "Yeah," and he kind of looks at me like, "Oh, okay." So you don't have to worry about me. No one's gonna look outside and chase me away like they used to do, so it makes me realize that I've come a long ways. But you know I've made some changes, and some strides. Even if it's just something little, like standing in front of that store like that and he remembers—I can walk out of that store like, "Yeah, I don't do that anymore. I'm not that kind of person anymore," you know. So there's still a lot of other areas in my life that I need to tighten up—and I'm gonna tighten up—but, at least I don't do that anymore.

REFLECTIONS

The people who participated in "Your Story and Mine: A Community of Hope" took major steps in their lives through education, religion, work, reconnecting with family members, leaving abusive family relationships, volunteering, and abandoning drugs and alcohol. Eventually they took another giant step and began to paint pictures of and write poems about their homeless experiences. They have gained even more perspective on their lives and have built greater self-confidence on their new journey.

Their Stories through Paintings and Poems

Using Art to Heal

Just as people have been telling their stories and those of others through words—oral and written—for years, they have also been drawing and painting their stories. Sometimes they write poetry—another avenue of sharing their thoughts, feelings, and ideas. Tens of thousands of years ago, people drew their stories on the walls of the caves where they lived. "The first rock drawings were etched and . . . the first cave-pictures of bears and other animals were scratched out" (Brodskaia 2007, 7).

However, over the years, drawing images was not only for the purpose of sharing stories. Cathy A. Malchiodi, art therapist and author, wrote: "Since ancient times, art has served as a means to repair and renew the self, and the world's wisdom traditions have affirmed imagery as a remedy for what ails the body and mind" (Malchiodi 2002, xi).

People have an innate, primal need or desire to tell their stories. Some love to tell them. Others need encouragement. Still others are extremely private. Providing the opportunity to these people to paint their life stories, or segments of them, opened up another option for self-expression, without the self-censorship that sometimes goes with the use of words. Art from the soul just is.

In her book *Drawing on the Artist Within*, Betty Edwards explored many creative individuals' written words.

Words alone were often inadequate to describe the creative process ... to be truly creative we must somehow turn ourselves away from usual modes of thought in order ... to look at the world from a different point of view. ... Verbal language can be inappropriate for certain creative tasks and ... words at times can even *hinder* thinking. ...

Thus, ... *direct perception*, a different kind of "seeing," is an integral part of the thinking—and hence the creative—process. ... Drawings, like words, have meaning—often beyond the power of words to express, but nonetheless invaluable in making the chaos of our sensory impressions comprehensible." (Edwards 1986, xii–xiii)

This chapter explores the participants' stories as they talk about their art and poetry. You can see some of their paintings in the photo gallery of this book. Also woven throughout this chapter are the mentors' reflections on the participants' creative endeavors, which enhance our understanding of the participants' stories and art about their personal experiences with homelessness.

We provided a supportive, nonjudgmental environment so that people could begin to paint their stories. Some painted about their memories of homelessness. Some painted self-portraits. Others painted images from their imagination. Just as they did not necessarily tell complete stories through words about all their home-less experiences, their paintings are also glimpses or vignettes of their lives while homeless—their memories, fantasies, and dreams. As Cathy Malchiodi has written, "Artistic self-expression can help you explore, release, and understand the source of emotional distress, ameliorate trauma, and repair and resolve conflicts. ... Your inner artist reveals only as much of yourself as you are ready to see and understand" (Malchiodi 2002, 150).

Mentors sat next to participants while they worked on their creative projects. We encouraged them, gave them support, and passed no judgment as to the right or wrong way to paint. We never required that they do any of the activities, nor did they need to respond to any questions we asked. However, we encouraged them to ask questions. While we cannot scientifically stipulate that this project changed these peoples' lives, we can safely say that based on their comments, the breakthroughs in their artwork, their lives and outlook on life, our observations, and Michigan State University graduate students' evaluations, they made many positive changes during this period.

Marion Heider, who provided individual support to the participants during the art classes, reflected on her experience in our roundtable discussion with video producer Peter Frahm. She said:

I was there to assist. The mood was cheerful and exciting, and people interacted with each other. The results were astounding—paintings of families, houses of childhood when life was easier. During these times, we all talked to each other and told stories about our lives. Several adults talked about themselves. I listened and asked questions about their lives and their children.

We shared stories about our families, and some men talked of their times in jail or when they were strung out on drugs and how that affected the families. We laughed about events in our lives, and I cried too when their children didn't see the parent for a period of time due to drugs or moving from place to place. We felt good when someone brought in new pictures of a family member.

I was impressed—everybody has a different kind of art, expressing something from their lives. If you asked each artist, "Can you tell me about that?" they would tell you something that they have not really told before, and they're very different one from one another. And you would ask them to tell you what that means, and they tell you a part of their life that was so bad and they were putting it down. They would need to talk about it, and I'm thinking, "That is so personal." They're just revealing their soul to you. I honored that very much and was very flattered that they talked about it.

Everybody talked to everybody else in the class. It is not that everyone was everybody's buddy, but I didn't see any hostility or disruption. I did not see anyone arguing or not talking to someone or not sitting next to someone. It was as if we were all friends. We all knew each other, and we were painting what we want to paint. Their humor and smiles also impressed me. It was almost as if sometimes they made fun of themselves. "Well, you know, I did it. I painted, and I was saying I couldn't paint." And I think I started to see a sense of pride in what they were doing.

After reviewing the photographs that Allyson, Erika, and I took throughout the duration of the project, I noticed a difference between the expressions on their faces in the wintertime, when they had just begun their art classes with Erika, and in the springtime, when they were painting their final pictures for the mural. Initially, their faces appeared locked. They did not smile. They wore hats and jackets inside during class to stay warm. They were still feeling cold from the outdoors. When spring came, their faces were open. They often smiled and giggled. They had also gotten over some of their fears of painting their stories.

Allyson said:

We all had so much fun. You could see in their eyes and the way they held themselves, but they also had to overcome obstacles in order to paint. I think getting them to believe in themselves just a little bit in the art piece was especially difficult. "Will I do this very simple design today? I can't draw. I can't do anything artistic. I'm never going to get this." The process of being scared started to change, and they began to try emotionally and physically. Eventually, we could not get them to close down for the day. "When can I draw again? When can I paint?"

Many of them painted for the first time despite their initial thoughts and fears that they could not paint. Symbolically and literally, this experience reflected their taking a new step in a positive direction. They stepped out of their immediate situations, reflected, and created. They transformed their raw feeling into art or poetry. They each concentrated diligently and quietly, with thoughtfulness and care.

They might have been engaged in difficult present-day dramas at the time of the project, but were not involved in past dramas and traumas of homelessness—those were the stories they painted. They conjured up the experiences, reflected upon them, and painted or wrote about them with some perspective over time. Their paintings revealed profound grief and trauma from childhood, adolescence, and young adulthood. They also painted their self-portraits—so they could see how they looked from their perspectives. On completing those paintings, their faces glowed with pride.

One of my most favorite poets from the time I was in high school is the British poet William Wordsworth, who wrote many poems about nature and emotions. In 1800, he wrote: "I have said that poetry is the spontaneous overflow of powerful feelings: it takes its origin from emotion recollected in tranquility: the emotion is contemplated 'till by a species of reaction the tranquility disappears, and an emotion, kindred to that which was before the subject of contemplation, is gradually produced, and does itself actually exist in the mind" (Wordsworth [1802] 1984, 611).

Years ago, when I had personally encountered my own inner roadblocks, one of my mentors suggested that I try to paint images that I saw within me that reflected my stories from childhood and adolescence, my struggles and challenges, pains and joys, as well as new images—dreams, fantasies, hopes, and desires. She told me that painting could prove valuable on my life journey, heal old wounds, free me of inner burdens, help me embrace my current life, and inspire and empower me to move my life forward. While I was verbal and could talk and write at length about my inner life, words often actually interfered with my ability to truly see and understand my feelings and spiritual world, which often heavily weighed me down emotionally. Painting lacked a rational, defensive component that writing had for me. Seeing what I grappled with internally, paying attention to those images, and acknowledging them and their significance could help objectify my life experiences so they would not be as raw, abrasive, or painful as the literal experiences.

I asked two artist friends if they would draw pictures to accompany a collection of poems I had written. They both independently said that I had to draw the images myself since these images were mine, inside my mind and heart. They could not see them, so could not possibly draw them even with my accompanying poetry. Initially disappointed when they each said no, I realize in retrospect that they were right.

Malchiodi talks about the value and significance of art:

> The simple act of making art nourishes the inner self and connects us with the outer world of relationships, community, and nature. It is a natural process of caring for the soul and experiencing it in all its dimensions. . . .
>
> Art therapy, the use of the creative process for emotional restoration and healing, grew out of the idea that images are symbolic communications and that art making helps us to express and transform difficult life experiences. It has expanded our understanding of how image making and imagination help during the dark night of the soul, carrying forward the ancient knowledge of art's healing powers as well as the work of Freud and Jung. Artistic expression is one of our elemental tools for achieving psychological integration, a universal creative urge that helps us strive for emotional well-being. (Malchiodi, *The Soul's Palette*, 4)

I followed my mentor's and friends' suggestions, which ultimately propelled me to draw or paint several hundred pictures within just a few years—often late at night into the early hours of the morning. I saw so many images within me during my waking hours, yet it was not humanly possible to photograph them. The images took on a life of their own, a momentum and sense of direction. They came with a rush and passion. They knocked on my mind's inner walls, and begged me to look at them and listen to their messages, let them out and draw them while fresh. They needed immediate gratification so I would not forget them—in a similar way that if we want to remember a dream, we need to write it down as soon as we wake up—otherwise, in seconds, it might disappear from our consciousness. Often, when waking up in the morning, I feel as if I have been to the movie theater all night long and am exhausted from all the intricate visual stories. I often tried to draw my dreams as well.

> When words are not enough, we turn to image and symbol to speak for us. They are a conduit to all we contain within and a way of reflecting and recounting where we have been, where we are, and where we are going. Artistic expression is far more than self-expression and has much more astonishing power. Artistic

creativity offers a source of inner wisdom that can provide guidance, soothe emotional pain, and revitalize your being. More important, it is a wellspring that enlivens, rejuvenates, restores, and transforms and it exists within everyone for health and well-being. (Malchiodi 2002, x)

Early on, I began drawing with a pencil that I let gently wander on the meandering lines of the textured surface of the paper. Slowly, faces emerged—almost like ghosts from the past that haunted me. Some dominated more than others. As time passed, I used a thin black marker. While on a family trip to the mountains of West Virginia, I used my sons' colored markers. Later, I found higher-quality markers, with thin tips on one end and thick tips on the other, that came in many colors. Working with markers rather than paints helped expedite the process, to get the images down on paper as quickly as possible. Eventually, however, I also worked with the water-based gouache paints that are the most brilliant of all paints.

I had no rules on what or how I drew or wrote and passed no judgment. Sometimes I painted images I saw in the daytime. Sometimes I painted my nighttime dreams that complemented my poems. Other times I incorporated words in the paintings. I sketched childhood memories, such as going on the weekend with my father to play tennis and swim at a nearby lake. We then went to a local family-owned ice-cream store, where we frequently shared a large coffee milkshake.

In another instance, one day, when feeling emotionally injured, I suddenly saw an image within my mind and painted a story poem about it—words and painted images. A great big black, amorphous blob like a gaseous cloud attacked and then enveloped a white daisy. The flower could not breathe. Its white petals and green leaves bled, then fell to the earth. All that remained was the green stem and yellow center of the flower. It had no memory. It could not recall why or how it was devastated—only that it had experienced a traumatic injury. It had been too little and frail to defend itself. Later, a small, fresh pink rose appeared.

I painted fanciful images—symbols of emotions—such as seagulls flying out of a young woman's mouth, some whose wings revealed their full wingspan, others with broken wings. Very colorful nature images often simultaneously appeared in poems, such as in "Healing the Soul" (1994). I then painted a picture and infused the poem in it.

At dawn, the gold sun rises,
Tingeing the sky with pink
And lighting Venus and the crescent moon.
The autumn wind whistles through the brass chimes,

Replacing the clanging, cacophonous symphonies
That echo through my inner castle walls.
White candles melt the moat's frozen water
Which have sealed off the truth
And orange-red rage for many years.
The aquamarine waves with many shades of blues and greens
And fresh, orange peaches beckon
Schools of fish and flocks of birds to migrate.
These harbingers of truth
Grant permission not to censor
The hidden messages of early childhood memories,
Which I feel, but cannot interpret yet.
But now, just as the orange, red and yellow nasturtiums revealed
The truth about the deceptive old gardener,
When they bloomed among the fallen old dark oak and maple leaves and pine needles
In the woods, and not in the garden beds
Where he was supposed to plant them,
In time, my truths emerge.
The birds, the fish, the peaches, the brass wind chimes,
The candles, and waves—symbols of gentility and validation,
Have eased my panicked, choking voices,
Slowly, permitting trust and faith.
Finally, as my soul begins to heal,
I understand that
I cannot see all or do all by myself.
I must trust others.
I must take one day at a time.
I am not alone.
Others have lived in exile for many years.
These new images and messages transform old fears
And empower me to begin to soar in peace.

These personal experiences from many years ago further empowered me in my discussions with the other mentors as we conceptualized "Your Story and Mine: A Community of Hope." They validated the process of providing a variety of options for self-expression that might help the participants heal from deep emotional wounds and lift roadblocks that had not permitted them to see a variety of options for solutions.

Malchiodi writes:

Symbols may appear in your dreams or be created consciously. Taking an image from your dreams or imagination and putting it on paper, canvas, or clay enhances your self-understanding and makes visible your personal myths and stories. Symbols in your art may reflect your neglected areas, bring attention to something you need to repair within yourself, or generate the energy needed for change. They naturally tell stories about who you are, where you come from, and where you are going. You never exhaust completely their meanings or healing aspects. (Malchiodi 2002, 78)

While designing our program, I tried to find similar ones that we could use as models. I did not find history museums that had specifically collaborated with homeless shelters. I did find information about art museums and libraries that offered after-school therapeutic art programs for at-risk children. An art program for adults with developmental disabilities, known as "Art from the Heart," is offered at Peckham Industries in Lansing, Michigan. Programs for prison inmates include artistic endeavors such as Arts in Prison, Inc. in Kansas, designed "to provide educational and personal growth opportunities through the arts for inmates, volunteers and community to motivate and inspire positive change." Many art-therapy programs are offered at homeless shelters. More recently, while reading Malchiodi's book, I learned about Raw Art Works (RAW), a community-based art-therapy program designed to inspire young artists to tell their stories, envision new possibilities, and transform their lives.

Now, I continue to surf the Internet to see what else I might find about museums and homelessness. Interestingly, I have found the work of photographers who have photographed and interviewed the homeless; their exhibits have appeared in many museums. For example, Boris Mikhailov was born in 1938 in Kharkov, Ukraine. He lives and works in the Ukraine and in Berlin. His stark, shocking photographs concentrate on the "social disintegration ensuing from the break-up of the Soviet Union—both in terms of social structures and the resulting human condition. Case History documents the social oppression, the devastating poverty, the harshness and helplessness of everyday life for the homeless" (Mikhailov n.d.).

Photographer Michael Nye, who lives in San Antonio, Texas, spent four and a half years interviewing and photographing the homeless. He now has a traveling exhibit of his images and the interviews. He writes:

Hunger is as old as history, and is wrapped into our genes as the great impulse to survive. Everyone knows the boundary between hunger and satisfaction. However, for many of us in this country of abundance, it is difficult to imagine someone so hungry and weak they would cry or lose the desire to live. . . .

People die and no one remembers their stories. Everyone in this exhibit knows something important and valuable, a wisdom about their experience that only they know. The fifty individuals represented in "Hunger" are teachers—and we are students. Stories are places where empathy and understanding begin. . . .

What we are given, what is planted in the first fields in our lives can be deeply mysterious in its generosity or insufficiencies. The poor in our communities are often the least heard and the most forgotten.

Listening is another way of seeing. Hunger is an issue of human rights. Everyone has the right to be heard, to be listened to, and to receive help when hungry. (Nye n.d.)

Recently, I read an article in the *New Yorker* magazine—in "The Talk of the Town," by Ian Frazier—about a theatrical program, Rehabilitation through the Arts, founded by Katherine Vockins. A dozen prisoners at the Woodbourne Correctional Facility (a medium-security state prison in Woodbourne, New York) performed their life stories for guests as part of "Theatricalizing the Personal Narrative."

The stories represent a truth, if not necessarily *the* truth, taken from the life of each speaker: "an emotional truth" as Dick Scanlan (the author of the book and the lyrics for "Thoroughly Modern Millie") describes it. He is one of the directors of the performance. . . .

Each prisoner recites his narrative, and it seems as if he had just thought of it, rather than having gone over it many dozens of times. . . . Violence, lost mothers, longed-for lovers, unanswered mysteries, regret, sorrow, and beloved children figure prominently. . . .

Scott says (Sherie Rene Scott, the star and co-author . . . of the Broadway hit "Everyday Rapture"), "Getting the story down takes technical skill, but doing it over and over becomes draining and frightening, and that's when you have to push through; that's when it becomes art." . . .

"Look at me now," Rick Morad, one of the performers, says. "I have changed through being in this program. . . . I've been in jail for over twenty years. I have a parole hearing in twenty-three months, and if I get out I don't know if I'll become an actor, but I do know I'll be a better man. This program works!" (*New Yorker*, August 1, 2011)

By participating in "Your Story and Mine: A Community of Hope," the participants also came to understand that they were not alone in their struggles. They were now part of a group of other people with comparable life experiences and a greater community in the Lansing area, bigger than their immediate family and friends. While they had been part of the homeless community, to some extent they were now outgrowing it, and discovering new friends and mentors from other spheres of their lives who were "homeless no more." They also knew that the stories they shared through words and paintings would travel throughout Michigan, elsewhere in the United States, and as far away as the Czech Republic.

Erika shared her thoughts about the participants and the project:

I started the project with a basic framework, but was pretty clueless, which ended up being a positive thing because I loved to see the participants and the nature of the project dictate what would come next and how to proceed.

Initially I thought the mural was going to be a collective statement, but as the project evolved, I realized that it was a collection of individual stories. Participants kept their individual identity. Yet, they were all together, all connected, stitched together. They were able to support each other. The project helped them to think about a world larger than themselves. When they're down and out, they start to look at life in a different way. If you have nothing, you look at life differently.

We had this big panel we were going to make, a portable mural that was going to tell this story of homelessness. What I expected was that different themes would develop, and that we would be working together on a collective statement about that and having a personal element of their story in it. What ended up was a collection of very individual stories. I felt that was really important—that they each had their own section, their own artwork unique to them, and that they weren't blended into this larger notion of homelessness. They maintained their own personal identity and story of homelessness. Yet, they were part of this larger society, and that is why we stitched them together because they are all part of the larger story of homelessness.

My role was the art instructor and overseer of the artistic component, where the participants expressed their life stories through artwork. We started out getting comfortable with art materials and then slowly introduced the idea using symbols to express life experiences and emotions. We worked on a timeline project that went in many different directions for each individual. Some of them focused on where they were at now. Others focused on where they wanted to be heading. Others told their whole story, beginning with their family of origin, what led to their homelessness, and the present.

We worked on self-portraits. I took photographs of them, and then we projected the photographs and traced their outlines and they painted their images.

They added the details that brought them to life. They were almost baffled. That seemed to be an important component because it hit on a sense of identity and feelings of invisibility in the homeless community. They are invisible to other parts of society in terms of establishing their individuality and even their existence.

I also noticed the support among these people. They look out for each other and take care of each other in unique ways. If someone is new to homelessness, someone is there to take the new person under their wing, to explain to them where to get food, where to get their needs met, what is bad about certain shelters. They have a concern for other people.

I think it is easier for these people to express compassion and empathy. They have been through some very difficult things in life. They know what it is like to be in a tough spot, to lose their home and to lose everything. Many of the participants are capable of being really empathetic. Being homeless is life changing and may be one of the lessons for me—that willingness to be vulnerable, to be with other human beings, emotionally and fully present. If something is touching about something that someone shares, it is okay to cry, to be vulnerable. I may have learned more from this experience than they did.

It is interesting to go back to the issue of self-abuse. I hadn't realized how important that painting their portraits really was in a way I hadn't thought of. It wasn't them. It was an image of them, a piece of artwork. Yet they were taking so much care to make a beautiful piece of artwork. Ultimately, it was an image of themselves, and that might be why some of them had such a hard time with it. Just about everybody who participated had some sort of early trauma in their lives. These really old themes came through a lot in their artwork and in their stories. When they experienced that trauma, it stuck with them. So maybe through talking about it and working on the artwork, they started to work with it differently. . . .

I know you cannot go back in time, but I kept wishing we could go back in time to these moments with these individuals and intervene. If we can help people closer to when the trauma is actually happening to offer some support, to intervene with mental support, then it might not have a grip on them in the way that it does.

A person with cognitive, mental, or developmental disabilities may not see a way out of the situation, but a solution might be apparent to someone who does not have those challenges. That's why it's really important for people to be supportive and say, "Well, have you thought about this? or that?" And even for people to keep a job, if you have mental health challenges and you don't know that you could get disability benefits . . . even if you do have disability benefits, it's challenging to exist on.

Human beings, among people who live in poverty, value human beings and relationships—they're the most important thing. And I think that's why sometimes even though relationships may be harmful, people maintain them.

In retrospect, I would make some changes to the classes. The more laid-back classes were more effective than the more structured classes. Furthermore, if they could take classes for a year, they could grow and find their own "voice" within the structured lessons. I think some of the lessons inadvertently limited the creativity of some of the participants by unknowingly setting expectations for the end result. In the short time that we had, I think it would have been more effective to allow more free painting and drawing and let the story come out of that. Initially, I did not think that their stories would just unfold. I thought the stories would need to be coaxed out, but I was not accurate in thinking this.

Erika taught several art classes to help them prepare for painting their self-portraits and a segment of their homeless lives. Most had not drawn before, and had certainly not told their stories through painted images. Many were amazed that they could actually paint when they thought they could not. Discover now their stories and vignettes about their homelessness as revealed through their paintings, and uncover their perceptions and feelings about their art. Read their poems that reflect their life stories or segments of them, and listen to the words of their mentors.

Experiencing Success

One morning, Wynette sat in class pensively. She told me that she had left her bag with family photographs on the bench at the bus stop near her apartment. She needed them for her art project. I asked her if I could drive her over to see if they were still there. She readily agreed to go. I told her I was concerned that her bag with photos might not still be there anymore.

"Oh, I know it's there. It's there. Nobody's going to take it," she said, reassuring me.

We drove to the bus stop in front of her apartment. When we arrived, she got out of the car and sure enough, she found her bag sitting exactly where she had left it.

"I told you it would be there," she said sweetly with a big smile on her face. We were both relieved.

We then returned to Advent House Ministries, where Wynette proceeded to lay out her photographs to make a collage of all her family members. She took great care deciding where she should place each photograph.

"Those pictures—they're just to tell about me, my kids, my dad, and my mom, and my sisters. Family is very important to me."

Both Allyson and Erika talked with Wynette about painting. Allyson said, "Wynette painted, after much protest. She thinks that she has to know how to paint, that there is a certain way to do things. I understand that. I think she feels that the painting is no good because she doesn't know how to do the details or create shadows. But, with a little motivating, and some help, she got down to it and did a great job."

Erika said, "Wynette began with a very stylized image she had found in the example of symbols, then moved towards painting her self-portrait."

Allyson added, "Wynette kept feeling like she was ruining her portrait. Erika helped trace her face, and I encouraged her to start with the broad strokes first. Do the easy parts, gain some confidence, and work your way up to the more difficult stuff. Wouldn't it be great if we all did that a little more in life? Or maybe that is just something I struggle with. I can sometimes get overwhelmed with the last steps when I should be focused on the first ones."

Erika explained that Wynette "also meticulously worked on an image of her old house, drawing it from memory. She at one time asked me to help. I did a little, but told her that she could probably do a better job, because she knew what the house looked like. She said, 'okay,' and with great focus painted a house on her own."

Wynette talked about her experience painting.

I painted a picture of a house. This is one of my homes when it got condemned. I just decided to paint it. This is me, my husband, and my seven kids while we were going out the door. The house got condemned because of the wiring and stuff like that and it wasn't up to code. They put a sticker on there and we had to leave the house and we went to a shelter. I liked that house. It was four bedrooms, really nice and big and roomy. We had to leave.

Well honestly, honestly I was really surprised when I made this picture. I was really surprised because I never did any kind of artwork, and I was more surprised than anybody because I was like, "I did that?!"

But I mean, art was not my favorite subject so I just, I was surprised, very surprised. I'm not an artist, so I don't think I would ever like to do it again. I don't know. I might. I would have to think about it. But I'm not for sure.

Finding the Inner Poet

Before I met Lewis, I had heard he wrote poetry, suffered from many emotional problems throughout his life, and had been in jail and prison—but that now he was married, with three children, and managed fairly well. He was particularly endearing and warm. Each time he came to an art class, he asked for a piece of paper to write a poem. He would say, "I'm a poet!" Each time, within minutes of extreme concentration and focus, he wrote an incredibly moving poem. One day, I took a risk and engaged in a discussion with him about art and poetry.

He said, "I don't do art. I can't paint. I just write poetry. I'm a poet!" This is what he always said when he came to class.

I said, "That's fine, but maybe you could just try to explore that option and paint one picture?"

Still, he was resistant. I began to personalize the experience. As we stood by a support post in the lower level of the Advent House Ministries building, I told him that for many years, I had also written poems and did not know how to paint. I told him that one day, I began drawing by using a pencil to outline the ridges and valleys on very rough paper, looked for forms and shapes, and then created characters and images. As Lewis and I stood there talking together, I pointed to the rough surface of the support post and asked him to imagine it was the surface of a piece of paper or canvas. I rubbed my finger along the post, similar to the rough paper I used, and made an outline of a face—with eyes, a nose, a mouth, and hair.

He was intent. His eyes glowed. He saw the face I was outlining. "Hey, you think just like I do!" His whole face was beaming!

I told Lewis that sometimes I painted pictures to accompany my poems. Sometimes, I just painted the images I saw within myself that I could not photograph. Other times, I literally wrote my poems into my paintings.

He said, "I'm going to paint a picture to go with the poem I just wrote."

Lewis realized he could incorporate a poem on the canvas side by side with the painting. I told him he had all kinds of options. He could make those choices and decisions.

He asked, "Do you think Erika has another canvas for me?" I told him I was sure she did.

Lewis sat down and painted several pictures. While we were not expecting Lewis to become a prolific artist, the significance of this story is that he was willing to try something new and different and ultimately gained satisfaction. He broke through his resistance and realized he could express himself in a new way. His wife,

LaKashia, was so excited and kept encouraging him, telling him that he was doing a terrific job.

Lewis talked to me about what it is like for him to write poetry. He has more than fifty poems that he has written over the years—while in prison and out of prison, and he continues to write today. He said,

> Writing poetry is an expression of feelings. Like if I can feel something, I can write it. Like if I feel like crying about something right now, I've learned to write it down right now and make them into poems.
>
> Because I couldn't say certain things in my household at my mom's and dad's, I used to write myself little poems after a while because I been angry or something. I almost used to think it was too unmanly. I thought people would laugh at me. I always wanted to do this. But, at that time, I was young and insecure and my friends are going to laugh at me. They're going to think I'm homophobia, which I am. And I never just wanted that for people to think I'm gay or something.
>
> And, now with this, I see that that was my reason for failure, because I held something that was worth a million dollars. I had this little bundle this whole time. Here I'm talking about I'm homeless. Basically, what I'm saying is, for years, I had this in me. I know that one day that this is going to pay off for me. But, I'm a late bloomer. Now, I'm starting to get my wings now, you know? Now, I'm starting to grow and prosper and feel better. And love.
>
> When I start to write a poem, it's like a trance. That's what it's like. It's like I'm almost putting myself into, like, a picture. I see it clearly. I write about what I see and feel at that moment.

The beauty of Lewis's poems is that they are raw, real, and primal. He wrote them himself; they come from his heart, mind, and soul and are based on his personal experiences and thoughts about his life and the world. They are written through his own eyes and not by someone else imagining Lewis's experiences. Since our project ended, he has written another 250 poems. He wrote the following two poems about homelessness while participating in "Your Story and Mine: A Community of Hope."

BEING HOMELESS
By Lewis H., 2009

My experience being homeless was traumatic,
yet the most meaningful times,
like being a father it allowed me to see

that one must fight, one must work.
One must stand like a rapper
battling freestyle for the crown.
Yes people It's going down.
Standing together as a force.
It's true that there was time
one never could know what about the times
when the only money we had was from selling drugs
searching my plugs
to only be robbed for every dollar
begging for extra money
to keep the gas paid.
But to try and still get your gas turned off.
Mind you it is frost bitten cold
and we also have a new born baby.
Maybe you can see
what it's like putting your clothes
in the window,
hot plates for a steamer,
Do I have experience,
or am I a dreamer?

REACH OUT
By Lewis H., 2009

As I woke up without a dollar
To my name, vast knowledge
of being homeless, and petty games,
so many children have followed
me how could I not be ashamed
To see a fine city of culture, and
Diversity be torn down, person
After person slipping away, young
Women giving their souls
Just to see her babies safe
And sound, how much going
Down does it take, another
Child dead, and the other
Child going to sleep with

A belly ache, staying
Self-Sufficient is strong
And good, who am I
To not help a homeless
Person in the neighborhood.

Painting a Hard Life

Erika worked closely with Robert. She said:

Robert had shared his story of when he was in his accident. He drew a picture of a coffin with the word "inevitable" in it. I was curious to know what that was, but I was also concerned. I wanted to make sure he was okay. He told me about how death is inevitable, how eventually, we all die—something about being aware of that, you live more, you love more, by being aware of it, the fact that we will all die.

He said that after his accident, he woke up and just wanted to die. And apparently, he had been in a coma for a couple of months and had died. He had a near-death experience. He didn't go into much detail. He didn't tell me. There was something in his eyes. He got something out of it, but that he couldn't really explain in words.

Over time Robert began to do things more on his own. On the last day, when he was finishing his painting, he had painted over the word "inevitable" through the process of painting the background. He asked if I had a pen or anything that he could use to go over it. I let him borrow a brand new Sharpie that I happened to have with me. He wanted me to write it, but I said that I was afraid I would mess it up. He then said that he could do it. I suggested he practice on a piece of paper first. He quietly said that he did not need to practice and proceeded to very neatly rewrite the word.

Although seemingly a small feat, it was indicative of his increase in confidence. At the end of this class, he asked that I take a picture of his finished piece, and asked if he could have a picture of it so he could look at it and say, "Look what I did!"

Robert painted for the first time. Despite his insecurity about it, he painted and actually enjoyed it. The idea was that a person can take a step in a new direction, such as painting, that can foster other positive steps.

Robert talked a lot about the spiritual component to being homeless, of having nothing and wandering the streets, spending time by the river and in

127

the woods in natural, public, off the beaten path where most people go, and discovering a spiritual component that maybe people who are busy with work are maintaining a job and family don't have.

I remember a really profound moment for me. This was a spiritual, personal experience for me when we went photographing along the river trail on the field trip to Old Town in Lansing. Robert had wanted to go to this special place where he used to sit. It happened to be across the river from where I had lived a few years before. My back yard butted up to the river, too, and I would sit down there, so that was a really special place for me as well. He was telling me how important the river was to him. He used to like to come down there and sit, and imagined all the people who had come before him for hundreds of years and had walked along the river and had had the same experience of being connected with that river. He's telling me this and he had no idea that I was also one of those people. I just had a connection to him, to the river and all the people who came before us.

It was where the Native Americans maintain gardens in Old Town. I had walked along that section of the river, and old laundry soap from a hundred years ago, and animal bones from animals who had gone down to the river to die. It was this universality of the river flowing, the life source, and this connection to history and humanity. It was a very brief, profound moment of connection.

We have a tendency early in life to separate ourselves from people who are really struggling, because that's them, over there. And it's never going to happen to me. It must be something that they did. Possibly, it was an unconscious something. Okay, I'm the instructor and you're the participant. That's not always the case. I felt in that moment when Robert and I were talking by the river that we were equals, and at that moment, Robert was helping me.

Robert talked about his experience painting:

Well, the drawing I did with these two hands and the chains—that was just for incarceration, trouble with the law. Erika helped me out with it. Erika's the one that sketched those, not me. I was telling her my stories. I just asked her if she could draw me a pair like that, a pair of hands with handcuffs around them. I've been in jail off and on. I mean probably the longest I've been in there is six, seven months, something like that. I don't want to be there again and stuff. Well, it's just not nice having your freedom taken away. I don't think anybody deserves to have their freedom taken away from them.

My painting here just symbolizes, I guess, hard life. Death is inevitable;

incarceration has been part of my life. I always have to learn how to smile now and cry later. Love, broken hearts, you know, trying to convey all this in a painting. I put love backwards. It's a broken heart. I guess because it seems like it's always been that way in my life. And my little military helmet in there—a good six years, mostly in the reserves. Just the spirituality, the inevitable death that we are all gonna face. I've always had my spiritual beliefs. I stick to them. Rest in peace to all the people that I've lost in my life, family and friends. You never know which way it's gonna get you. I've been close myself, a bad accident.

Robert also worked hard and meticulously on his self-portrait and was very proud of his painting. I remember how skeptical he was at the beginning of the project about the painting component. He had said he was not an artist and could not paint. I think even he was surprised at what he could do.

Sharing Artwork

David came to a jobs class at Advent House Ministries in February 2009. He was shy and tentative but had brought some of his paintings to share. His artwork flourished in class and at home, and he converted his closet into an art studio. A talented guitar player and songwriter, he has performed on his guitar at Perspective 2 in Old Town during open mike night on the recommendation of Brandy, one of his classmates. One day, Brandy and David were talking with Marion about how they could improvise together, either outdoors when the weather gets warmer or at some other places. They mentored and helped each other.

David received art supplies from Advent House Ministries and purchased others from money he has earned from his jobs—so he no longer has to sell his blood for art supplies. He told Erika that he wanted to start painting to supplement his income. Erika said:

I think this sums up all of it—the playing for the first time in front of an audience, building his self-confidence, fixing his tooth, getting a job, and becoming a "closet painter." Not only does he have an income now, he is using part of it to pay back the people who helped him by making them paintings.

As an artist, and not as an "art teacher," I connected to David. He has the mind and spirit of a painter/artist. One day in class, we talked about the state of mind that a person gets into sometimes when they are painting and creating, and that there is a need to do something to wind down before going back into everyday life. We talked about how sometimes we snap at people who interrupt us while we are painting alone. He said that sometimes he feels angry and agitated when he is painting. This shows great strength in spirit to be able to create something beautiful while experiencing strong emotions.

We did not use many words to talk about all this, but there was an understanding between the two of us that I could see in his eyes—it is not really something one can talk about, but something one feels. I gave him some suggestions to help him change gears so that he could separate from the creative work when he needed to go to work or whatever. Somehow, I think having someone else understand and relate to that was important for him. . . .

David told me about his Bible studies. He wanted to be a preacher and go around and share what he had learned that was very helpful early on in his own personal life that was Christianity. He wanted to share that with other people he thought might be looking for help during difficult times. It was not as if he thought he wanted to be a preacher and live in a nice house. He wanted to be a preacher and continue to spread the word to people who are homeless. It was like he hadn't even given thought of another way of doing that.

David talked about his experience painting:

I like art, I like music. I started drawing. I maybe took one art class, but I've always drawn for a long time, maybe longer than I've played the guitar. I started drawing when I was in my twenties. I left some of the artwork in Grand Rapids. My nephew probably got all the artwork. Sometimes I see him when I'm in Grand Rapids.

I found out about this program, "Your Story and Mine," because people at Advent House saw my drawings and asked me if I wanted to be in the art program. I was coming there for the job club day.

At Advent House, they said, "You ought to paint, 'cause you draw so good. You ought to try painting." I told them I didn't have a place to paint—easels and putting your paintings all over the place.

Some of my pictures, I just draw out of my head, my inner self. I just started drawing stuff. I like to draw people a lot. Before I took art class years ago, maybe like fifteen years ago, but I couldn't draw people. Now I can draw just about anything I put my mind to. But it's another gift that I have that I picked up. It relaxes me to draw different stuff. I mostly draw people, animals, angels, an Indian with arrows in his quiver, my roommates sleeping on the couch. Sometimes, I might of drawn my dreams.

I got a divorce from my wife. My brother took me and we went to Arizona and Idaho. So, I did a lot of traveling. And that's where I picked up the guitar and started playing. I liked the traveling 'cause I needed to clear my head after my divorce. I had been married fifteen years. I married when I was eighteen years old. I have three kids. They're young adults now, in their twenties.

I write songs a little bit, and I was playing the guitar on the street corner for a while just to make some money in Lansing. I didn't do too bad, I guess. I went out and got a license. Otherwise you're panhandling. So, I paid five dollars for a license to play. I first started playing the guitar 'cause I was hungry. I play better when I'm hungry. When you feel hollow, you aren't full of stuff that gets in your way.

I got one song about liberty that me and my brother wrote:

Liberty, she used to stand like a beacon in the bay
For all the passing ships that pass by the way.
Some found a way to freedom for a while,
But even a spring of water can lose its natural prime
If it's misused it will become dried. . . .

That's a couple of lines of it.

There was disappointing whispers from the crowd,
When they thought liberty had fallen.
Some said, "What does it cost to keep her torch lit?"
Others said, "it cost more to let it go out." . . .

I don't remember any more of it. Me and my brother wrote it together. He came up with one line, I came up with another line for it. He plays the guitar. I play the guitar, too. He lives in Twin Falls, Idaho. I just taught myself how to play the guitar out of books and just followed along in the books—shows you, this is a G— and spent time playing, learning different picking styles of the guitar 'cause Willie does a roll and . . . you roll your fingers and play it, so we practice a bunch of different stuff. Listening to Willie, and so I play kind of like his style and plus I play some blues too.

I worry about not having a job. I know that I can play music, but I don't think I could make any money at all. 'Cause I had some people who wanted to record me; a man out in Haslett give me his card just before winter started to come on. But I didn't call him or pursue that because I don't have any money to make demos.

Yeah, I got all my songs. I keep them in a notebook. But, like I said, I probably got to write them out all over again, so I get the spelling right of the songs. Because I just jot them down. I'm illiterate, so I don't know if I got stuff spelled right, so that's another thing I need to do before I get to that. I always thought I'm too old to be a performer, you know, like forty-nine.

I recently had a gig. Somebody said there was an open mike. I was at the Advent House for the art thing, and I was playing with my back to them, and they said, "You need to go to this open mike." It only cost twenty dollars to get in. So I went and paid the twenty dollars and went to do it. I think it was the Unicorn, down by 319 on Grand River in Old Town. I had never been there before. I didn't know what it felt like. Because I played for people on the street and for other people, so I didn't know what I was really feeling from it. But I told somebody I want to do open mike nights at some other places, but I haven't checked that out yet to see where they do it around town. Somebody said there are a lot of places where they have open mike night.

I've been playing for fifteen years, learning to play. When I come to Lansing I played a little more because I was hungry and somebody said, "You know you could go out and make some money playing your guitar." So I went out there to make a little so I could eat. It helps pay for food. I have my own guitar. Well I had it when I came here, when I left Idaho. My brother picked one up for like fifty dollars at a second-hand store.

I didn't do any music or art as a kid. I don't know why I'm tapping into them. I guess I'm expressing what's in my mind and in my life and drawing I guess.

Well I wrote another song when I was here. It's called "Jesus Drives a Buick."

Jesus drives a Buick with portholes in the side,
Just like his wounded side afloat
But that's cause the Buick has portholes.
I don't know if they call them portholes or what,
They're in the side of the car, and
Jesus drives a PT Cruiser, you know,
The kind the one made by Chrysler Town and Country, you know?

I wrote one song about my wife, my ex-wife, when I was hungry. It's called "Mother of Children That Are Full Grown."

I want to bury the hatred God only knows.
We should be as proud as peacocks today

Because our baby had a baby,
Her name is sweet Desire.

I'm now able to get my meals at the place where I live. Yah, they put food in the house. They go to the Red Cross once in a while and get food. But, like I said, I'm pretty new at it because I really didn't open up until I came here. You know with my music and stuff. Because they didn't believe in me at home. It's something that I want to pursue is the music, and probably the artwork too. I think it's the way of visions more than anything else—things that I see and things I'm thinking about in my inner self is through the pictures and stuff. Maybe in the spiritual sense maybe. Sometimes, I sing out of the Bible and play the guitar, the psalms, stuff like that for inspiration.

Well, I make up my own music or play what I've heard—a little of both, I think. I make up my own songs if I'm doing it by memory, if I'm singing and praising God with songs, yah know, it's just repeating some of the psalms, and probably some of my own words are in there too. But I would have to be and know what my mood was for that day. I couldn't remember what I sang. Yah know, in the spirit of that time and place when I was singing that song.

David's music and art continue to flourish together. They go hand in hand. One day, David asked Allyson if we could go to the Capitol. He had always wanted to play the guitar on the Capitol steps. So the three of us took a little road trip. I took photographs of David playing and singing while Allyson sat and listened. We then went back to Advent House, where he began painting a picture based on his experience there and the photographs I had taken of him.

Discovering Your Talent

Erika talked about Jackie's art:

Jackie just jumped right in the first day. I heard her from across the room ask me to help her draw rocks. In my head I thought, "I can draw rocks! I love drawing rocks." I looked at her painting and she had a very well-developed Southwestern landscape. She told me it was Nevada. I asked her if Nevada rocks looked similar to New Mexico rocks.

We had a great conversation about rocks, similarities and differences. The conclusion we came to was that if I helped her, they would end up as Colorado or New Mexico rocks. She decided she would just paint them from her memory since she had spent so many nights as a child looking at the rocks in Nevada. How could I paint what was in her mind? Through my fumbling around trying to paint the rocks from her memory, she realized that she could do it on her own and had confidence to do so. I love that my inadequacy had a part in Jackie having confidence in her own ability. Jackie also stated on more than one occasion that painting really helped her to relax. She said that she'd walk into class feeling frazzled, and leave feeling relaxed, and she'd say, "What just happened?"

The experience that Jackie had with Erika was similar to the one I had had with my two artist friends. At first, neither Jackie nor I had the confidence to paint our internal experiences and thoughts. We wanted a "real" artist to paint the images we saw inside ourselves.

Jackie talked about her art:

I didn't know I could paint! I had never painted before. I've drawn. I like fiddling, making crafts, and at least I used to do a lot of that before I had kids. It just wasn't really a priority after you have kids, so I just kind of pushed it in the background and just tried to deal with day-to-day things. When you've got a little girl, and then when you have two little girls, you just don't think about that. I mean also with the husband I had.

The first two paintings I just did 'em freehand. The first one—because they were telling you it was about, like, your times of homelessness. So I thought, "Well, there's so much of it in my life, so many years off and on of it that I could have been painting for a couple years on it if I did."

So I thought, "Maybe I'll just do scenery kind of things and have like little painting ideas for my mind, or little things I could remember of what it kind of looked like, of places I had been during different times of homelessness. About the only one I didn't paint too much of was California, because they're really almost kind of green too, but also there was deserty area as well.

So I just put, like, a desert scene for my first one, and I stuck me a little lone coyote out there. I'm talking about the beginning, and so that's the deserty scene is more like when I was a child. I mean even emotionally in my family I felt very alone, so that was a very lonely—it's pretty—but kind of a very lonely scene. That's why I put the little coyote alone.

Well the farmhouse, I just wanted to put in some of how Tennessee looks. It's humid and hot up there, but I really loved it. I mean it's lush, it's green, you've got waterfalls everywhere, because I lived right up there at the Smoky Mountains, so I was in a really beautiful area. It was hard to leave. It really was because I had roots there—I had grown my own roots of, I guess, not just my family, it was just like emotional roots.

I didn't put people or anything in the Tennessee one. To me it doesn't seem so alone. It's more lively, serene. I did have some bad parts with my marriage, so I just kind of mixed it all together and put it all together in there, so there's a lot of different mixed feelings in there from happy to sad. And then I tried to put the family life in there, that's why I put the little farm. I don't have a farm. It just fit in there well. It's kind of just my idea of the family life in there and that started mine.

Now the last painting I'm doing has got me and my girls. I've got three girls now, so as my four-year-old daughter says, "It's a woman's world" or "It's a girl's world," because we have no boys. I've got me in there. Everybody's doing a portrait, so I put me and the girls in there. Then I've got a book, showing education, because that'll be a big thing for many years. Then, I also put some water because there's a lot of water in Michigan, and then I'm doing the background scenery with some trees and snow.

I mean most people know that where would you be without an education? Think about it. If you didn't finish high school, where would you be? You'd be struggling. I mean the economy is getting worse. I know there's a lot of people that do have a good education that are hurting out there because they've lost their jobs and stuff, but you're going to have a better chance at it—a better chance at having a better career. I'm tired of nickel-and-diming it. I really am trying to. I budget. You're gonna have to do that for the rest of your life. I know that, but it'd be nicer, if something goes on, you have your emergency fund, or having a home—that's such a big thing. I think the prettiest house that I have ever in my entire life lived in is the house I'm living in right now, at the Veterans of Foreign War for Children.

Finding Yourself through Art

Erika talked about Dora's art:

Dora painted very fluffy, delicate "free paintings" at the beginning and throughout the classes. She did not talk much about her story until the last class she was there. She created an image of a tree and also images of her mother on either side. It was painted in Dora's delicate style. She told me the story of her mother finding a $100 bill in her purse on a day they were starving and crying. Dora said from that day on, everything changed for them. She cried as she told me this story. I think it was important for her to take the story she had shared with me, and in her oral history, and make a tangible object out of it [the painting] so that she could see it.

Dora talked about her life and her art:

I wanted to participate in the "Your Story and Mine" project because I could speak up and I can say whatever I want to, now. And I wanted people to know, you don't need a man to be happy. You don't need anybody to be happy. You can make yourself happy. And I feel like not a lot of people hear that, and a lot of people feel that because we have kids together—because of the kids. No, you don't, you know, you don't have to be abused by anybody. You don't have to be verbal abused by anybody. You don't have to put up with that. Men too, men get abused as well. Their story just doesn't get out like a woman's, and that's what drew me to do this documentary, 'cause I was sad for a long, long, long time, and now I'm not. I'm happy. Today, I'm happy.

Today, I'm safe and secure. I'm me again since about two years ago, at forty. I don't feel like I'm forty-two and I don't act like I'm forty-two. I'm really playful and a clown. You know what I mean—because I didn't get to do all those things when I was young. I was ruining my life when I was younger, so I didn't get to be a kid, so now that I'm forty-two, I'm being a kid and it's nice, its good.

Asking for Understanding

When you see somebody walking down the street while you're driving your car, your nice car passed 'em or whatever, instead of looking at them like, "Damn, there goes a homeless person. Look at that person looking in the trash," "Why don't they go do this" or "Why don't they go do that?" You don't know what that person's background is like. You don't know that person. Understand that it can happen to you. Be caring and be willing to help. Understand where that person is coming from, how they're living their life, because it could happen to you. Always share, be willing to share and give. Have a good heart and help.

Loren wrote this poem about when he was homeless:

WHEN I WAS HOMELESS

By Loren

Being homeless is a combination of a lot of things
Lack of education, bad job market, inflation
and a host of a lot of other things
No matter what the cause may be
it is a very rough thing to have to go through

When I was homeless, I had to endure
a lot of hardships
Weather. Being Cold. Sleeping in my car.
80 degree weather or if it was summer not being
able to have somewhere to shower
Or having a hard time finding something to eat
Or a change of clothes

I have slept places unbearable
Sleeping in my car
under stairs in an apartment complex in the
corner hoping no one saw me
In apartment complex basements

One thing I've learned
is how to survive
It made me a lot more
aware of myself and my
circumstances
and how life decisions can affect you

When you are down and out
and you think things can't get any better
you keep your eyes on the prize and
pray for good weather
Take one day at a time and
fill up your cup
Then work really hard . . .
that is how

you

come

up

REFLECTIONS

Interestingly, by participating in this project, these formerly homeless people developed an appreciation for new avenues to express their life stories—words, art, and music. They each were courageous and gained inner strength and confidence as they left behind fears about painting. We hoped that if they could try something so new as painting, they could also explore other options in their lives and try to go in new directions.

Looking back on this journey, I realize now that several of these people resisted drawing at first. Some, like Wynette, were afraid they could not do it, since they had never done it before. Lewis was certainly not going to paint—after all, he was a "poet!" and not an artist; yet with a little encouragement, he painted several pictures. I remember how clearly Robert said, during one of the classes designed to prepare people to participate in the project, that he did not know how to paint and that he would not paint. He was not afraid to tell his painful story, which he graciously and willingly did. He just did not want to do it through painting—at least not at first. Erika helped him work through his resistance .

Once they each found themselves actually painting their self-portraits and stories of homelessness, they were proud and in such awe and surprise. I believe we all gained a new sense of hope—reflected in the title of our program, "Your Story and Mine: A Community of Hope."

Resilience from Memory, Hopes, and Dreams

The world breaks everyone, and afterward, some are strong at the broken places.

—Ernest Hemingway, *A Farewell to Arms*

The Making of Resilience

Those who have been homeless struggle with layers of problems and traumas as children, teenagers, and adults, and the painful memories of these experiences—some remembered, some repressed. But these people also strive, as we all do, to create and realize their dreams—some concrete, some abstract. They have been primarily familiar with one way of life stacked with negative experiences. Roadblocks have chronically interfered with their ability to move their lives forward. However, by remembering past pain and feelings, crying and grieving, sometimes we heal our old wounds and more space becomes available in our inner worlds for hopes and dreams and courage. If we share and transform the pain through words, art, and music, our emotional burden may lighten as we then access new, brighter thoughts for the future.

While some people realize they want and need to find a new path, and must abandon their old destructive habits to find it, they cannot necessarily conceptualize the new journey of their lives, because it is unfamiliar. It does not resemble anything they have ever known in their personal history or their parents' history or that of their ancestors. They are understandably afraid.

So, how does a human being who has suffered as much as these people have, even begin to dream or envision a new life or create a new self-definition? Without a map, how do they find a new way? What is resilience and who are the resilient?

According to psychologist Al Siebert,

> Resiliency means being able to bounce back from life developments that may feel totally overwhelming at first. When resilient people have their lives disrupted they handle their feelings in healthy ways. They allow themselves to feel grief, anger, loss and confusion when hurt and distressed, but they don't let it become a permanent feeling state. . . . This is why resilient people usually handle major difficulties easier than others. They expect to rebuild their disrupted lives in a new way that works for them, and the struggle to overcome adversity develops new strengths in them. (Siebert 2005, 5)

From the very beginning of this book, I have talked about my fascination with, and respect for, people who are resilient, and I often wonder why and how some people rebound after experiencing trauma and tragedy while others stay stuck in their grief. I had the wonderful privilege of meeting and talking with Darlene A. G. Groomes, an associate professor of human development and child studies at Oakland University in Rochester, Michigan. Darlene specializes in research on adaptation to disability and evaluation of programs that serve individuals with disabilities—specifically the relationship between hardiness/resilience and effective adaptation. She offered this perspective on the people who participated in "Your Story and Mine: A Community of Hope":

> The individuals' lives in these particular stories traversed many experiences that are filled with fear, roadblocks, and hardship. They have bounced back and shown promise of adaptive behavior, not only because of the successful literacy program in which they participated, but also because of the steps they have taken to commit toward accepting themselves for who they have become.
>
> These individuals have transformed because they have aligned their personalities with levels of personal competence to meet goals of literacy, shelter, and life with less fear. These individuals are successful because at the heart of their being lies a person willing to act despite experiences that are difficult and, at times, dangerous. The act of moving beyond fear and aligning the self with goals that can be met, and which inform future acts in face of challenge, creates resilience. Like a rubber band, these individuals make an effort to bounce,

rather than to snap and to let defeat have an effect on the accomplishment of their goals.

The mentors involved in this project offered their thoughts about resilience as well. Toni said that some children survive profoundly difficult experiences. "Some who are hung by their heels outside their window are extremely resilient. Other children become like a Sybil. They are extremely fragile and break apart into many pieces. They just never get out of it. Some people have more inner resources. Maybe they are born with them. I do not know."

Allyson also talked about the importance of mentors in childhood and adult-hood. "There is research now about a resilience gene in your DNA—you may be better predisposed at resilience than others. It gives you a better shot at handling the situation with everything you are facing."

I wonder if hopes and dreams are the result of negative or positive experiences, or if perhaps they have an independent life and direction of their own. How do these people conceptualize their dreams and become motivated to pursue them? Does the pain become too much and the soul cannot accommodate any more sorrow? How does a person begin to take steps to move in a new direction?

A change of attitude, if possible, can help, according to Shakti Gawain: "When we are negative and fearful, insecure or anxious we will tend to attract the very experi-ences, situations, or people that we are seeking to avoid. If we are basically positive in attitude, expecting and envisioning pleasure, satisfaction and happiness, we will attract and create people, situations, and events which conform to our positive expec-tations. So the more positive energy we put into imaging what we want, the more it begins to manifest in our lives" (Gawain 1978, 7).

According to psychologist Al Seibert, hope is an important ingredient for healing and having dreams. He says:

> From ancient times, people have recognized that a spirit of hope helps them bear times of great suffering, illnesses, disasters, loss, and pain. They learned that the spirit of hope could lead to being healed. And it makes sense. Now we know that positive feelings and support groups increase immune system functions and enhance healing. A wounded or sick person feeling hope could rest, be receptive to being tended by family, clan or tribal members, and receptive to the healing effects of poultices, herbal teas, or medicines given by healers. (Siebert 2005, 107)

One of my friends from adolescence, who is now an artist in New Mexico, told me that one of her mentors shared these inspirational words: "Try to discover what kind of flower you are and then find the best garden in which to plant yourself." These words have echoed through my mind for years.

The people in our project have transitioned from homelessness to "homeless no more." With ongoing emotional support from staff at Advent House Ministries, they continue to learn how to discover their present, past, and future time and place—who they are, where they have come from, what their challenges and goals are, and what their futures may hold. As they begin to solve some of their problems and learn to be kind to themselves, they slowly realize some of their dreams, which reinforces their new journeys as they transplant themselves into their new gardens to grow and bloom. Many have also learned to have hope and patience and not expect instant gratification. Having their own home creates much stability for them as they continue their journeys in life.

Erika said, "I think they have been through some overwhelming things for one individual to face, and a lot of us would probably think we can't survive. Yet they have survived. These people can actually be looked at as survivors and incredibly resilient—even that they exist, considering everything they have been through. It's almost like a miracle. It's incredible that they even exist. There's a resilience, just for even existing."

As they get more stable housing, an education, and jobs, increasingly it is possible for them to redefine themselves and think more positively about their families and their lives. As they revitalize themselves, they can continue to have even more positive experiences.

As Groomes explained further:

These individuals have worked hard to accept themselves and their less than optimal life experiences. As a result of their adaptation, they have made a choice, reflect, and move forward on the path of resiliency. Perhaps it is this choice, one's conscious effort to move forward in the face of adversities, that brings success.

My own research has supported this thinking—and the findings of famed psychologists like Seligman, Snyder, and Taylor who have examined how things go right. Quality of life and well-being often remain elusive to those who cannot link one's thoughts of success, in the tiniest of increments, to experiences that challenge the human heart and mind. Choosing to define the self in terms of positive strengths can lead to success.

The participants also talked about their need to grow in healthy ways:

David said, "I just have to rely on some people who want to help me. There's a big difference between people who want to help and people that criticize."

Loren said, "Everyone needs love. Everyone needs a chance, no matter what kind of mistakes you made in your life. You can still overcome those mistakes."

Lewis also developed a greater understanding about himself—where he has been and what he needed to do to transform his life so that he and his wife and children can all grow in a healthy way. Making such a conscious, profound choice empowered him to move forward. His poem "Are You Willing to Open Your Heart?" (2009) vividly and brilliantly exemplifies his memory, pain, grief, hopes, and dreams, and says, "My eyes feel they need to cry." This line affected me so profoundly that it became crystal clear that this would become the title of this book. Lewis wants and needs to remember his old wounds. His creative endeavor of writing poetry further affirms his grieving process and his need to cry, so he can heal from all his life traumas. Out of all his pain come hope and dreams.

ARE YOU WILLING TO OPEN YOUR HEART?

Lewis H., 2009

Being homeless has taught me to enjoy life, but to reach beyond one meal a day.
It also has given me the chance to open my eyes
and see what it's like for other countries
who do not have clean water for their crops.

Finally my eyes feel they need to cry.
I feel the hunger pains.
Thoughts of what it's like to lay down and die.
When I be free from my sins,
Will the system allow criminals to be rehabilitated once again?
Will I be nothing but a petty, homeless, worthless drug dealer again?
Wow! This is hard to say. Even I have a dream of owning a house one day.
I was taken away from my mother and father.
I've been a ward of the state.
I was ten.
Every time I got kicked out of school, it was never to return again.
I graduated from high school at seventeen.
Funds ran low.
So did the job and independent living.
My foster parents kicked me out.
Nowhere to go that month in Michigan. It was piled with snow.
I was initiated into a gang,
taught to sell drugs and

how to bang,

how to never be homeless when you're in the gang,

but if you're trying to get your life on track and homeless, with a child,

how are you gonna eat?

Everyone who owns houses wanna preach questions.

Will that feed my wife's belly?

Or go back to the street?

Jailhouses? To and from prisons?

Then another black man kicked out into the snow. It's like horrors.

Hear my screams under a bridge bundled together, asking for help.

Are you willing to open your heart? Are you willing to open your heart?

Lewis grieves the past traumas as a child, teenager, and young adult. He reveals his raw feelings of loss, abandonment, disappointment in himself and the system, failure, and humiliation. He acknowledges what he did and what others did to him—the state took him as a little boy from his parents, his foster parents kicked him out, schools expelled him, he lost jobs, and funds ran out. He spent time in jail and prison. A gang initiated him. While living under a bridge, homeless, he nearly froze. He makes clear the conundrum he faces of having to change his source of income, feed his child, and get his life on track simultaneously. In the past, he repeated familiar patterns of failure, but now takes ownership of his actions.

By questioning what will happen when he's "free from [his] sins", i.e., "Will the system allow criminals to be rehabilitated once again? Will I be nothing but a petty, homeless, worthless drug dealer again?" he allows for the possibility of change and rehabilitation. While trying to "get his life on track," impressively he says, "Being homeless has taught me to enjoy life" and "to reach beyond one meal a day." He is clearly motivated, particularly when he has a child he needs and wants to feed. "If you're trying to get your life on track and homeless, with a child, how are you gonna eat?" This is a major breakthrough for him—and how he asks for help: "Are you willing to open your heart?" He wants people to listen to his plea for empathy and compassion. Now, he has the opportunity to dream.

Like the others, Lewis chose to redefine himself and plant himself in a new environment, a very different garden from his original ones. Like all human beings, he and the other "formerly homeless" all have dreams—ones that are reasonable, realistic, achievable, and so familiar. They struggle as many of us do between what is an avocation and what is a vocation. They want to continue their newfound belief in themselves. Their goals have become clearer.

Alex Kotlowitz writes in his book about Lafeyette and Pharoah's experience upon seeing a rainbow in Chicago. At first, Lafeyette pooh-poohs his younger brother's desire to chase the rainbow to look for the gold.

> Pharoah knew there might not be anything at the rainbow's end, but he wanted the chance to find out for himself. That would have shown Lafeyette. At the least, he figured, he could have made a wish....Not until weeks later did he disclose what his request to the heavens would have been.
>
> 'I was gonna make a wish.... Hope for our family, like get Terence out of jail, get a new house, get out of the projects.' When he disclosed his appeal, he had to stop talking momentarily to keep himself from crying. It hurt to think of all that could have been.
>
> Lafeyette too conceded that he'd wondered about what they would have found at the rainbow's end.... But maybe Pharoah was right. Maybe they could have found something there. Heaped with disappointments, fourteen-year-old Lafeyette wanted to believe. He wanted to be allowed to dream, to reach, to imagine. He wanted another chance to chase a rainbow. (*There are No Children Here*, 285)

The people who participated in "Your Story and Mine" have each expressed their dreams. They want to go to school. They want to work. They want to own their own homes, with a yard, and not have to keep moving. They want a car that does not break down. They want to travel and shop. They want to remarry. They want their children to have a better life and education than they had, and want them to realize their dreams. They want to pursue their religious lives. They want to volunteer and help others positively. They want a peaceful life. They want to relax and "hang" with their families. They want to enjoy the holidays. They no longer want to be afraid of pursuing their talents in music, art, and writing. They want to publish their poems. They want to perform and publish their music. They want to earn money from their creative endeavors. They want to make a positive impact on this world. They want change for the good of this country. They want independence and self-sufficiency.

Are their dreams any different from those of any other human beings? From yours? Mine? Our friends'? Our families'? Read on. Listen to their dreams.

Celebrating

Wynette said:

On Election Day, I watched TV at home and read about it in the newspaper the next day. I thought Barack Obama was the best candidate because he was the first black presidential candidate. My kids cried. I was happy. Some were glad. Some were mad. Some of my family had a big party. I hope my grandchildren will remember this day when it comes around again. I hope everything that he said that he will do changes everything for us.

If I had a day to myself to spend it the way I wanted to, I would do crossword puzzles, watch soap operas, watch wrestling, see Kashia, one of my daughters, and one of my grandkids. Someday, I would love to get married again. Five years from now, I hope to move anywhere. My biggest wish is to have a good Christmas. I never hope for anything. Yah, I do sometimes, I hope I can get back with my kids' dad.

Experiencing Hope

Lewis said:

I'm a late bloomer. I'm starting to get my wings, now, starting to grow and prosper and to love. Jesus Christ left us with the commandment to have and to love. And that's when you start blooming in life, when you have our children. People need that. When you try to strive and be better for them. That's when you start blooming in life. It's like, "Wow, now I get a chance to have people hear me." And people say, "You talk too much." And maybe I talk too much because people haven't heard me enough.

I'm still being inventive. I want to own a house too, Ms. Martha. I want to own something. I'm thirty-five years old now. I will be thirty-six. Imagine that. Time passed on. I felt like I'm just even blessed to breathe this air. And, it's like God is saying, "Hey, I'm giving you chances. I'm giving you chances to make an impression on somebody." Even you, like right now, you're making an impression on me. And I'm able to express myself instead of yelling at my wife and she's sitting there like a wall, not even listening. And I've got a recorder here and you writing down some of that stuff.

Everybody reading the Hallmark cards. "Oh, that is sooo beautiful. Hey, I could do that." And I say, "Wow. Why don't I do this for a living, write some Hallmark cards for Christmas and sell some?"

I plan to further this writing effort as a career. First off, I'm going to start with a poetry book. Then I'm going to work my way up to a nonfiction book. And then I'm going to make a fictional book. Then I'm done. I want to have a house for me and my wife and my kids. I want to make sure that I have money put away for my kids so they never have to worry about having to pay for college because it would be paid for. I want my kids to grow up being successful in life. I don't ever want them to experience what I have experienced. For kids to see what they see—I see why they grow up so fast.

Dreams

Robert said:

If I could have it the way I like it, it would be a free place to live, just like God intended it to be. No one paying rent to anybody. You could live where you want, you can pick up and go where you wanted to. It's an ideal way of life. But apparently, white man came over and destroyed all of that and said that they wanted to own properties and everything.

I'd really like to go back to living my life before the accident. The constant day-to-day pain that I'm in kind of wears you down and everything, and it's just hard.

I'm not really sure yet what I'd like to be doing if I could. Not really sure. Just going to keep doing what I'm doing right now, and that's going to church and being part of the groups like the GED class and a couple of classes that are preaching-oriented, and stuff like that. It's nice to be around other people that you get a different twist on life. You know, being around better people more— being around Christian people.

Trusting Your Gift

David explained that

Right now, I'm looking for work. But in the back of my mind I'd like to pursue this other stuff, like getting my songs published. There's people that make billions of dollars doing that. So, maybe that is what I need to pursue, because there is no work. You know people say, "There's no money in that. Why would you want to do that?" But I got to do something.

I'm pretty new at this. I had a lot of other people tell me that's not a job, but it could be. What do I have to lose? I didn't even know I had the art gift. Nothing exciting has really happened in my life, except for this, my artwork, and the picking up in my music.

I know they got a lot of tapings that they do, 'cause you hear it on the campus, and I just want to know where they do that. They record these artists and then they play them on the campus radio. The only reason I wouldn't do this in front of my family, it's like they're jealous because I have a talent, a gift. It's like, "Oh we've heard you, get out of here." I don't care if they find out about it. I don't know why people are like that 'cause they can't play an instrument.

Maybe it's my outlet. Maybe it's the way that I need to get to do something, 'cause I did pray about it and I asked God what to do, and he showed me midsummer, sent this guy by me once, and then another guy came by with the same company and said, "You need to call us."

This may be your way to get off the street, but I listened to too many other people. Too many said, "You don't got talent. You ain't got no voice." But other people told me I did. I got to believe in myself and not other people. Just because I grew up with them all my life doesn't mean they know me and who I am. I stopped talking to them because I believe they are trying to put a damper on my gift. I wanted to put my guitar down and not play.

Well, I came here to start over with a spiritual beginning and not to be afraid to use my talent, because people get a lot of joy out of my singing. And if they don't, I guess I don't need to play for them—like my family. They didn't understand what I was doing. I think I got a . . . I don't want to say a calling, but maybe I need to pursue this field and play my music and let the spirit move me into what I need to do. Yah, it makes me feel good, too. Yah, I think I just got to relax more. I could probably write if I just put my mind to it and do it. I just have to rely on some people who want to help me. There's a big difference between people who want to help and people that criticize it.

Yah, I think I had a fear of budding, you know, and coming to bring my gift out, but I know I got to pursue and do it because I think I was held back long enough. I shouldn't let anything stand in my way; this is what I'm supposed to do. I don't believe in dreams, but I believe in miracles, though, so I might as well pursue this thing and do it.

Developing Roots

Jackie said:

I would like to drive a nice car. Well, for one, they're more comfortable. They got good air-conditioning and it's yours. I want a good car that doesn't die on me, doesn't break down, that runs good. It doesn't have to be new, I guess, just as long as it's a good running vehicle. I have my vain moments too. I mean I do like to clothes-shop, at least I used to before I had kids. I haven't done that for like five or six years, but that would be nice to do that again.

So I'm hoping that going to school—that's our main thing—is I want to be able to put away money so that my kids can go to school themselves, and so that way they can achieve their higher education, they can do what they want, or believe, or dream in, when they're younger.

I want a house so bad that's ours that I don't have to move from. I can't tell you, if I had a dollar for every time I moved I would be probably as rich as Bill Gates. We've moved so much, and I just—that's just my thing. I don't care if it's not the best looking thing. I like doing things and I would fix it up and make it ours. I'd like to have a home that's paid for so I don't have to worry about having a mortgage on it—or something that my kids will always have, because I never had that. So that's a really big thing. It's nice.

I'm happy I'm there, but that's kind of sad. I mean most people when they talk about their story, or their family, they talk about, they have made roots. I want my children to do that. I want them to be secure, because they might not grow up to be like me. And if they have more of a foundation to start their life, then maybe they have a better opportunity to make something good of themselves, so, that's what I hope.

Encouraging Empowerment

Bill said:

Five years from now I would love to be helpin' people get outta that pit. To give 'em encouragement that there is hope, to try to motivate them. And not have people do that pity party, "Why me? Why me? Why me?" Joyce Meyers says you can be pitiful or powerful, and I want people to think that they can be powerful people.

And when they get into that pity mode, you wanna say, "Go help someone less fortunate." And it makes you feel good. But, I wanna encourage people to not give up. I wanna deal with that type of people. And I don't wanna be the savior, or the answer, or solve the world's problems.

But, somehow my life, or my experiences, might be able to make somebody think about the road they're going down. Hopefully, some part of my story might open someone's eyes. I can't save everybody. I thought I could at one time, when I first got into the homeless thing. I got burned out. Was trying to solve everybody's problems and startin' more of my own. Getting depressed and frustrated, and I had to draw a line where you stop tryin' to help people and you start Bill time. Doing things that I like, 'cause I can really easily get quite involved and just not shut off. And I can keep going until I get burned out.

I try to take care of myself along the way. I go through my periods where I get depressed. And I wanna isolate myself. Typically, when I do that, then I know that I'm not focusing on me. And I'm not gathering things around me that need to be positive. Because having a lot of people that are having negative things going on around you, you can easily get sucked. It literally can suck the life out of ya dealing with this type of situation.

I just need to know for myself, to have positive people around me. You just can't have people around you all the time that are going through problems, that are talkin' negative constantly. I have to put people in my life that are positive, like the people from church—people that are doing well, people that honestly care about me, people that I deal with, that know what I am going through. They are there to help support. I have support people in my life. These are people that are doing well that I can talk to.

Ideas for the Future

Dora said:

I would like to change. I want to be somebody and I am gonna be. That's why I'm going to school, and that's the only thing that I would change that my education continues, even when I am a nurse or whatever. I want to continue my education and fill my brain with things that I never knew about.

I'd travel to Atlanta, Georgia. I love it there. I would love to live there—the people, and just the shopping, the celebrities that live there, the weather, the houses that I've been in. Huge houses. In ten years, well, let me tell you. I have a pond in my back yard with some fish, a couple little ducks. I want yellow ones, so I'll probably have them painted yellow. I would have a boat. I would have a car. I would probably adopt children. You know my life would be really good. Happy—not necessarily with a man, but alone, because that's how I choose to want my life. You know that's what I want to do.

Thank you for the documentary. I loved it. I like doing this and I hope that the people that get to see this watching it get something out of it. I don't know what they are going to get out of it, but I hope it's something positive.

Helping Others

Loren had a lot to say:

I want to be able to help people. I want to go actually go to like the State Capitol internship with some Representatives. I'd like to go out to the nation's capital, the White House, and the U.S. Capitol, and shadow some cats and get to know them and show you how things are done. Eventually, I'd like to be a politician. Well, the way I've lived my life, I feel that I could help. I'm aware of what's going on, on the ground level, right there in the battle, in the heart of things. So, I would like to help people with jobs, getting educated with jobs, any kind of job. I'd like to definitely help people as far as stopping this homelessness and that sort of thing.

But, individually when you meet somebody, I'd like to be able to just let them know there's hope out there, somebody cares. I'm here to help because I understand what it's like out there.

So, for people who have never experienced homelessness, or even have low income or poverty, I would tell them to "Keep your house. Make all your payments on time! You don't want to experience this. You can make it through it, but you don't want to experience it."

I see people now—more and more people are having kids, down like at the Volunteers of America. That's really rough on kids having to come up in that situation, but there ain't nothing they can do about it. They're with mom and dad.

But I would tell them, I would explain to them, what it's like being home-less. What I'm trying to say that "Don't think that your rug can't get snatched out from under you," and with the housing market right now, a lot of people are experiencing it. Always care about other people and think about what it could be like. Always think about what it could be like on the other side, and under-stand, especially with the way the economy is now, people are a lot closer to that situation. A lot of people are coming out to the food shops, where they feed for free, but always remember that it can happen to you and your family.

When you see somebody walking down the street while you're driving your car down—your nice car past 'em or whatever—instead of looking at them like, "Damn, there goes a homeless person," "Look at that person looking in the trash," "Why don't they go do this?" or "Why don't they go do that?" You don't know what that person's background's like. You don't know that person. Understand where that person's coming from, how they're living their life, because it could happen to you. This is one thing I like and I would just say, always share, be willing to share and always be willing to give, and have a good heart and help.

One good thing I like is the people at the mission. They bring their kids in and they help serve food, and their family members, or even if it's all adults, people are in touch, they see what it's like out there. They're helping, and it reminds them that these people out here need help, but also what it's like on the other side. You don't want to be on that other side, because it's cold outside, and it's a cold world. It's tough. So I would just say my advice to anybody that got it, don't lose it. Stay in touch. Let your kids serve somebody that's homeless: they're helping and they're giving back. They're seeing how you can help society out. Then for adults, and especially for teenagers, how you can . . . your life can slip from you—quick. I was in high school, and I never thought I'd have to go through none of this. And just the simple mistake that you make.

Thank you for having me, for taking the time to listen to my story. I really appreciate saying my point of view, and letting people know what I've been through.

Reflections

We all have dreams and hopes, even if we cannot always visualize or believe in them. Sometimes, some of us experience depression and thoughts of doom and gloom. Even under the best of circumstances, we do not always believe in ourselves or think we can attain our goals. Sometimes, we encounter internal barriers or external roadblocks. We get stuck. We engage in counterproductive behaviors and seek negative attention. We get lost in the mire.

When we dream again, we feel happy, satisfied, and fulfilled. These people's dreams and hopes are positive, noble, beautiful, and profound. If we only read about their dreams and hopes and did not know whose dreams they were, would we know what difficult journeys they have traveled? Would we know they were any different from anyone else? Would we know that they had once slept on the streets, in fields, in woods, under a bridge, or in cars when it was freezing cold outside? Would we have known that they had eaten out of a dumpster or had had only one or even no meals in a day?

Learning about their dreams helped me realize how similar we all are as human beings. As I began to get to know them, I felt an unusual sense of peacefulness and camaraderie with them. Perhaps I was growing more at ease and overcoming some of my own prejudices, fears, and preconceived ideas about them. Perhaps I realized we actually had more in common than I originally thought. Perhaps I was no longer afraid.

At the end of the "Your Story and Mine: A Community of Hope" program, Toni, Allyson, and Erika organized a field trip with the group to Old Town, a revitalized older section in Lansing. They gave each participant a disposable camera to take photographs of people and places and brought everyone a picnic lunch. It is not a dangerous area, but as we walked around I had this "feeling," and thought that if anyone tried to bother any of us that the participants would defend us. Perhaps, because of their life experiences, they knew how to take care of themselves, and could and would protect us.

Marion shared these observations about that day:

> The day we went to Old Town with cameras showed a group of people with laughter, daring delight in climbing down the banks to the river. Everyone participated and no one was left out or not laughing somewhere on the adventure.
>
> Robert acted the part of someone sleeping in a box outside. Though the idea isn't funny, there was something this group understood that it was "okay" to laugh. It was a day of people having fun, yet recognizing sleeping in a box is not fun, and Lewis showing us where he slept was not fun. It was a thing in the past. I really believe that group could relate to such a thing and some of us could not. But, generally the day brought laughter. Maybe because everyone had a camera of their own to use for whatever pictures they wanted to take. I saw a success in sharing with people the chance to laugh.

While we walked by the river, Lewis showed us where he had lived under a boardwalk for six months. He was proud now, realizing how far he had come since those days.

Then, Lewis politely stopped a young woman who was dressed in a business suit and high-heeled shoes and asked her if he could take her photograph. She smiled and said, "Yes." Then, she asked him if he was part of a tour group. He said, "No, we're part of a homeless project." She said, "That's cool!" I just chuckled to myself. Each took the other at face value.

I thought again about what Steve Lopez had said about his relationship with Nathaniel Ayers. He got to know one individual in depth. We had all become a little familiar with several people who had moved themselves off the streets.

Perhaps hearing about their hopes and dreams and hanging with them in Old Town helped make these people more real to the other mentors and me. As human beings, we each have a story, dreams, and hopes. We can spend an afternoon together, walking around the town without instruction, eating a picnic lunch, having fun and laughing, and having faith together in pursuit of our dreams. We were all part of the same project. We were all dependent on one another to make the project work and complete it. And we all succeeded. I believe I can speak for all of us when I say we all felt good about our experiences together. Now, as I look back on our journey, I smile—and as Lewis said, "My eyes feel they need to cry." Many more continue to travel the path taken by Lewis and all the others. Hopefully, they, too, will find a new road, but are learning that first "You'll just have to hit rock bottom."

References

ACLU (American Civil Liberties Union). 2005. "Racial Profiling: Definition." https://www.aclu.org/racial-justice/racial-profiling-definition.

Agee, James, and Walker Evans. 1939. *Let Us Now Praise Famous Men*. New York: Ballantine Books.

Ayer, Eleanor H. 1997. *Homeless Children*. San Diego: Lucent.

Baumohl, Jim, ed. 1996. (For the National Coalition for the Homeless). *Homelessness in America*. Phoenix: Oryx Press.

Beegle, Donna M., with Debbie Ellis and Rimia Akkary. 2007. *See Poverty . . . Be the Difference! Discover the Missing Pieces for Helping People Move out of Poverty*. Tigard, OR: Communication Across Barriers.

Blau, Joel. 1992. *The Visible Poor: Homelessness in the United States*. New York: Oxford University Press.

Bonanno, George A. 2009. *The Other Side of Sadness: What the New Science of Bereavement Tells Us about Life after Loss*. New York: Basic Books.

Boyd, Brian. 2010. *On the Origin of Stories: Evolution, Cognition, and Fiction*. Cambridge, MA : Harvard University Press.

Brodskaia, Natalia. 2007. *Naïve Art*. New York: Parkstone International.

Brown, S. 1986. Presentation at the Second National Conference on Children of Alcoholics, Washington, DC, 26 February.

Busch, J. W. 1985. "Mentoring in Graduate Schools of Education: Mentors' Perceptions." *American Educational Journal* 22, no. 2: 257–65.

CBS, *60 Minutes*. 2011. "Homeless Children: The Hard Times Generation." http:// www.cbsnews.com/stories/2011/06/26/60minutes/main20072626_page2. shtml?tag=contentMain;contentBody.

CDF (Children's Defense Fund). N.d. "Ending Child Poverty." http://www. childrensdefense.org/policy-priorities/ending-child-poverty/.

Children's Bureau. U.S. Department of Health and Human Services. N.d. http:// archive.acf.hhs.gov/programs/cb/pubs/cw006-09/cw006-09.pdf.

Coles, Robert. 2010. *Handing One Another Along: Literature and Social Reflection*. New York: Random House.

Courage to Change, One Day at a Time in Al-Anon II. 1992. Virginia Beach, VA: Al-Anon Family Group Headquarters.

Criswell, Sara Dixon. 1998. *Homelessness*. Overview Series. San Diego: Lucent Books.

Day, Angelique. 2006. "The Power of Social Support: Mentoring and Resilience." *Reclaiming Children and Youth* 14, no. 4 (Winter): 196–98.

Diblasio, Frederick A., and John R. Belcher. 1993. "Social Work Outreach to Homeless People and the Need to Address Issues of Self-Esteem." *Health and Social Work* 18, no. 4.

Didenko, Eugenia, and Nicole Pankratz. 2007. "Substance Abuse Is Much More Common among Homeless People Than in the General Population." National Coalition for the Homeless. http://www.nationalhomeless.org/factsheets/ addiction.pdf.

Edwards, Betty. 1986. *Drawing on the Artist Within: An Inspirational and Practical Guide to Increasing Your Creative Powers*. New York: Simon and Schuster.

Eleoff, Sara B., et al. 2010. *Children Living with Relatives Struggle with Physical, Mental Health Issues: Study Shows about 2.8 Million Youths in "Kinship Care"*. American Academy of Pediatrics. http://phys.org/news192000502.html.

Erikson, Kai T. 1976. *Everything in Its Path: Destruction of Community in the Buffalo Creek Flood*. New York: Simon and Schuster.

Flowers, Ronald B. 2001. *Runaway Kids and Teenage Prostitution: America's Lost, Abandoned, and Sexually Exploited Children*. Westport, CT: Praeger.

Fraiberg, Selma, E. Adelson, and V. Shapiro. 1975. "Ghosts in the Nursery: A Psychoanalytic Approach to Problems of Impaired Infant-Mother Relationships." *Journal of the American Academy of Child Psychiatry* 14: 387–422.

Frankl, Viktor E. 1959. *Man's Search for Meaning*. Boston: Beacon Press.

Frazier, Ian. 2011. "The Talk of the Town." *New Yorker*, August 1, 21–22.

Gardner, Howard. 1993. *Multiple Intelligences: New Horizons in Theory and Practice*. New York: Basic Books.

Gawain, Shakti. 1978. *Creative Visualization: Use the Power of Your Imagination to Create What You Want in Life*. New York: Bantam Books.

Geewax, Marilyn. 2012. "Preparing for a Future That Includes Aging Parents." http://www.npr.org/2012/04/24/150587638/preparing-for-a-future-that-includes-aging-parents.

Gottschall, Jonathan. 2012. *The Storytelling Animal: How Stories Make Us Human*. Boston: Houghton Mifflin Harcourt.

Hemingway, Ernest. 1929. *A Farewell to Arms*. New York: Charles Scribner's Sons.

Hopper, Kim. 2003. *Reckoning with Homelessness*. Ithaca, NY: Cornell University Press.

James, Doris J., and Lauren E. Glaze. 2005. *Mental Health Problems of Prison and Jail Inmates*. Special report prepared for Bureau of Justice Statistics, Washington, DC. http://bjs.ojp.usdoj.gov/index.cfm?ty=pbdetail&iid=789.

Jencks, Christopher. 1995. *The Homeless*. Cambridge, MA: Harvard University Press.

Kotlowitz, Alex. 1991. *There Are No Children Here: The Story of Two Boys Growing Up in the Other America*. New York: Anchor Books.

———. 1998. *The Other Side of the River: A Story of Two Towns, A Death, and America's Dilemma*. New York: Anchor Books.

———. 2004. *Never a City So Real: A Walk in Chicago*. New York: Crown.

Kozol, Jonathan. 1975. *The Night Is Dark, and I Am Far from Home*. Boston: Houghton Mifflin.

———. 1985. *Illiterate America*. New York: Anchor Books.

———. 1987. *Rachel and Her Children: Homeless Families in America*. New York: Crown.

———. 1992. *Savage Inequalities: Children in America's Schools*. New York: HarperPerennial.

———. 1995. *Amazing Grace: The Lives of Children and the Conscience of a Nation*. New York: Crown.

Lankford, Susan Madden. 2009. *Downtown U.S.A.: A Personal Journey with the Homeless*. San Diego: Humane Exposures Publishing.

Liebow, Elliot. 1993. *Tell Them Who I Am: The Lives of Homeless Women*. New York: Free Press.

Lopez, Steve. 2008. *The Soloist: A Lost Dream, An Unlikely Friendship, and the Redemptive Power of Music*. New York: Berkley Books.

Lowenthal, Barbara. 1999. "Effects of Maltreatment and Ways to Promote Children's Resiliency." *Childhood Education* 75, no. 4 (Summer): 204–9.

Malchiodi, Cathy A. 2002. *The Soul's Palette: Drawing on Art's Transformative Powers for Health and Well-Being*. Boston: Shambhala.

Man, Cadillac. 2009. *Land of the Lost Souls: My Life on the Streets*. New York: Bloomsbury.

Meichenbaum, Donald. N.d. *Important Facts about Resilience.* The Melissa Literacy Institute for Violence Prevention and Treatment. www.melissainstitute.org.

Mikhailov, Boris. N.d. Photographs of the Homeless. Saatchi Gallery, London. http://www.saatchi-gallery.co.uk/artists/boris_mikhailov.htm.

Miller, Alice. 1990. *The Untouched Key: Tracing Childhood Trauma in Creativity and Destructiveness.* New York: Anchor Books.

Morrell, Jessica P. 2007. *Voices from the Street: Truths about Homelessness from Sisters of the Road.* Portland, OR: Gray Sunshine.

Moynihan, Daniel P. 1969. *Maximum Feasible Misunderstanding: Community Action in the War on Poverty.* New York: The Free Press.

NAEH (National Alliance to End Homelessness). N.d. "Commercial Sexual Exploitation of Children (CESC) and Youth Homelessness." http://www. endhomelessness.org/content/article/detail/4299.

NCA (National Children's Alliance). N.d. "Child Abuse Research, Education, and Resources." http://www.nationalchildrensalliance.org/index.php?s=17.

NCFH (National Center on Family Homelessness). N.d. "Homeless Children, America's New Outcasts." www.familyhomelessness.org.

NCH (National Coalition for the Homeless). 2009a. "Why Are People Homeless?" http://www.nationalhomeless.org/factsheets/index.html.

——— . 2009b. "HIV/AIDS and Homelessness." http://www.nationalhomeless.org/factsheets/hiv.html.

——— . 2009c. "Substance Abuse and Homelessness." http://www.nationalhomeless.org/factsheets/addiction.html.

——— . 2009d. "Minorities and Homelessness." http://www.nationalhomeless.org/factsheets/minorities.html.

——— . 2009e. "Mental Illness and Homelessness." http://www.nationalhomeless.org/factsheets/Mental_Illness.pdf.

——— . 2009f. "Who Is Homeless?" http://www.nationalhomeless.org/factsheets/who.html.

NCHV (National Coalition for Homeless Veterans). 2009. "Homeless Veterans." http://www.nationalhomeless.org/factsheets/veterans.html.

NCL (National Coalition for Literacy). N.d. http://www.national-coalition-literacy.org/wae_adult.html.

Newman, Tony. 2002. *Promoting Resilience: A Review of Effective Strategies for Child Care Services.* Prepared for the Centre for Evidence-Based Social Services, University of Exeter, UK.

NIAAA (National Institute on Alcohol Abuse and Alcoholism). N.d. "Alcohol Use

Disorders in Homeless Populations." http://pubs.niaaa.nih.gov/publications/Social/Module1oDHomeless/Module1oD.html.

NLCHP (National Law Center on Homelessness and Poverty). N.d. "Homelessness and Poverty in America." http://www.nlchp.org/hapia.cfm.

Nye, Michael. N.d. *About Hunger and Resilience*. http://www.michaelnye.org/hunger/abouthunger.html.

Orwell, George. 1954. *A Collection of Essays*. New York: Doubleday.

Parker, Kim. 2012. *The Boomerang Generation: Feeling OK about Living with Mom and Dad*. Washington, DC: Pew Research Center. http://www.pewsocialtrends.org/2012/03/15/the-boomerang-generation/2/.

Payne, Ruby K. 1998. *A Framework for Understanding Poverty*. Highlands, TX: RFT Publishing.

ProLiteracy. 2012. "The Impact of Literacy." http://www.proliteracy.org/NetCommunity/Page.aspx?pid=265&srcid=264.

Rose, Steven R., and Marian F. Fatout. 2003. "Contemporary Social Issues Affecting Children and Adolescents in Family Systems." In *Social Work Practice with Children and Adolescents*, 50–67. Boston: Pearson Education.

Rossi, Peter H. 1989. *Down and Out in America: The Origins of Homelessness*. Chicago: University of Chicago Press.

Sethi, Aman. 2012. *A Free Man: A True Story of Life and Death in Delhi*. New York: W. W. Norton & Company.

Siebert, Al. 2005. *The Resilience Advantage: Master Change, Thrive under Pressure, and Bounce Back from Setbacks*. San Francisco: Berrett-Koehler Publishers.

Sidel, Ruth. 1996. *Keeping Women and Children Last: America's War on the Poor*. New York: Penguin Books.

Simos, Bertha G. 1979. *A Time to Grieve: Loss as a Universal Human Experience*. New York: Family Services Association of America.

Snow, David A., and Leon Anderson. 1993. *Down on Their Luck: A Study of Homeless Street People*. Berkeley: University of California Press.

Terkel, Studs. 1986. *Hard Times: An Oral History of the Great Depression*. New York: The New Press.

Tiny [Lisa Gray-Garcia]. 2006. *Criminal of Poverty: Growing Up Homeless in America*. San Francisco: City Lights Foundation.

Toth, Jennifer. 1993. *The Mole People: Life in the Tunnels beneath New York City*. Chicago: Chicago Review Press.

UDHR (The Universal Declaration of Human Rights). 1948. Article 25, par. 1. http://www.un.org/en/documents/udhr/.

US DOJ (United States Department of Justice). 2009. "Facts about Children and Violence." http://www.justice.gov/defendingchildhood/facts.html.

Vanderstaay, Steven. 1992. With photographs by Joseph Sorrentino. *Street Lives: An Oral History of Homeless Americans*. Philadelphia: New Society Publishers.

Whitfield, Charles L. 1987. *Healing the Child Within: Discovery and Recovery for Adult Children of Dysfunctional Families*. Pompano Beach, FL: Health Communications, Inc.

Wordsworth, William. [1802] 1984. Preface to *Lyrical Ballads* (1802). In *William Wordsworth: The Major Works, including The Prelude*, 595–615. New York: Oxford University Press.

Wright, James D. 1989. *Address Unknown: The Homeless in America*. New York: Aldine Transaction.

Zastrow, Charles, and Karen K. Kirst-Ashman. 2001. *Understanding Human Behavior and the Social Environment*. 5th ed. Belmont, CA: Wadsworth.